D1084005

THE DAEMONIC IN THE POETRY OF JOHN KEATS

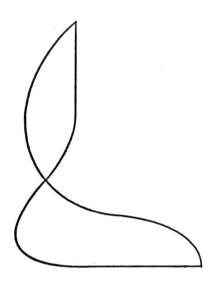

THE DÆMONIC IN THE POETRY OF JOHN KEATS

CHARLES I. PATTERSON, JR.

UNIVERSITY OF ILLINOIS PRESS
Urbana   Chicago   London

For
Royal Gettmann
and for my father
Charles Ivey Patterson, Sr. (1887–1969)

PREFACE

The idea of this study originated fourteen years ago during an attempt to explain how Keats, notably skilled at depicting sensory experience, also repeatedly expressed the beauty which "hath terror in it," as Wordsworth had termed it in *The Prelude*. Keats's reference to "my demon Poesy" in *Ode on Indolence*, echoing a conception of the poet in Plato's dialogues, was of some help; but alone it was not enough, for it did not explain the nature of the pertinent passages in the poetry itself. But I discovered from a brief discussion in Lemprière's *Classical Dictionary* (a copy of which Keats owned) and from passages in his poetry that Keats was aware of the pre-Christian Greek conception of a nonmalicious daemon who is neither good nor evil but who dwells outside the pale of human restrictions in a realm of greater joy and beauty. Soon after, I found in Keats's copy of *Palmerin of England* that he had frequently underlined and scored accounts of similar creatures and their effects on human beings in this romance of chivalry. I began to see that frequently in his poems Keats deliberately attempted to create the effect of a realm of superior joy beyond mortality. The light thereby thrown upon most of Keats's major poems and some others seemed enormous; passages became more meaningful and more functional within the poems, and baffling questions of interpretation began to be answered.

This aspect of Keats's poetry and its import have not been

traced out heretofore. In his book *Aesthetic and Myth in the Poetry of Keats* (1965), Professor W. H. Evert includes a chapter entitled "My Demon Poesy" that points out demonic aspects of Keats's imagination; but Professor Evert has not differentiated between the evil demonic in Christian theology and the nonmalicious Greek and Celtic daemonic in legend and fairy lore. Therefore my interpretations of individual poems diverge markedly from his. Moreover, Professor Werner Beyer has not made this distinction in *Keats and the Daemon King* (1947), in which his chief aim was to establish the poet's debt to Sotheby's translation of Wieland's *Oberon*.

The claim is not made here that knowledge of the Keatsian daemonic will overturn all established interpretations of the pertinent poems, but I think that it may drastically alter customary views of *La Belle Dame sans Merci, Lamia, Ode on Indolence*, and *Endymion*. A major evidence of the value of apprehending the daemonic in Keats is that it enhances and augments existing readings of poems like *Ode to a Nightingale, Ode on a Grecian Urn, The Eve of St. Agnes*, and *To Autumn*, the last of which is the apex of the anti-daemonic in his poetry.

I wish to thank the University of Georgia for released time and for generous help with clerical expenses. Thanks are due to too many persons for all to be mentioned, but I must record here my special gratitude to the late Mabel A. E. Steele, former Curator of the Keats Collection at Harvard University, a gracious lady always generous with her time and resources; to Professors Jack Stillinger at Illinois, W. H. Evert at the University of Pittsburgh, and Richard Harter Fogle at North Carolina for encouragement and many very helpful suggestions with the manuscript, although any errors are mine alone; and to Professor Royal A. Gettmann at Illinois, who encouraged this study by his belief in its pertinence and who long ago enlightened my mind as did no other ever.

Charles Patterson
September 15, 1969

CONTENTS

CHAPTER ONE

THE NATURE
AND SOURCES OF
THE DAEMONIC
IN KEATS'S POETRY

The particular nature and function of the daemonic element
in Keats's poetry, hardly noticed at all until recently, have
never been traced out in full. The few critics who have discussed it in part, chiefly Mario Praz, Werner Beyer, and
W. H. Evert,[1] have not differentiated between the Christian
conception of demons as supernatural evil creatures and pre-
Christian Greek and Celtic conceptions of daemons[2] outside
the pale of humanity but neither evil nor malicious. Various
modes of the latter and of their daemonic world, especially
mental reactions and feelings attributable to such creatures,
are what Keats used; and he employed them in crucial ways
in major and minor poems throughout his career. An accurate perception of these elements and their function in Keats's
poetry provides answers to important questions concerning
the nature of his art and helps to solve difficult problems in

[1] Mario Praz, *The Romantic Agony*, tr. Angus Davidson, 2nd ed. (London,
1954); Werner Beyer, *Keats and the Daemon King* (New York, 1947); and
W. H. Evert, *Aesthetic and Myth in the Poetry of Keats* (Princeton, 1965).
[2] The two different spellings to indicate the different meanings are frequently,
though not always, maintained. When Keats used the word, and that was seldom, he spelled it *demon* while almost invariably expressing non-Christian
meanings.

1

the exegesis of complex poems. Although he refers directly to only a few supernatural creatures as daemonic, in his poetry he depicted a good many as such in their effects upon mortals; and the daemonic experiences and daemonic states of mind which they engender in human beings continually appear in his poems as central factors. His uses of this element in the poems are chiefly of three kinds: allusions to it in sonnets and verse epistles; dramatizations of it and its effects on the characters and action in narrative poems, especially *La Belle Dame sans Merci, Lamia,* and *Endymion;* and powerful juxtaposition of it against the customary levels of consciousness in his odes. His attitudes toward the daemonic vary over a wide range—all the way from intense and engulfing preoccupation with it, to a teetering in the balance between affirmation and denial of it, to temporary rejection of it altogether, and, finally, reduction of it to a minor position within the manifold beauty that poetry can express. His long preoccupation with it and varied uses of it helped him to produce lyric and narrative poetry of distinctive charm and power.

The word "daemonic" is used here not to indicate Keats's intense preoccupation with the act of writing poetry, although that intensity deserves such a designation, as he suggested in the phrase "my demon Poesy" in *Ode on Indolence,* where he is evidently alluding to a conception of the daemonically inspired poet which is mentioned in Plato's dialogues but which is much older. Professor Claude Finney states that Keats learned from B. R. Haydon "a variation of Platonic theory of demonic inspiration," and letters between the two men during the spring of 1817 afford some evidence.[3]

[3] Claude L. Finney, *The Evolution of Keats's Poetry* (Cambridge, Mass., 1936), I, 213. On May 10, 1817, Keats wrote to Haydon, "I remember your

But in the present study the word "daemonic" is used in part to denote a special aspect of Keats's preoccupation with some of the particular objects that constitute the matter of his poetry and in part to denote the qualities which those objects take on as a result of the intensity of his preoccupation with them. In the first sense the word indicates a special mode of intense perception; in the second sense it indicates the extraordinary qualities of the objects when known through that mode of perceiving. Both are highly significant in Keats's development of most of the protagonists of his narrative poems and the speakers of his odes. The first sense of the word helps to explain why they perceive what they indicate during daemonic states and why they react to it as they do; the second sense of the word helps to describe and to clarify the particular nature of what they perceive at such times. The important matter is not Keats's daemonic intensity while creating his poems but the daemonic characteristics and reactions of his protagonists while under occult agency and the heightened, remote, rare beauty and terror which Keats's imagination produced while dealing with these characters. Three of his five principal narrative poems have nonmortal heroines—*Endymion*, *La Belle Dame sans Merci*, and *Lamia*—and the emphasis in all three is centered on the daemonic effects these suprahuman females have upon the human lovers who become involved with them and upon the outcome of the involvement. This daemonic element was continually in conflict throughout Keats's poetic life with its direct opposite in his fecund imagination: his persistent love of the actual world,

saying that you had notions of a good Genius presiding over you—I have of late had the same thought." He then asks whether it is "too daring to Fancy Shakespeare this Presider," evidently echoing parts of a letter from Haydon during the previous March. H. E. Rollins, ed., *The Letters of John Keats* (Cambridge, Mass., 1958), I, 141–142, 124; henceforth cited as *Letters*.

the common lot of all, and his great ability to depict it in images that are concrete, vivid, and powerful. Sometimes, in revulsion against the daemonic, he accentuated the beauty of the actual to a degree that can be called anti-daemonic, and it rose in triumph above the daemonic in his poetry before the end. The conflict between the two continually tended to enrich him rather than to tear him apart, and it gave to his best poems an excitement both emotional and intellectual until the end of his career.

As mentioned earlier, the first source of the daemonic in Keats's poetry is one of several pre-Christian Greek conceptions of daemonic creatures before Christian theology debased all daemons together into hellish beings and fallen angels; and there is external and internal evidence that Keats knew enough about them to set his imagination in motion. Before the Christian era there was a belief in Greece that a good daemon and a bad daemon watched over each individual, and this belief survived with modifications for a time in the Christian period. Keats may be reflecting something of it in the opening quatrain of his sonnet *Why Did I Laugh To-night:*

> Why did I laugh to-night? No voice will tell:
> No God, no Demon of severe response,
> Deigns to reply from Heaven or from Hell.
> Then to my human heart I turn at once.[4]

More significant to an understanding of Keats's daemonic were conceptions of other Greek daemons mentioned as long-standing common knowledge by the lesser disputants in Plato's dialogues. These daemons were conceived to be suprasen-

[4] Keats's poems will henceforth be quoted and cited by line numbers as given in H. W. Garrod, ed., *The Poetical Works of John Keats*, 2nd ed. (Oxford, 1958), except where otherwise indicated.

sible and suprahuman creatures intermediate between gods and men, at times messengers between them, at times agents of the gods in their relationships with men.[5] They were thought to have assisted in the creation and subsequently to have been set over men to govern them and to bring to them a spontaneous and free life not possible under their own governance. Belonging neither to the world of mortals nor to the world of the gods, these daemons were outside the pale of human limitations of any kind—moral, physical, social, or legal—and therefore were neutral creatures, neither good nor bad, neither moral nor immoral. They lived in a state of intense joy and ecstasy without limit or restraint and therefore superior in joy and beauty to the actual world of humanity. The whole matter is put very clearly in two passages from Plato's dialogues, "Statesmen," and "Laws IV," and is discussed in the dialogues in various other places:

> Blessed and spontaneous life does not belong to the present cycle of the world, but to the previous one, in which God superintended the whole revolution of the universe; and the several parts of the universe were distributed under the rule of certain inferior deities . . . and each one was in all respects sufficient for those of whom he was the shepherd . . . and I might tell of ten thousand other blessings, which belong to that dispensation.

> There is a tradition of the happy life of mankind in days when all things were spontaneous and abundant. And of this the reason is said to have been as follows: . . . God, in his love of mankind, placed over us the demons, who are a superior race, and they with

[5] Extensive bibliography and informative discussions of various conceptions of the daemonic appear in Robert H. West, *The Invisible World* (Athens, Ga., 1939); and in James Hastings, ed., *Encyclopedia of Religion and Ethics* (New York, 1925). See also Reginald Scot, *The Discoverie of Witchcraft* (London, 1886—a reprint of the 1st ed., 1584), pp. 411–542.

great ease and pleasure to themselves, and no less to us, taking care of us . . . made the tribes of men happy and united.[6]

While echoing these ideas concerning neutral as well as good and bad daemons, Robert Burton, whom Keats read repeatedly, also mentions that they copulate and marry with human beings, that they far excel men in worth, and that they are mortal and can die just as human beings do.[7] Quite understandably, human beings at times long to project themselves figuratively into something like a daemonic realm, where the limitations and barriers to utmost joy seem to fall away in ecstatic experience unequaled by anything in the actual world. It is easy to see how this conception would capture the imagination of the young Keats battering away at the bounds that restrict joy and beauty; and he used various modes of it to explore how far man in his drive for fulfillment could break loose from the plane of empirical phenomena and the common consciousness and thereby enjoy apparently suprahuman delight. Keats repeatedly chose to depict, in narrative poems and in odes, protagonists who strive to gain entrance into a daemonic realm of superior joy and ecstasy. This quest and its objective are significantly different from those of the Platonic and neo-Platonic lover of the Beautiful seeking to ascend to union with the Absolute or Ultimate Beauty, as voiced by the major speakers in Plato's dialogues and echoed by hundreds of neo-Platonists subsequently. The latter quest is spiritualizing, ennobling, humanizing, and at its end tranquilizing; the former is just the opposite of these: emotional,

[6] *The Dialogues of Plato*, tr. B. Jowett (New York, 1937), II, 299, 485. Some of these notions were later voiced by various neo-Platonists. Keats expresses ideas akin to these frequently, for example, *I Stood Tip-toe*, 185–187, and *Sleep and Poetry*, 29–34.
[7] Robert Burton, *The Anatomy of Melancholy* (London, 1924), pp. 116–124 and *passim*. Burton's account is puckish and garbled.

supersensuous, intense, sequestering the seeker in over-whelming excitement. Some neo-Platonic systems, for example that of Plotinus, envisage the lover of Ultimate Beauty as passing through a stage of daemonic ecstasy en route toward the Ultimate, but he is supposed to progress beyond emotional intensity toward a union with the Ultimate that is tranquil and calm; the daemonic quest, on the other hand, is directed toward ecstatic joy itself as its final objective. In the Platonic quest for the Ultimate the Beautiful merges with the Good near the end; in the daemonic search for utmost joy this merging with the Good cannot take place, for the daemonic pertinent here is neither good nor evil but neutral to both.

The term "daemonic realm" is used herein simply as a metaphor for a particular area or activity of the human consciousness influenced by much that wells up from the unconscious; for, of course, Keats did not literally believe in daemons but used the idea of a daemonic world as an objective correlative to an inner proclivity within man. The term denotes trance-like states of mind like some of those which psychologists and psychiatrists now discuss. The daemonic state in Keats's poetry is a sharply focused trance in which a person still perceives specific objects and situations vividly and concretely, but with a daemonic intensity and fixation upon only those qualities and aspects of these objects that are desirable to him. During this intensity he views them in his mind's eye in a kind of neutral way as to their relationship to good and evil and to human transience, as if recapturing something of the Greek notion of a spontaneous and superior joy prevalent in primordial times; he views them with a markedly heightened sense not only of their beauty but of their remoteness, strangeness, and fearfulness and may feel drawn into closer relationship with them for a brief time. Although

Keats's letters indicate that he had read *The Sorrows of Werther*, there is no evidence that he had any knowledge (even at second hand) of Goethe's autobiography, *Dichtung und Wahrheit* (1811–33), and the pertinent fourth part was first published after Keats's death; but a few passages from it make this concept of the daemonic seem remarkably clear—and, indeed, remarkably Keatsian. Goethe elevates it into a universal principle, as Keats came more and more to do; but Keats conceived it as operating primarily within the mind of man, while Goethe stated that it also exists and acts outside man in animals and in the universe. Like Goethe, Keats thought of it "after the example of the ancients." Like Goethe, Keats dealt with its fearfulness in imaginary creations of his pen, in which he worked out its various implications for humanity. And there is a resemblance to Goethe's Faust in Keats's protagonists and the speakers of his odes reaching beyond earthly existence for greater experience than the human lot affords. In translation these passages from *Dichtung und Wahrheit* read as follows (Goethe is using the third person to speak of himself):

> He believed he could detect in nature—both animate and inanimate, spiritual and non-spiritual—something which reveals itself only in contradictions, and which, therefore, could not be encompassed under any concept, still less under a word. It was not divine, for it seemed without reason; not human, for it had no understanding; not diabolical, for it was beneficent; not angelic, for it took pleasure in mischief. It resembled chance, in that it manifested no consequence; it was like Providence, for it pointed toward connection. All that restricts us seemed for it penetrable; it seemed to deal arbitrarily with the necessary elements of our existence; it contracted time and expanded space. It seemed to find pleasure

only in the impossible and to reject the possible with contempt.

To this entity, which seemed to intervene between all others, to separate them and yet to link them together, I gave the name daemonic, after the example of the ancients and of those who had perceived something similar. I tried to shield myself from this fearful entity by seeking refuge, in accordance with my usual habit behind an imaginary representation. . . .

Although this daemonic element can manifest itself in all corporeal and incorporeal things, can even manifest itself most markedly in animals, yet with man especially has it a most wonderful connection that creates a power which while not opposed to the moral order of the world still does so often cross through it that one may be considered the warp and the other the woof. . . .

However, the daemonic appears most fearful when it becomes predominant in a human being. During my life I have observed several. . . . They are not always the most eminent men either in their intellect or their talents . . . but a tremendous power seems to flow from them; and they exercise a wonderful power over all creatures, and even over the elements; and who can say how far such influence may extend? All the combined forces of convention are helpless against them.[8]

---

[8] *Dichtung und Wahrheit* (Vierter Teil, Zwanzigstes Buch), ed. Georg Witkowski, *Goethes Werke*, X (Leipzig [193–]), 317–319. The translation is essentially mine with some help from that of J. Oxenford (Boston, 1882), II, 321–323, and with many helpful suggestions from Professor Calvin Brown. I gratefully acknowledge that my colleague Professor Arra Garab first called this passage to my attention. The German text is as follows:
"Er glaubte in der Natur, der belebten und unbelebten, der beseelten und unbeseelten, etwas zu entdecken, das sich nur in Widersprüchen manifestierte und deshalb unter keinen Begriff, noch viel weniger unter ein Wort gefasst werden könnte. Es war nicht göttlich, denn es schien unvernünftig; nicht menschlich, denn es hatte keinen Verstand; nicht teuflisch, denn es war wohltätig; nicht englisch, denn es liess oft Schadenfreude merken. Es glich dem Zufall, denn es bewiess kein Folge; es ähnelte der Forsehung, denn es deutete auf Zusammenhang. Alles, was uns begrenzt, schien für dasselbe durchdringbar; es schien mit den notwendigen Elementen unsres Daseins

These statements reveal the daemonic as especially powerful when operating within the consciousness of man, where it brings a startling relaxation of the mind's usual ability to order, unify, guide, and shape experience. Along with unearthly joy, daemonic experience brings either a step toward another kind of ordering of human experience or a step toward no ordering of it at all, toward conscious anarchy. Though never so inclusive and penetrating as Goethe's in prose, Keats's discussions of the theory of it in poems come out at this same point. Here is most likely the single basic reason for his caution in imaginative exploration of daemonic experience in his poems and for his final rejection of it as a major avenue to human fulfillment—the risk of disintegrating the mind's ability to order and form experience in the ways necessitated by the conditions of earthly life.

It has perhaps become apparent already that as a mode of perception daemonic knowing is akin to what Keats called

---

willkürlich zu schalten; es zog die Zeit zusammen und dehnte den Raum aus. Nur im Unmöglichen schien es sich zu gefallen und das Mögliche mit Verachtung von sich zu stossen.

"Dieses Wesen, das zwischen alle übrigen hineinzutreten, sie zu sondern, sie zu verbinden schien, nannte ich dämonisch, nach dem Beispiel der Alten und derer, die etwas Ähnliches gewahrt hatten. Ich suchte mich vor diesem furchtbaren Wesen zu retten, indem ich mich nach meiner Gewohnheit hinter ein Bild flüchtete. . . .

"Obgleich jenes Dämonische sich in allem Körperlichen und Unkörperlichen manifestieren kann, ja bei den Tieren sich aufs merkwürdigste ausspricht, so steht es vorzüglich mit dem Menschen im wunderbarsten Zusammenhang und bildet eine der moralischen Weltordnung wo nicht entgegengesetzte, doch sie durchkreuzende Macht, so dass man die eine für den Zettel, die andere für den Einschlag könnte gelten lassen. . . .

"Am furchtbarsten aber erscheint dieses Dämonische, wenn es in irgend einem Menschen überwiegend hervortritt. Während meines Lebensganges habe ich mehrere teils in der Nähe, teils in der Ferne beobachten können. Es sind nicht immer die vorzüglichsten Menschen, weder an Geist noch an Talenten . . . aber eine ungeheure Kraft geht von ihnen aus, und sie üben eine unglaubliche Gewalt über alle Geschöpfe, ja sogar über die Elemente, und wer kann sagen, wie weit sich eine solche Wirkung erstrecken wird? Alle vereinten sittlichen Kräfte vermögen nichts gegen sie. . . ."

"Negative Capability"—that cognitive process in which the poet is continually losing most of his self-identity from being so often "in for—and filling some other body," [9] when the presence of the object being known so fills the consciousness as almost to blot out the consciousness of self, or as Coleridge described it, the process by which a powerful mind *becomes* that on which it meditates.[10] Both "Negative Capability" and daemonic knowing entail this near loss of self-identity and sense of being united with and possessed by the object that is being known. But a highly significant difference is evident. When this knowing capability remains centered on objects in the actual world, it results in a closer union of the self and its world; on the other hand, when this intense cognitive power is focused on something not of this world or upon something that impels the consciousness out of this world, the process frequently results in a startling separation of the self from the world of men and things as the emotion-charged mind creates for itself a daemonic world. In this state there is powerful ambivalence. On the one hand, there is intense ecstasy, joy, and well-being as the particular object of this knowing takes on the magical qualities of rare, strange, and remote beauty;

[9] *Letters*, I, 387. Cf. I, 193. A useful discussion of this matter as Keats understood it is W. J. Bate's monograph, *Negative Capability* (Cambridge, Mass., 1939), and Professor Bate also devoted a chapter to it in his definitive biography, *John Keats* (Cambridge, Mass., 1963), pp. 233–264. The idea was deeply imbedded in the philosophic thought and aesthetic theory of the period. It frequently appears in Coleridge's *Biographia Literaria* and other writings and in Hazlitt's essays (one source of Keats's knowledge of it). Schelling developed it at length in his *Transcendental Idealism*, a useful discussion of which can be found in George Mead, *Movements of Thought in the Nineteenth Century* (Chicago, 1936). The basic idea of "Negative Capability" is a cardinal principle of Zen Buddhist poetry in the Orient, as recently discussed by Lucien Stryk in "Zen Buddhism and Modern American Poetry," Supplement to *Yearbook of Comparative and General Literature*, XV (1966), 187–188.

[10] T. M. Raysor, ed., *Coleridge's Shakespearean Criticism* (New York, 1960), I, 188.

on the other hand, there floods through the consciousness, simultaneously or moments later, the aura of something desolate, sequestered, and apart. Although the remoteness and apartness add to the magic and strangeness of the beauty for a time, this magical beauty quickly fades, leaving the participant in an aftermath of varied feelings about these expiring daemonic ecstasies. At times he feels an overwhelming compulsion to experience them again at any cost and a consequent strong aversion to the ordinary world:

> in their stead
> A sense of real things comes doubly strong,
> And, like a muddy stream, would bear along
> My soul to nothingness. . . .
>
> *Sleep and Poetry*, 156–159

But at times this "sense of real things" that "comes doubly strong" in the aftermath of daemonic experience is doubly welcome, and these ordinary things then acquire a heightened value and beauty of their own by contrast—a response that can be designated the anti-daemonic, for it is often accompanied by strong aversion to the daemonic itself. A passage from Keats's verse epistle *To J. H. Reynolds, Esq.* (1818) indicates the nature of the anti-daemonic and at the same time clearly shows Keats's realization that the daemonic realm, which is neither earth nor heaven nor hell but a neutral region outside, was not the area where the imagination could do its best work for humanity. The reasons he gave here are highly significant:

> O that our dreamings all of sleep or wake
> Would all their colours from the Sunset take:
> From something of *material sublime*,

                        .   .   .   .
                        For *in the world*
We jostle. . . .
                            Things cannot to the will
Be settled, but they tease us out of thought.
Or is it that *Imagination brought*
Beyond its proper bound, yet still confined,—
Lost in a sort of Purgatory blind,
Cannot refer to any standard law
Of either earth or heaven?—It is a flaw
In happiness to see beyond our bourn—
It forces us in Summer skies to mourn:
It spoils the singing of the Nightingale.
                            67–85 (italics added)

This was a remarkable insight for a young poet of twenty-three groping toward a sound understanding of the relationship between himself and his world. Keats clearly indicates here that when he was teased "out of thought" he was not automatically impelled into a world of spirit or of abstractions, but into a daemonic world, where his imagination ("brought/ Beyond its proper bound") could not sustain itself for long, since it could not refer to any polar points of knowing, to "any standard law/ Of either earth or heaven." He does not mean "standard law" in a legal or moral sense. And yet he did not fearfully or moralistically abandon the dimension of beauty which the daemonic could add to his poetry; he learned to use it in a sane and manly way that would not spoil the singing of the earthly nightingale. He seemed to think that in the genuine poetic mind there is an inherent safeguard; for in another verse epistle, *To My Brother George* (1816), while depicting the "enchanted portals" and "golden halls" of "a Poet . . . in such a trance," he concluded the passage with these lines:

> Yet further off, are dimly seen their bowers,
> Of which, no mortal eye can reach the flowers;
> And 'tis right just, for well Apollo knows
> 'Twould make the Poet quarrel with the rose.
>
> 43–46

Because of this safeguard in the structure of his mind, neither the earthly nightingale nor the earthly rose was spoiled for Keats by his daemonic excursions, which add richness and range to the total poetic experience his works afford. He always kept the daemonic under the control of his intellect, although he used it more deftly and skillfully in his later poems. His controlled use of it does much to protect him now from damaging charges of aestheticism. His full awareness that the imagination could be destructive when pressed beyond the limits of its validity is revealed in quite another way in his heavily scoring and underlining certain passages in a copy of *Palmerin of England*, the old Portuguese romance of chivalry translated by Anthony Munday and Robert Southey.[11] In one passage therein a knight who is attempting to rescue his lady from enchantment in a magic chamber, where she lies still and immobile amidst marble statues,

---

[11] The original was written in Portuguese by Francisco de Moraes about 1544. Keats had in his possession a borrowed copy of a translation made from a French text by Anthony Munday during 1581–87 and later "corrected," according to the title page, by Robert Southey (London, 1807), who maintains in his preface that he retranslated more than half of it. The copy is now in the Keats Collection at Harvard University on loan from its present owner, Mr. Arthur A. Houghton, Jr. The passage referred to here is in Volume IV, pp. 177–181. I have discussed the copy and Keats's scorings and marginalia in "The Keats-Hazlitt-Hunt Copy of *Palmerin of England* in Relation to Keats's Poetry," *Journal of English and Germanic Philology*, LX (January, 1961), 31–43.

becomes so enthralled himself that he goes into a state of helpless daemonic fascination before her: "[He was] now so passionately afflicted that his judgment and reason clearly abandoned him, and he determined to remain there in that strange
dwelling place beside his lady, not remembering that he had
no other food than his own *imaginations, which would sooner
destroy than support him.*" Keats underlined the italicized
words here and vertically scored the margins of the page, according to a note written by Leigh Hunt at the bottom. Obviously, Keats was not only fascinated by the daemonic but also
was fully cognizant of the limits of its validity and aware of
its dangers. He realized that it *could* be destructive, but
through good sense and good judgment he prevented its becoming so.

Although there are similarities and overlappings, daemonic
experience can be distinguished from dreams, mystical experience, and visionary experience, terms which have been used
loosely to describe much of Keats's poetry. Daemonic experience is different from mystical experience, for in the latter
usually the mind is not focused on a specific concrete object—
such as a nightingale, a Grecian urn, an elfin mistress, a
goddess, a pale maiden in Hell, a lover—but is directed toward something metaphysical or abstract, like "pure Being,"
the world soul, spirit, essence, nirvana, or deity. The mystic
believes that he is intuitively apprehending great truth, witnessing a spiritual revelation, or achieving union with cosmic
consciousness; but in daemonic experience there is always a
concrete object of desire, there is nothing really metaphysical
or spiritual, there is no intuitive perception of truth during the
experience although generalizations may be made upon it
later, and there is no feeling of union with cosmic consciousness. The union of the self and the object in daemonic experi-

ence is more empathic and emotional than it is intellectual and spiritual, and it is a union with a particular thing or concrete object of contemplation or something to which the concrete object is a means of approach, for instance the world of the nightingale and the world of the Grecian urn in Keats's odes. Mystical experience is said to be indescribable; on the other hand, daemonic experience is easily describable, for it is vivid, sensory, and detailed, although greatly enhanced; and the persons who experience it often feel a compulsion to describe it. Visionary experience, while closer to what Keats presents in his "other world" passages, is still significantly different, and the term is not sufficiently accurate to indicate clearly what he is expressing. Visionary experience is usually either the act of envisioning something not actually present to the senses, something entirely apart from fact and phenomena, or the act of apprehending intellectually a complex new conception of reality, with the various elements of the conception ordered and interrelated within the whole, such as Blake's apocalyptic vision of perfected man which he described as a possible future stage of human life, or Shelley's vision of the regenerated world to be achieved through man's filling his consciousness with Intellectual Beauty. Keats's daemonic experience, on the other hand, is not an intellectual vision and does not consist of such intellectual components. It is almost entirely aesthetic and emotional, and it always entails concrete objects, although transfigured, altered, and enhanced during the experience; but it is not an organized, ordered conception of things or a vision of future human perfection. On the contrary, the Keatsian daemonic experience brings a relaxing of the ordered and conceptual, centers on the immediate present even when involving myth or previous culture, focuses on the particular, and eschews a conceptual scheme of any kind. It is more nearly of the nature of a primordial time rather than of a possible future time of human perfection. In daemonic experience there is more of a feeling of participating in something than of merely witnessing or visualizing something. Of the many kinds of experiences called visionary, some that occur during a trance or state of ecstasy and entail the vivid and particular are closest to daemonic experience, but even in these there is not the feeling of participation and involvement, as in daemonic experience, but rather the effect primarily of observing and witnessing, such as the religious devotee's vision of Heaven, or a saint, or the Virgin. During daemonic experience a person has more traffic and activity— physical, emotional, and mental, or involving all three—with the object of his preoccupation during the time. In sum, since visionary experience includes such a tremendous range, the term and the concept are not specific enough to denote what Keats tries to express. Similarly, "dream" is an even less suitable term; it covers far too much ground, although a person may have a daemonic dream in which he drastically remakes and reshapes what he dreams that he is participating in, as Keats did in a dream of Dante's Francesca da Rimini (*Letters*, II, 91). But not as many daemonic experiences occur during sleep as during what Keats termed a "waking dream" in *Ode to a Nightingale*, and there are too many different kinds of experiences called dreams for the term to be very helpful in a discussion of this aspect of Keats's poetry. Daemonic experience is essentially what it is, and the concept does more to indicate its particular nature than the others that have been used for the purpose. Keats severely condemns visionaries and dreamers together in *The Fall of Hyperion* (I, 161–162).

Ever since Matthew Arnold quoted passages from Keats's

Ode to a Nightingale to exemplify what he called the element of Celtic magic in poetry,[12] various critics have pointed out some of the unearthly beauty and terror in Keats's poetry without mentioning that they may be related in some way to pre-Christian Greek and Celtic conceptions of a daemonic realm of suprahuman joy and ecstasy. Keats undoubtedly gleaned something of his knowledge of this conception of the daemonic from his copy of Lemprière's *Classical Dictionary*, which Charles Cowden Clarke said that Keats virtually "learned," for this book contains a brief account of the matter. He could have obtained other information about it from two handbooks of classical mythology, Spence's *Polymetis* and Tooke's *Pantheon*, which together with Lemprière gave him a considerable knowledge of Greek and Roman myth.[13] Douglas Bush says that Keats in his poetry treats Greek myth at times more nearly in the Greek manner than any other Romantic poet.[14] Keats could hardly have failed to hear some of his friends, like Clarke, Hunt, or Shelley, discuss daemonology; Shelley was known to be discussing various aspects of Plato at Hunt's, where he left copies of *Alastor* and *Hymn to Intellectual Beauty*, during a period when Keats was often there, December, 1816. Frequent references in Keats's letters make certain that he read about nonmalicious Greek daemons in Burton's *Anatomy of Melancholy* during 1819, and he acknowledged taking the plot of his *Lamia* from Burton's account of the story, which Keats printed at the end of his poem. But the knowledge of the matter which he gained from these

[12] Matthew Arnold, *On the Study of Celtic Literature* (London, 1867), first presented as four lectures at Oxford and then published in *Cornhill Magazine*, March–July, 1866.
[13] Bate, *John Keats*, pp. 26, 177.
[14] Douglas Bush, *Mythology and the Romantic Tradition* (Cambridge, Mass., 1937), pp. 81–129.

sources was supplemented by others, for there is extensive evidence that he derived much of his familiarity with this concept of the daemonic from his reading of the romances of chivalry, especially *Amadis of Gaul* and the already mentioned *Palmerin of England*, the latter of which he marked and scored in a copy which he kept from late 1817 until his death in 1821. His underlinings and scorings show that he was especially interested in the passages depicting persons in a daemonic state of mind and the sort of world visualized by them during that time. His knowledge of fairy lore, much of which had flowed into the romances, also contributed to his understanding of the matter, for in these stories creatures from a realm outside the human pale often make raids into the actual world and carry persons away, some of whom never return from the region of the fairies, while others overcome the barriers to their return and flee back safely to the world of mortals, as is also the case in the romances of chivalry and in the popular ballads indebted to them (for example, *Thomas Rhymer*). Keats made use of this basic plot, involving both its outcomes, repeatedly; it seemed to be the story he liked most to tell. A major source of Keats's knowledge of fairy lore was Sotheby's translation (1780) of Wieland's *Oberon*, and Professor Werner Beyer has established Keats's familiarity with it beyond doubt.[15]

But knowledge of the sources of the daemonic would have meant little to Keats or to his art without his strong inclination for daemonic experience itself as an increased dimension of poetic life. In the depths of his being Keats obviously

---

[15] *Keats and the Daemon King*. This book is devoted primarily to the influence of Sotheby's translation of *Oberon* on Keats's poetry generally and does not include an attempt to clarify the nature of the daemonic and its function in his poetry, for Beyer makes no distinction beween the Christian and non-Christian conceptions of daemonic creatures and their world.

possessed what Robert Graves has designated the "white goddess," a universal power both creative and destructive that inspires the poet.[16] It is akin to the subliminal archetype which Jung called the *anima*, deep in the collective unconscious shared by all men. In Keats it was more than usually strong, for at times it welled up from the depths and dominated his imagination to a degree almost inexplicable before Jung's analysis of the unconscious. The *anima* archetype is an already existing pattern in the mind for apprehending the idea of the feminine in an all-embracing image that unites not only all the desiderata of woman but also her fearful and dangerous aspects, such as her power to engulf and again possess man utterly, as she once did when she carried him in her womb. The term "archetypal image" in modern literary criticism usually denotes the external object that activates an inward potential. The *anima* reveals itself in a man's love life in the form of boundless fascination, overevaluation, and infatuation; and it is projected symbolically as "a great illusionist seductress . . . [drawing man] into the paradoxes of life." "The anima can fascinate, hypnotize, and even capture the consciousness—one could become anima possessed." [17] Something like this is clearly the case with Keats's knight in *La Belle Dame sans Merci* and with Lycius in *Lamia*. With these proclivities active within him, Keats could, through daemonic fixation on the dark mysterious side of his mind, relax his will and consciousness and take possession of subconscious materials reaching back to the primordial, which he

[16] Robert Graves, *The White Goddess: A Historical Grammar of Poetic Myth* (London, 1948).

[17] Carl G. Jung, "Archetypes and the Collective Unconscious," in Herbert Read, ed., *The Collected Works of Carl G. Jung*, tr. R. F. C. Hull, IX, Part II (New York, 1959), 26–32, 68–70. Cf. Morris Philipson, *Outline of Jungian Aesthetics* (Evanston, Ill., 1963), pp. 52–63.

found symbols to render forth with unearthly power. These materials seem almost to have possessed *him* at times, but he always pulled them up short and brought them under the control of a basic framework of thought and art in his poems. From the first he evidently knew that he had to be wary of the white goddess and of the *anima*, for they could become as destructive as flame to the moth. But Keats was a wise and discerning moth in the face of his flame. Though fortunately he had not come exactly to fear the fire in the year 1819, which ushered in the period of his greatest poetry, he had come to know the proper distance from the blaze. Perhaps it is profoundly significant that an earlier meaning of the word *anima* was "a flame" (Jung, *op. cit.*, p. 26).

His external knowledge of the daemonic together with his inner affinities with it and subconscious proclivities for it did more than anything else to give a rich complexity to his poetry, which otherwise would have operated too exclusively on only one plane of being and would therefore have been less rewarding and exciting. The daemonic proclivity enabled him not only to throw over his poetic fabric at times a mysterious beauty close to terror, but also by contrast to set off in high relief the ever-present beauty of the actual world, as these two different types of beauty wrestled in conflict in his imagination throughout his career. Best of all, the daemonic element gave to his poetry another dimension than the actual without the vagueness of abstract idealism, for the daemonic provided for him another realm of experience outside that of the common consciousness and yet one quite different from the ideal, as his poems repeatedly indicate.

CHAPTER TWO

THE FUNCTION
OF THE DAEMONIC
IN *ENDYMION*

Most interpreters of Keats's poems have steadfastly designated his *Endymion* an allegory of a young poet's quest for
ideal beauty.[1] Others have swung to the opposite extreme and
have proclaimed Endymion's quest simply the pursuit of
erotic experience.[2] More recently, and quite cogently, the
poem has been interpreted by Stuart M. Sperry as an account
of a search for visionary experience and eventual immortality
in conflict with the claims of humanity and mortality.[3] There

[1] For example, Sidney Colvin, *John Keats* (New York, 1925), p. 205; Robert Bridges, *Collected Essays*, Part IV (Oxford, 1933), p. 87; Ernest de Selincourt, *The Poems of John Keats* (London, 1951), p. xl; C. D. Thorpe, *The
Mind of John Keats* (New York, 1926), pp. 55–56; J. M. Murry, *The Mystery
of Keats* (London, 1949), p. 144; and Claude L. Finney, who unreservedly and
unequivocally labels it a neo-Platonic poem, *The Evolution of Keats's Poetry*
(Cambridge, Mass., 1936), I, 298–299.

[2] Chief among them are Amy Lowell, *John Keats* (Boston, 1925), I, 318,
456, 365; and Newell Ford in two articles and a monograph: "*Endymion*—a
Neo-Platonic Allegory?" *ELH*, XIV (March, 1947), 64–76; "The Meaning of
'Fellowship with Essence' in *Endymion*," *PMLA*, LXII (December, 1947),
1061–76, in which the key passage used to support transcendental and neo-
Platonic readings of the poem is interpreted as containing no Platonic or neo-
Platonic meaning whatsoever; and *The Prefigurative Imagination of John Keats*
(Stanford, Calif., 1951), pp. 9–86. Cf. E. C. Pettet, *On the Poetry of Keats*
(Cambridge, 1957), p. 153.

[3] Stuart M. Sperry, "The Concept of Imagination in Keats' Narrative Poems,"
unpublished doctoral dissertation, Harvard University, 1959, pp. 34–93. Cf.

are other interpretations, some of them far afield from the text;[4] but all three of the basic views indicated above reveal in varying degree something of what is expressed in *Endymion*, especially the third one as voiced by Sperry, which is probably the most responsible and accurate exegesis yet to appear. However, all of them omit a significant part of what the total structure and fabric of the poem set forth. The daemonic element in the poem supplies what is needed to modify, supplement, and unite the contributions of previous fruitful interpretations into a view of the poem that is more comprehensive, specific, and accurate.

For Endymion's quest begins at the very outset and continues until near the end chiefly as a search for daemonic experience—for experience out of this world, beyond the actual and its limitations, beyond the moral and immoral into joy and ecstasy without stint. Daemonic ecstasy was envisioned in some neo-Platonic systems as one stage of ascent toward the ideal, but the expectation was that the participant would progress through it into the spiritual. Endymion never does so. His major concern continues to be daemonic ecstasy itself. Despite Professor Ford's persuasive denial,[5] Endymion does enunciate a quest for the ideal in the passage equating happiness and "fellowship with essence" (I, 777–857), for the typical framework of escalation, the light imagery, and the symbolic representation of the ideal (Cynthia) are clearly dis-

---

his "The Allegory of *Endymion*," *Studies in Romanticism*, II (Autumn, 1962), 38–53. See also the excellent study by Boyd McWhorter, "Keats's *Endymion* Reconsidered," unpublished doctoral dissertation, University of Texas, 1960.

[4] For example, J. R. Caldwell, *John Keats' Fancy* (Ithaca, N.Y., 1945), pp. 95–31; and H. Clement Notcutt, *An Interpretation of Keats's Endymion* (New York, 1964; 1st ed., 1919).

[5] See note 2 above. Keats could hardly have escaped absorbing some knowledge of neo-Platonism from his considerable reading in Spenser, Shakespeare, and Drayton; and he surely must have heard Shelley talking of Plato at Hunt's.

cernible throughout the passage. But at the apex of the scale the love of Cynthia, which is to represent the final step into union with the ideal, is continually turned into a pursuit of daemonic experience by the intensity of the young Endymion. Therefore, what transpires in the actual working out of the ascent to the ideal in the poem is that the quest for the daemonic continually usurps and superimposes itself upon the quest for the ideal. This usurpation by the quest for the daemonic persistently blurs the quest for the ideal throughout and gives it the puzzling quality that has baffled many readers, especially those who attempt to maintain a neo-Platonic interpretation to the end. The passage that most encourages this recurrent endeavor Keats added to the poem while it was going through the press. In a letter to his publisher, John Taylor (January 30, 1818), he requested that the second half of line 778 in Book I and the first half of 779 be changed to read "fellowship divine/ A fellowship with essence," for the passage originally had neither of these phrases that have loomed so large ever since.[6] In the letter Keats stated: "You must oblige me by putting this in, for setting aside the badness of the other, *such a preface is necessary to the subject*" (italics added). Whether the word "subject" meant the whole passage (I, 777–857) or the whole poem, I think that Keats made these emendations in a belated effort to bolster the neo-Platonic element and bring the main action in line with the lame, tacked-on ending (unsatisfactory to nearly all interpreters), in which Cynthia is incongruously brought back

[6] The lines originally read:
> Wherein lies happiness? In that which becks
> Our ready minds to blending pleasureable:
> And that delight is the most treasureable
> That makes the richest Alchymy.
>
> I, 777–780

into the picture after the quest for her has been emphatically rejected. I believe that Keats made the emendations *because* he knew full well that while he was composing it the poem had taken quite a different course from the one promised in the passage as it originally stood and yet a course of development which he had found no effective way to conclude, thus necessitating his belated attempt to strengthen the neglected strain. For the truth is that throughout the story Endymion repeatedly mistakes the daemonic for the ideal, turning Cynthia into a daemonic agent rather than an effective representation of the highest neo-Platonic essence, until his final rejection of his pursuit of her and manly resignation to the world of actuality near the end. The chief thing he learns during this long process of initiation is that the daemonic is *not* the ideal, as he has been mistaking it to be. The central conflict in the poem is therefore between the daemonic and the actual, for this fundamental opposition embraces the others. The conflict between ideal and actual is easily resolved after the inclusive one between the daemonic and actual is settled by Endymion's recantation of the daemonic and discovery of the ideal in the actual. In discussions of neo-Platonism the highest neo-Platonic ideal is never found in the actual. In Keats's poem this pervasive and inclusive juxtaposition between daemonic and actual is functional all through the narrative. It provides a more specific and accurate description of the object of Endymion's real quest, dictates its outcome, and clarifies the significance of final events more satisfactorily than heretofore; and it helps to define the ideas that form the base of the poem and to shape the incidents that constitute its plot, as becomes apparent when the effects of this conflict are traced throughout the structure of the action.

I

The poem begins with the poet, in his own person, firmly enunciating in the introduction the ever-present and compelling beauty of the actual world:

> A thing of beauty is a joy for ever:
>
> .   .   .   .
>
> Some shape of beauty moves away the pall
> From our dark spirits. Such the sun, the moon,
> Trees old, and young sprouting a shady boon
> For simple sheep. . . .
> Now while the early budders are just new,
> And run in mazes of the youngest hue
> About old forests; while the willow trails
> Its delicate amber; and the dairy pails
> Bring home increase of milk.
>
> .   .   .   .
>
>   let Autumn bold,
> With universal tinge of sober gold,
> Be all about me when I make an end.[7]

After the introduction this strain is immediately picked up and extended in the description of the forest of Latmos, the feast of Pan, and the famous hymn to Pan, who is certainly a proper god to be invoked in praise of the joys of the ordinary world in which men live from day to day. This description is in the pastoral tradition, but Keats is putting it in concrete images which make it more down-to-earth and less conventional than most pastoral poetry. The hymn to Pan reads in part:

---

[7] Book I, 1–57. Passages in *Endymion* are henceforth cited by book and line numbers only, as given in Garrod's 1958 edition of *The Poetical Works*.

> O thou, to whom
> Broad leaved fig trees even now foredoom
> Their ripen'd fruitage; yellow girted bees
> Their golden honeycombs; our village leas
> Their farest blossom'd beans and poppied corn;
> The chuckling linnet its five young unborn,
> To sing for thee; low creeping strawberries
> Their summer coolness; pent up butterflies
> Their freckled wings; yea, the fresh budding year
> All its completions. . . .
>
> I, 251–260

These good things of earth serve to set off in sharp contrast the present condition of Endymion, for he gives no attention at all to the festivities in praise of the manifold "completions" of the actual world. During the hymn to Pan he sits with an aged priest around whom are old men discussing the afterlife and "the fragile bar/ That keeps us from our homes ethereal." This discussion does not indicate a concern with the ideal in Endymion's mind, for he takes no part in it and pays no heed to their talk or to the hymn to Pan. He is unmindful of the actual and of the heavenly: "all out-told/ Their fond imaginations,—saving him" (I, 392–393). Subsequent events bear out fully the implications of this beginning. At the conclusion of the hymn Endymion is unaware of the cessation of the mass of sound and of everything else in his immediate surroundings, for he is obviously in a state of daemonic prepossession:

> Now indeed
> His senses had swoon'd off: he did not heed
> The sudden silence, or the whispers low,
> Or the old eyes dissolving at his woe,

Or anxious calls, or close of trembling palms,
Or maiden's sigh, that grief itself embalms:
But in the self-same fixed trance he kept,
Like one who on the earth had never stept.

I, 397–404

The daemonic characteristics of this trance are easy to recognize, and their identity is indicated by their cause: his unawareness of his immediate sensory world and lack of interest in the people about him stem not from his having achieved union with a spiritual entity such as the Platonic "One"; on the contrary, his condition derives from his contemplating with daemonic intensity a smaller object of thought: the mysterious feminine creature whose three visits with him in dreams he is soon to relate and whose identity he does not know for sure. His consciousness has gone out of himself and his immediate world but has not gone into any other, that is, has not united with any object of thought large enough to constitute for the mind another world that is satisfactory and durable. He has impelled himself into a neutral region that is neither earth nor heaven nor hell, as later events reveal.

Immediately after this appearance of Endymion on the scene, his daemonic prepossessed condition is set off in sharp contrast against a second presentation of the wholesome, satisfying joys of the ordinary world; and his acknowledgment of their powerful appeal initiates the conflict that continues to the end of the poem. His sister Peona appears and ministers to him with loving care. She is the chief spokesman for the validity of the joys of the lowly world of here and now, and her attachment to it is so complete that she cannot comprehend the lure of the daemonic and occult. She gives Endymion relief from his spell at once:

Her eloquence did breathe away the curse:

.   .   .   .

So she was gently glad to see him laid
Under her favourite bower's quiet shade,
On her own couch, new made of flower leaves,
Dried carefully on the cooler side of sheaves
When last the sun his autumn tresses shook,
And the tann'd harvesters rich armfuls took.
Soon was he quieted to slumbrous rest:

.   .   .

And as a willow keeps
A patient watch over the stream that creeps
Windingly by it, so the quiet maid
Held her in peace: so that a whispering blade
Of grass, a wailful gnat, a bee bustling
Down in the blue-bells, or a wren light rustling
Among sere leaves and twigs, might all be heard.

I, 412–452

So effective are these ministrations of Peona that Endymion is immediately brought round to a calmer state of mind in which he vows to give over his fierce pursuit of joys beyond the ordinary and to find contentment in the pleasures of the life about him:

Thus, in the bower,
Endymion was calm'd to life again.
Opening his eyelids with a healthier brain,
He said: 'I feel this thine endearing love
All through my bosom. . . .
Can I want
Aught else, aught nearer heaven, than such tears?
Yet dry them up, in bidding hence all fears

That, any longer, I will pass my days
Alone and sad. No, I will once more raise
My voice upon the mountain-heights. . . .
                    again I'll poll
The fair-grown yew tree, for a chosen bow:
And, when the pleasant sun is getting low,
Again I'll linger in a sloping mead
To hear the speckled thrushes, and see feed
Our idle sheep.'

                                        I, 463–486

To encourage these resolves and this renewed calm in Endymion, Peona takes her lute and plays a lay

More subtle cadenced, more forest wild
Than Dryope's lone lulling of her child.

                                        I, 494–495

However, although she immediately sees "Endymion's spirit
melt away and thaw," Peona fears that he is only pretending
this placidity and returning interest in shepherd life in order
to cover up a wild fascination for something unsanctioned by
gods or men:

                    'Brother, 'tis vain to hide
That thou dost know of things mysterious,
Immortal, starry; such alone could thus
Weigh down thy nature. Hast thou sinn'd in aught
Offensive to the heavenly powers? Caught
A Paphian dove upon a message sent?
Thy deathful bow against some deer-head bent,
Sacred to Dian? Haply, thou hast seen
Her naked limbs among the alders green;

And that, alas! is death. No, I can trace
Something more high-perplexing in thy face!'
I, 505–515

Peona's dominant trait is contentment with the common lot. Although she never shows anywhere in the poem an understanding of the daemonic or of its powerful appeal, she has here stumbled close to the truth of what is troubling Endymion.

The lines of the developing conflict between the daemonic and the actual now become more clearly defined as Endymion, seeing that Peona has penetrated partway into his real interest, decides to make a clean breast of it and to ease himself of his "secret grief" while at the same time reaffirming his rededication to his role as king of the Latmian shepherds in the world of everyday life. Therefore, he relates to Peona his first dream meeting with the moon goddess (I, 572–681). Significantly, this mingled bright moon and feminine creature is set forth in terms which convey very little of the effect upon him of anything ideal; the goddess is clearly an object of ecstatic longing, strongly sexual, with whom Endymion in the dream achieves aesthetic empathy, the sense of union and loss of self-identity which Keats later designated "Negative Capability":

> she did soar
> So passionately bright, my dazzled soul
> Commingling with her argent spheres did roll
> Through clear and cloudy. . . .

Since this creature, either moon or goddess, is not of this world, Endymion's union with her carries him out of the earthly plane into her starry region, where he is "not fearful,
I, 593–596

nor alone,/ But lapp'd and lull'd along the dangerous sky" (I, 645–646) until he dreams (in a dream within the dream) that he falls asleep. When he awakens, he is in one of the typical postdaemonic states of mind: that state in which "the stings/ Of human neighborhood envenom all" (I, 621–622) and all ordinary human pleasures have lost their savor. He proclaims:

> 'all the pleasant hues
> Of heaven and earth had faded: deepest shades
> Were deepest dungeons; heaths and sunny glades
> Were full of pestilent light; our taintless rills
> Seem'd sooty, and o'er-spread with upturn'd gills
> Of dying fish; the vermeil rose had blown
> In frightful scarlet. . . .
>   If an innocent bird
> Before my heedless footsteps stirr'd, and stirr'd
> In little journeys, I beheld in it
> A disguis'd demon, missioned to knit
> My soul with under darkness; to entice
> My stumblings down some monstrous precipice:
> Therefore I eager followed, and did curse
> The disappointment. Time, that aged nurse,
> Rock'd me to patience. Now, thank gentle heaven!
> These things, with all their comfortings, are given
> To my down-sunken hours, and with thee,
> Sweet sister, help to stem the ebbing sea
> Of weary life.'
>   I, 691–710

"These things" in line 707 above refers to the preceding "deepest shades," "sunny glades," "taintless rills," and "vermeil rose" *now relieved of the blight that had been thrown over them by the aftermath of the daemonic* in the protagonist's mind when time, "that aged nurse," had freed him from the lingering daemonic influence, allowing these concrete objects in the actual world to reassume their lower-pulsed but very real beauty and thus become "comfortings." These and the human love steadily radiated by Peona "help to stem the ebbing sea/ Of weary life" filled with boredom and monotony to one who has known the glory of the daemonic. In his postdaemonic condition he was initially so disenchanted with actuality that he wanted the "innocent bird" to be a "disguised demon" leading him even to destruction if necessary for escape. Peona, seizing upon his slight progress toward reorientation to the actual, urges him on, partly by shaming him concerning the passivity of his mysterious preoccupation and partly by encouraging a resumption of active participation as a shepherd king in the life of his time:

> 'Yet it is strange, and sad, alas!
> That one who through this middle earth should pass
> Most like a sojourning demi-god, and leave
> His name upon the harp-string, should achieve
> No higher bard than simple maidenhood,
> Singing alone, and fearfully,—how the blood
> Left his young cheek; and how he used to stray
> He knew not where; and how he would say, *nay*,
> If any said 'twas love. . . .
> —Endymion!
> Be rather in the trumpet's mouth,—anon
> Among the winds at large—that all may hearken!
>
> .   .   .   .
>
> Then wherefore sully the entrusted gem
> Of high and noble life with thoughts so sick?

Why pierce high-fronted honour to the quick
For nothing but a dream?'

I, 722–760

The passage reveals again that Peona does not comprehend the powerful appeal of the daemonic clothed round with unearthly beauty; she thinks it only the shadowy lure of a "dream" world that has been troubling him. But she has achieved a signal victory; even though she does not understand what had nearly enslaved him, her human love and concern have brought him partway out of his state of daemonic prepossession into the light of day, and he begins to find value there, as the next lines show:

> Hereat the youth
> Look'd up: a conflicting of shame and ruth
> Was in his plaited brow. . . .
>   amid his pains
> He seem'd to taste a drop of manna-dew,
> Full palatable. . . .

I, 760–767

The now well-established and strongly accentuated opposition in the poem between the lure of the daemonic and the appeal of the actual, with the protagonist beginning to move toward the latter, provides the over-all context needed for perception of the meaning and significance of the famous passage concerning "fellowship with essence," which comes next. That is, juxtaposed against the quest for daemonic pleasure, the search for value and reality indicated in the passage appears to be an ascending search for these chiefly in the areas of the normal human consciousness and its customary objects, not in a realm apart from humanity, until at the top of

the scale he admits his "stedfast aim" to love an immortal
and to explore that experience (I, 848). Endymion is trying to
have things both ways: he is trying to turn from engulfing
daemonic ecstasy to the satisfactions of customary human
experience and yet continue his search for something higher
though not yet fully understood. Also he is trying to make
Peona think that he has already given up his out-of-this-world
prepossessions. The passage is in the form of a long speech by
Endymion to Peona, ostensibly an attempt by him to quiet her
fears for him and to convince her that he still has his balance,
that he still has genuine interests in the actual world of men,
and that these interests still yield some satisfactions.

Coming immediately after the last quoted passage, his
speech begins:

> 'Peona! ever have I long'd to slake
> My thirst for the world's praises: nothing base,
> No merely slumberous phantasm, could unlace
> The stubborn canvas for my voyage prepar'd—
>
> .   .   .   .
>
> yet my higher hope
> Is of too wide, too rainbow-large a scope,
> To fret at myriads of earthly wrecks.'
>
> I, 769–776

Then he puts the fundamental question with which the passage deals—the question of what constitutes happiness. It is a
question that has been prepared for and anticipated in Peona's
continual plea that he give up his occult longings and try to
find happiness in the activities of ordinary life:

> Wherein lies happiness? In that which becks
> Our ready minds to fellowship divine,

> A fellowship with essence; till we shine,
> Full alchemiz'd, and free of space.
>
> I, 777–780

Although the key phrases here were last-minute emendations (see note 6 above) sent to the publisher while the poem was in press, Endymion at this point in the story could understandably express this expectation; in the course of the action he learns that he can never be "free of space," for he finds the ideal only in the actual at the end. But now the wording of the phrase suggests that he meant the mind's "fellowship with essence" to consist in vaguely mystical cognitions without a precise object or definite content, and this unfortunate effect is heightened by the ensuing "Behold/ The clear religion of heaven," which refers not to the heaven of mystical Christianity but to the early Greek religion, with its conception of a world that is alive, beautiful, and concrete, filled with living creatures of all kinds inhabiting tree, mountain, and river. Fifteen lines later there is another potentially misleading statement that again blurs his description of aesthetic empathy ("Negative Capability").[8] Having termed this union a "oneness" in line 796, he then adds carelessly, "and our state/ Is like a floating spirit's," which again makes the whole matter seem vaguely mystical and "flighty."

But the great bulk and core of the passage presents a conception of the various gradations of happiness derived from experiencing the "essence" of the chief beauties and joys in this world of phenomena and humanity so intensely and fully that they nearly blot out the consciousness of self. There is nothing at all that can be called a mystical flight in it until the last stage, the fifth, comes up with its symbolism of the

[8] See Chapter I, note 9.

moon and light. But the four earlier stages are nonetheless neo-Platonic, except that love is placed higher than friendship, for altogether they constitute the usual escalation, which is virtually always a plan of ascent in this world to something higher that is out of it. One thing that is amiss, though, is that Endymion has become too deeply involved too early with what is supposed to symbolize the ultimate ideal in the fifth stage, the moon goddess; and this factor operates strongly to deflect the escalation into the daemonic instead, as will be seen.

There are four stages in the "fellowship with essence" in this world.[9] The first (lines 781–786) is made up of the cognition of beautiful objects in nature to the point of self-oblivion—"a rose leaf," "music's kiss," and the sound of wind. The second (lines 787–797) consists of a similar experiencing of the beauties in art and myth:

> Then old songs waken from enclouded tombs;
> Old ditties sigh above their father's grave;
> Ghosts of melodious prophecyings rave
> Round every spot where trod Apollo's foot;
> Bronze clarions awake, and faintly bruit,
> Where long ago a Giant Battle was;
> And, from the turf, a lullaby doth pass
> In every place where infant Orpheus slept.

[9] Professor Ford was surely correct (see note 2 above) when he designated "essence" in the passage to mean the constituent reality of concrete objects and "oneness" to mean aesthetic empathy, but he did not sufficiently take account of their arrangement in a somewhat typical Platonic or neo-Platonic escalation and of Endymion's declared intention to seek a love union with an immortal (I, 848–849), who turns out to be Cynthia, a symbol of light and the last "leap" in the escalation out of this world and into ultimate reality. Professor Finney (*The Evolution of Keats's Poetry*) does not distinguish between stage four (mortal love) and stage five (immortal love or love of the ideal), but this distinction is very clearly made in the poem (I, 843–857).

Feel we these things?—that moment have we stept
Into a sort of oneness. . . .

I, 787–796

That is, when we deeply feel these things, we achieve a "oneness" of our minds with the concrete, actual, ever-present beauty of our world in a cognitive union that is richly satisfying and destructive of self-preoccupation—i.e., "self-destroying" (I, 799). That this oneness is self-destroying is re-emphasized by what comes next, giving the third stage, which is friendship carried to the point of self-abnegation:

> But there are
> Richer entanglements, enthralments far
> More self-destroying, leading, by degrees,
> To the chief intensity: the crown of these
> Is made of love and friendship, and sits high
> Upon the forehead of humanity.
> All its more ponderous and bulky worth
> Is friendship, whence there ever issues forth
> A steady splendour. . . .

I, 797–805

The fourth and highest stage in the mortal world is noble and pure-minded love between the sexes, which is most "self-destroying" of all in its power to carry the lover out of himself through union with the beloved into union with love itself, affording an insight into its essential substance:

> but at the tip-top,
> There hangs by unseen film, an orbed drop
> Of light, and that is love: its influence,
> Thrown in our eyes, genders a novel sense,
> At which we start and fret; till in the end,

Melting into its radiance, we blend,
Mingle, and so become a part of it,—
Nor with aught else can our souls interknit
So wingedly: when we combine therewith,
Life's self is nourish'd by its proper pith.

I, 805–814

This essence of love as stated here at its apex is still conceived as existing in the mortal sphere; it is assigned neither to the vague world of dreams nor to the world of absolutes apart from men and objects. "Essence" does not necessarily mean "absolute," for Aristotle had his essences right here amidst minds and objects. Neither the immediate context of the passage concerned nor the over-all context afforded by the main line of the action in the poems indicates that Keats meant anything "other worldly" here.

In addition, what Endymion says next about the matter shows—fully and conclusively, I think, in conjunction with the previous evidence—that Keats kept his conception of the essence of love, *up to this point in the passage*, within the normal human sphere of minds and objects, for it is not represented as an emanation from an entity outside that sphere:

For I have ever thought that it [love] might bless
The world with benefits unknowingly.

I, 826–827

And immediately thereafter he strongly implies that in essence love is a part of the great organic power that brings the swelling fruitage, richness, and ripeness in the world later celebrated in his *To Autumn*, a poem which in its full implications is one of his strongest rejections of all that is abstract:

Just so may love, although 'tis understood
The mere commingling of passionate breath,
Produce more than our searching witnesseth:
What I know not: but who, of men, can tell
That flowers would bloom, or that green fruit would swell
To melting pulp, that fish would have bright mail,
The earth its dower of river, wood, and vale,
The meadows runnels, runnels pebble-stones,
The seed its harvest, or the lute its tones,
Tones ravishment, or ravishment its sweet,
If human souls did never kiss and greet?

I, 832–842

This concept of a great organic totality unfolding in myriad forms is the metaphysic that supports the world view Keats later set forth in *Hyperion*. That the love he speaks of above is earthly, though it has the power to make man participate in some kind of immortality, appears certain from the next lines, in which Endymion in effect glances back over it and designates it earthly while preparing to reject the pursuit of fame, which Peona has urged upon him, and to proclaim that there is still another kind of love, far more worthwhile than fame, which must surely give even greater benefits and "measure of content," he thinks, than the love described in the fourth stage of the "fellowship with essence."

This disclosure, in fact an admission of something which she had suspected but which he had almost dispelled from her mind, startles Peona (I, 850), as it may startle all who have been equating the fourth stage in the scale with his love of the moon goddess; for his love of her is only now brought in *after* the love which he had discussed up to this point and, be it noted, brought in rather hypothetically. His now-admitted love of the goddess is represented as something which he only *hopes* to discover to be a great reality, and on this basis he is attempting to justify to Peona his love for an immortal, which he later admits is "impious" (II, 183–184), as Peona knows and he ignores:

> 'Now, if this earthly love has power to make
> Men's being mortal, immortal; to shake
> Ambition from their memories, and brim
> Their measure of content; what merest whim,
> Seems all this poor endeavour after fame,
> To one, who keeps within his stedfast aim
> A love immortal, an immortal too.
> Look not so wilder'd. . . .'
>
> I, 843–850

All this will now become clear: he means that genuine earthly love, the fourth stage of the fellowship with essence, enables men's mortality to partake of immortality through allowing men to participate in the great process of real being, in the total living reality unfolding in the universe. Since this is so, he argues, the externals of earthly fame, which Peona has urged him to pursue, are inconsequential to a man like himself who is grasping at something even higher than earthly love, who is keeping his steadfast aim upon "A love immortal, an immortal too," as he says above. That is, he is seeking an instance of love that is immortal because it entails union by a mortal with an immortal creature. This is to be his step beyond the earthly and into the ultimate ideal, the Absolute. But at this point something becomes startlingly apparent that has been the case from the beginning: whatever she is in mythology, Keats does not at all successfully delineate the immortal Cynthia here *as symbol*. Nor does he ever, before or after. To Endymion and to most readers she remains until near the end an object of daemonic fascination strongly sexual, hardly suggesting values beyond herself at all. We cannot know how much this deficiency resulted from Keats's well-known lack of full control of his poem and from his groping by means of it toward things not yet clear to him; but the idea that Endymion's pursuit of Cynthia was chiefly a mistaken one seems deliberately intended and sustained until its emphatic rejection near the end of the poem (IV, 636–655). Keats had read much idealized eroticism in Renaissance poetry, but he had not learned to turn the trick himself. We can sense that Endymion is to some extent turning her into a daemonic agent, but on the other hand we cannot discover how much of her intended import he is missing in his pursuit of her. At her lofty point in the scale of ascent the daemonic repeatedly enters and superimposes itself upon the ideal, with the result that the main action takes a different direction from here on. The Cynthia-Endymion love story becomes an interplay of the daemonic (centering in his pursuit of Cynthia) against the actual (represented by Peona and the Indian maid). Therefore the humanizing episodes that intervene (Alpheus-Arethusa, Glaucus-Scylla, Indian maid–Endymion) do not logically constitute steps in an escalation that leads toward union with Cynthia, but one that appears to lead distinctly *away* from such a consummation. From the time when Cynthia is given the symbolic position at the top of the escalation but without satisfactory accreditation in that position, this poem in basic content and development becomes almost entirely daemonic and anti-daemonic rather than neo-Platonic; and as thus considered the episodes in the humanization of the hero fit into the whole functionally, as they patently do not when the continuance of a neo-Platonic interpretation beyond this point in Book I is forcibly insisted upon in the clear absence of a sufficiently compelling symbol at the top of the escalatory framework. Well has it been said that Keats changed his plan of development after beginning the poem;[10] whatever the causes, he used the neo-Platonic materials only part of the way or in a different way from the established pattern. But the failure of Cynthia to "come through" as an effective symbol of the ideal all along is in line with Endymion's emphatic rejection of his pursuit of her as "a nothing" just before the end. When looked upon primarily as a neo-Platonic poem, it must of necessity be deemed an abortive one, but it is much more effective and significant when viewed as a poem depicting a conflict between the daemonic and anti-daemonic, the latter including the actual.

The love of Endymion for Cynthia is "impious" (II, 184) in its intrinsic nature (mortal for immortal) and daemonic in the degree and effects of its intensity, completely dissociating him from his usual interests and preoccupations. It brings him a Dionysian frenzy of involvement with the loved object itself that possesses him utterly, not a resulting serene contemplation of the spiritual entity which that object is supposed to symbolize. Prior to telling Peona about the scale of the "fellowship with essence," Endymion has three times experienced this engulfing involvement and afterward has felt the deadly aftermath, when the usual objects and pursuits of mortal life lose their appeal. In the neo-Platonic ascent one does not despise the earthly stepping stones when passing on to the higher sphere to which they lead, certainly not in the works of Keats's major teacher in these matters, Edmund Spenser. But Endymion does not yet understand the significance and conse-

---

[10] Sperry, "The Allegory of *Endymion*," pp. 45, 46, 52.

quences of this daemonic love disguised as heavenly, as he will learn to do in the course of the action of the poem. Now he is engrossed in his effort to justify his impiety to his shocked sister:

> Look not so wilder'd; for these things are true,
> And never can be born of atomies
> That buzz about our slumbers, like brain-flies,
> Leaving us fancy-sick. No, no, I'm sure,
> My restless spirit never could endure
> To brood so long upon one luxury,
> Unless it did, though fearfully, espy
> A hope beyond the shadow of a dream.
>
> I, 850–857

Here he is pleading on good ground as far as he understands; both daemonic experience and actual experience are concrete and vivid—not indistinct and shadowy, like abstractions or something seen in dreams. The significant difference is that actual experience does not bring the deadening aftermath in which everything else pales into the unpalatable, as is the case with daemonic experience. As he has stated, genuine earthly love brings fulfillment that is "self-destroying" but does not cloy—"unsating food" he has called it (I, 816). He understands, as Peona does, that this daemonic love may be dangerous for mortals and is "impious" (II, 183–184), but he thinks he can "get by" with it unscathed. Throughout one of Keats's major sources, Lyly's prose play *Endimion, the Man in the Moon*, the protagonist's love for the goddess is steadily represented as something which he knows to be beyond his mortal sphere and therefore forbidden.[11] It is similarly represented in

---

[11] On one level of the complex allegory in Lyly's play she represents Queen Elizabeth.

Keats's poem, with terrible consequences built into the heart of the experience itself. Endymion's rejection of the pursuit of Cynthia is usually termed a puzzling failure to find the ideal in the "heavenly." In truth, it is a rejection of the daemonic. He *has* to reject the daemonic in order to escape destruction and consequently has to reject the pursuit of *her* for she has become the object and cause of his daemonic enthrallment, even though he himself has transformed her into that. Near the end of the poem after Endymion's full initiation into knowledge of the effects of daemonic experience, he voices his emphatic recantation:

> O I have been
> Presumptuous against love, against the sky,
> Against all elements, against the tie
> Of mortals each to each, against the blooms
> Of flowers, rush of rivers, and the tombs
> Of heroes gone! Against his proper glory
> Has my own soul conspired. . . .
> *There never liv'd a mortal man, who bent*
> *His appetite beyond his natural sphere,*
> *But starv'd and died.*
>
> IV, 638–648 (italics added)

But between that scene late in Book IV and the present one concluding Book I there are significant developments in Endymion's subsequent experiences that lead step by step to that surprising event and make it fully probable and acceptable; for it is in truth a recantation of the daemonic in favor of the claims of humanity and the beauty of the human world. Here at the end of Book I Endymion knows only that his three experiences with the moon maiden have been brief and bewildering though ecstatic. One of them (I, 943–971), which suggests the core of the later poem, *La Belle Dame sans Merci*, takes place when an unknown feminine voice lures him to a cave "secreter/ Than the Isle of Delos" and promises him "sigh-warm kisses" and other erotic delights if he will enter. But shortly after he enters, all vanishes, just as happens to the knight in *La Belle Dame*.

Book I ends quite understandably with Endymion's reiterating his promise to Peona to give up these esoteric pursuits and to feel more interest and satisfaction in the universal things of earth:

> Ah! where
> Are those swift moments? Whither are they fled?
> I'll smile no more, Peona; nor will wed
> Sorrow the way to death; but patiently
> Bear up against it: so farewel, sad sigh;
> And come instead demurest meditation,
> To occupy me wholly, and to fashion
> My pilgrimage for the world's dusky brink.
> No more will I count over, link by link,
> My chain of grief: no longer strive to find
> A half-forgetfulness in mountain wind
> Blustering about my ears: aye, thou shalt see,
> Dearest of sisters, what my life shall be;
> What a calm round of hours shall make my days.
>
> I, 970–983

II

After a brief invocation Book II of the poem begins with direct reference to this vow. The poet asks the crucial question about it and gives the answer:

> Brain-sick shepherd-prince,
> What promise hast thou faithful guarded since
> The day of sacrifice? Or, have new sorrows
> Come with the constant dawn upon thy morrows?
> Alas! 'tis his old grief.
>
> II, 44–48

That is, Endymion has not yet been able to keep the vow, but has fallen back into his occult longings. In this, the first scene, he follows a butterfly to a fountain by a cavern's mouth, where the nymph who inhabits the fountain pities him and then prophesies:

> thou must wander far
> In other regions, past the scanty bar
> To mortal steps, before thou cans't be ta'en
> From every wasting sigh, from every pain,
> Into the gentle bosom of thy love.
>
> II, 123–127

Small wonder, then, that he is now cruelly torn between the worth of the actual world, which he can dimly perceive but cannot share, and the surging pull of his daemonic love, that still beckons:

> But this is human life: the war, the deeds,
> The disappointment, the anxiety,
> Imagination's struggles, far and nigh,
> All human; bearing in themselves this good,
> That they are still the air, the subtle food,
> To make us feel existence,[12] and to show

---

[12] Cf. Keats's journal letter to George and Georgiana Keats, February 14 to May 3, 1819: "Call the world if you Please 'The vale of Soul-making.' Then you will find out the use of the world. . . . I say '*Soul-making*' Soul as dis-

How quiet death is. Where soil is men grow,
Whether to weeds or flowers; but for me,
There is no depth to strike in: I can see
Nought earthly worth my compassing. . . .
I'd rather stand upon this misty peak,
With not a thing to sigh for, or to seek,
But the soft shadow of my thrice-seen love,
Than be—I care not what. O meekest dove
Of heaven! O Cynthia, ten-times bright and fair!

.   .   .   .

O be propitious, nor severely deem
My madness impious; for, by all the stars
That tend thy bidding, I do think the bars
That kept my spirit in are burst[13]—that I
Am sailing with thee through the dizzy sky!
How beautiful thou art! The world how deep!
How tremulous-dazzlingly the wheels sweep
Around their axle! Then these gleaming reins,
How lithe!

II, 153–191

These last lines show that Endymion, through intense
concentration on his memory of the goddess, has conjured her
up before him and has gone into an ecstasy of daemonic union

---

tinguished from an Intelligence—There may be intelligencies or sparks of the
divinity in millions—but they are not Souls till they acquire identities, till each
one is personally itself. . . . How then are Souls to be made? How then are
these sparks which are God to have identity given them—so as ever to possess
a bliss peculiar to each one's individual existence? How, but by the medium of
a world like this. . . . Do you not see how necessary a World of Pains and
troubles is to school an Intelligence and make it a soul? A place where the
heart must feel and suffer in a thousand diverse ways!" (*Letters*, II, 102).
[13] Cf. *I Stood Tip-toe*, 190–191: "Ah! surely he had burst our mortal bars;/
Into some wond'rous region he had gone." Cf. also *Endymion*, II, 124–125,
quoted above: "past the scanty bar/ To mortal steps."

with her in an engulfing, trance-like state. But almost immediately this glory is shattered:

> 'When this thy chariot attains
> Its airy goal, haply some bower veils
> Those twilight eyes? Those eyes!—my spirit fails—
> Dear goddess, help! or the wide-gaping air
> Will gulph me—help!'—At this with madden'd stare,
> And lifted hands, and trembling lips he stood.
>
> II, 191–196

He now finds himself back by the cavern's mouth, where in actuality he had been all the time, "froze to senseless stone" but for a voice that commands him:

> 'Descend,
> Young mountaineer! descend where alleys bend
> Into the sparry hollows of the world!
>
> .   .   .   .
>
> He ne'er is crown'd
> With immortality, who fears to follow
> Where airy voices lead. . . .'
>
> II, 202–214

The intermingled daemonic beauty and terror of "the fearful deep" into which he descends is at first described in verse reminiscent of the "darkness visible" of Milton's Hell in *Paradise Lost:*

> Dark, nor light,
> The region; nor bright, nor sombre wholly,
> But mingled up; a gleaming melancholy;
> A dusky empire and its diadems;
> One faint eternal eventide of gems.
>
> II, 221–225

Thereafter the rendering of this nether region resembles descriptions of underground chambers and passageways which Keats scored in the old Portuguese prose romance *Palmerin of England*.[14] Endymion passes through a "marble gallery," a "mimic temple," beyond which he glimpses a statue of Diana, and many winding passages, before he wearily sits down on the marble floor beside "the maw/ Of a wide outlet, fathomless and dim" (II, 271–272). As "new wonders ceas'd to float before" him and "thoughts of self came on," a new development emerges in Keats's uses of the daemonic in *Endymion* and a major turning point in the structure of its action; for here Endymion experiences for the first time the anti-daemonic. There surges up in him, now cut off from sensory contact with his usual world, an extraordinarily powerful longing to feel sensation, to revel in the normal, pleasing, wholesome, ordinary world of natural phenomena. This response is strikingly different from the usual aftermath of a daemonic experience, in which a person finds that the plain joys of our common lot have faded into the unpalatable; now Endymion feels an overpowering longing for them that is augmented by a new element of revulsion against the daemonic experience itself:

> What misery most drowningly doth sing
> In lone Endymion's ear, now he has raught
> The goal of consciousness? Ah, 'tis the thought,
> The deadly feel of solitude: for lo!
> He cannot see the heavens, nor the flow
> Of rivers, nor the hill-flowers running wild
>
>   .   .   .   .
>
>   nor felt, nor prest

[14] See Chapter I, note 11.

Cool grass, nor tasted the fresh slumberous air;
But far from such companionship to wear
An unknown time, surcharg'd with grief, away,

    .   .   .   .

Warming and glowing strong in the belief
Of help from Dian: so that when again
He caught her airy form, thus did he plain,
Moving more near the while. 'O Haunter chaste
Of river sides, and woods, and heathy waste,
Where with thy silver bow and arrows keen
Art thou now forested?'

II, 281–305

Catching sight of the statue of Diana again, he apostrophizes her as one continually "finding in our green earth sweet contents" and implores her to help him to get back to that earth:

        'Ah, if to thee
It feels Elysian, how rich to me,
An exil'd mortal, sounds its pleasant name!
Within my breast there lives a choking flame—
O let me cool it the zephyr-boughs among!
A homeward fever parches up my tongue—
O let me slake it at the running springs!
Upon my ear a noisy nothing rings—
O let me once more hear the linnet's note!

    .   .   .   .

O think how I should love a bed of flowers!—
Young goddess! let me see my native bowers!
Deliver me from this rapacious deep!'

II, 314–332

Thus, robbed of the sensations that make up his feeling of well-being in the everyday world, he yearns for them again. Heretofore, in his juxtaposing the joys of the daemonic against those of the actual world, Endymion has never admitted that the latter could bear up in worth against the former; now he places such high value upon the latter that we can properly designate it the anti-daemonic, a revulsion against the Dionysian, frenzied ecstacies of the daemonic and a strongly increased satisfaction with the ordinary world of men and things.

His new-found preference for the joys of common humanity is based purely on aesthetic grounds, *not* on moral considerations, although a distinct spiritual gain eventually results from it. In the structure of the action this incident marks the point at which the protagonist begins to get the better of his daemonic prepossessions; he backslides considerably after this, but from here on he makes progress toward acceptance of our mortal lot and final rejection of the daemonic in the end. This is the beginning of the humanization of the hero as set forth in the poem, and it indicates the particular nature of his spiritualization during the rest of the action—a spiritualization that derives nothing from his quest for a neo-Platonic ideal or from his pursuit of Cynthia, whether or not the latter is taken to represent the former. He is spiritualized through his relationships with humanity in the world of the actual.

This paradoxical power of the daemonic to impel Endymion toward its opposite—the anti-daemonic, in which the plain beauty of actuality assumes new value—helps to set off sharply the significance of his meeting with Alpheus and Arethusa and also the more important encounter with Glaucus and Scylla, two highly important later incidents in the plot. The relationship of these to the anti-daemonic would be seen more clearly if Keats had not brought in two other incidents first: the Venus and Adonis story, and then Endymion's sexual consummation with the unknown maiden. These incidents are indeed pertinent and functional, however. The Venus-Adonis story is inversely parallel to the Endymion-Cynthia story now in progress, for just as mortal Endymion pines for immortal Cynthia, so immortal Venus had pined for mortal Adonis and therefore quite understandably asks her son Cupid to favor Endymion's love and prophesies success for him: "Endymion! one day thou wilt be blest" (II, 573). He does become blessed eventually, though not quite in the way suggested here.

This prophecy encourages Endymion to continue his daemonic quest, for shortly afterward in the bower to which he was carried by an eagle he yearns for his goddess love with renewed zeal (II, 686 ff.). His ensuing sexual consummation in a dream with the unknown maiden is subtly in harmony with the preceding story of the love of Venus for mortal Adonis, for the unknown maiden is obviously the moon goddess Cynthia in disguise, and she now voices the same consuming passion for Endymion (II, 774–815) that Venus had voiced for Adonis, although she refuses to reveal to him her identity. Endymion clearly shows before the consummation that he does not know whether she is mortal or immortal (II, 753–755); and because he is in a swoon afterward, he does not hear her admissions of Olympian connections in her passionate ravings. The whole episode therefore has an important relationship with the now-emerging anti-daemonic element in the poem, for the episode shows that he can still love a supposedly mortal maid and is not yet hopelessly enslaved beyond recall in the remote corridors of the daemonic. He is suspended between two worlds, and these two worlds in opposition are now becoming clearly distinguishable as the actual against the daemonic rather than the actual against the ideal. Keats speaks of the incident in beautiful lines that suggest the elemental nature of the kind of experience which poetry can capture:

> 'tis a ditty
> Not of these days, but long ago 'twas told
> By a cavern wind unto a forest old;
> And then the forest told it in a dream
> To a sleeping lake, whose cool and level gleam
> A poet caught. . . .
>
> II, 829–834

When Endymion awakens, he is clearly shown to be suspended between these two worlds, recalling the previous joys of the actual (now somewhat faded) but still preferring the daemonic:

> Endymion sat down, and 'gan to ponder
> On all his life: his youth, up to the day
> When 'mid acclaim, and feasts, and garlands gay,
> He stept upon his shepherd throne: the look
> Of his white palace in wild forest nook,
> And all the revels he had lorded there:
> Each tender maiden whom he once thought fair,
>
> .   .   .   .
>
>   Then the spur
> Of the old bards to mighty deeds: his plans
> To nurse the golden age 'mong shepherd clans:
>
> .   .   .   .
>
>   and his wanderings all,
> Until into the earth's deep maw he rush'd:
> Then all its buried magic, till it flush'd

High with excessive love. 'And now,' thought he,
'How long must I remain in jeopardy
Of blank amazements that amaze no more?
Now I have tasted her sweet soul to the core
All other depths are shallow. . . .
                              other light,
Though it be quick and sharp enough to blight
The Olympian eagle's vision, is dark.'

                                    II, 886–911

But at this point he hears the sound of the rushing waters of the river god Alpheus pursuing the nymph Arethusa, whom he loves, and pleading with her to yield. Following the sound, Endymion soon hears Arethusa, fearful of displeasing the goddess Diana if she yields, resisting Alpheus' entrancing plea in words which reveal that she is in precisely the same situation as Endymion himself—torn between the daemonic lure of the river god and the quiet appeal of the satisfactions of her ordinary life before she knew any other:

                        —Alas, I burn,
I shudder—gentle river, get thee hence.
Alpheus! thou enchanter! every sense
Of mine was once made perfect in these woods.
Fresh breezes, bowery lawns, and innocent floods,
Ripe fruits, and lonely couch, contentment gave;
But ever since I heedlessly did lave
In thy deceitful stream, a panting glow
Grew strong within me: wherefore serve me so,
And call it love? Alas, 'twas cruelty.
Not once more did I close my happy eye
Amid the thrushes' song.

                                    II, 963–974

In this expression of the power of the daemonic to bring about a higher evaluation of the anti-daemonic, there is a significant advance over the previous one, spoken by Endymion; for here is expressed for the first time the idea that daemonic ecstasy may not be worth its price, since that price must be paid in lessened capacity for the ever-present joys of the ordinary world, which Keats considered indispensable for mortals.

Although Alpheus and Arethusa are nonmortal creatures, they live among human beings in the mortal world, not amid the Olympian hierarchy; and Endymion instantly feels a deep and moving human sympathy for them in their plight:

> On the verge
> Of that dark gulph he wept, and said: 'I urge
> Thee, gentle Goddess of my pilgrimage,[15]
> By our eternal hopes, to soothe, to assuage,
> If thou art powerful, these lovers' pains;
> And make them happy in some happy plains.'
>
> II, 1012–1017

This sympathy proves to be "other light" that is not darkness and "other depths" that are not shallow, if we may borrow his own recent words, for it turns his attention temporarily from his daemonic quest to the world of mortals and thereby helps to prepare him for the more powerfully humanizing encounter

[15] Endymion may mean that Cynthia is the goddess of his pilgrimage (see III, 43, and II, 573–575), but Cynthia's earthly self, Diana, the major mode of this triform goddess, has just served in that capacity at a crucial time (II, 302–332, 339–343), and she (among other functions) was the goddess of young men in their growing up. Keats's copy of Lemprière's *Classical Dictionary* explains the identity of the threefold goddess fully in the discussions of both Diana and Hecate. However, Venus also appears to be directing events in the poem (II, 437, 573–575, and *passim*), and increasingly assumes this role, which at one point she claims (III, 903–909), as the poem progresses and Cynthia appears more and more to be an object of daemonic prepossession. After all, this is a love story, and Venus is the goddess of love.

with Glaucus in Book III, in which he not only feels sympathy with a human creature in daemonic enthrallment but also participates actively in his rescue.

III

After an inept opening to Book III, Endymion's wanderings through the undersea world (already foretold, II, 123–127) are presented in appealing lines of simple verse which stress the desolate apartness there from the human world, as if to set off in sharp contrast the humanizing effect of the meeting with Glaucus soon to come:

> Far had he roam'd,
> With nothing save the hollow vast, that foam'd
> Above, around, and at his feet; save things
> More dead than Morpheus' imaginings;
> Old rusted anchors, helmets, breast-plates large
> Of gone sea-warriors; brazen beaks and targe;
> Rudders that for a hundred years had lost
> The sway of human hand. . . .
>
> III, 119–126

Thoughts of the moon itself, of his moon goddess, and of his "nearer bliss" with the unknown maid mingle in his mind as he pursues his solitary way through the strange region. Then comes his first sight of Glaucus suddenly blotting out his memories of the goddess, whose beauty he is about to swear to. Keats's description suggests that Glaucus blends with the waving mosses and cavernous shadows of the underwater world as if he were a part of the rock formation and flora there. Keats's skill in presenting all this goes far to minimize the incredibility of it for the moment:

He saw far in the concave green of the sea
An old man sitting calm and peacefully.
Upon a weeded rock this old man sat,
And his white hair was awful, and a mat
Of weeds were cold beneath his cold thin feet;
And, ample as the largest winding-sheet,
A cloak of blue wrapp'd up his aged bones,
O'erwrought with symbols by the deepest groans
Of ambitious magic: every ocean-form
Was woven in with black distinctness; storm,
And calm, and whispering, and hideous roar,
Quicksand, and whirlpool, and deserted shore.

III, 191–202

Awakening as from a trance and with the cry "Thou art the man," Glaucus announces that Endymion is destined to free him from his cold, watery prison. Endymion's initial aversion and defiance melt away when the gray-haired creature weeps. He begins to tell Endymion his story in spare, plain, unadorned narrative verse of high quality which helps to indicate by its nature the kind of simple happiness that the speaker is recalling:

I was a fisher once, upon this main,
And my boat danc'd in every creek and bay;
Rough billows were my home by night and day,—
The sea-gulls not more constant; for I had
No housing from the storm and tempests mad,
But hollow rocks,—and they were palaces
Of silent happiness, of slumberous ease:

. . . . .

But the crown
Of all my life was utmost quietude:

More did I love to lie in cavern rude,
Keeping in wait whole days for Neptune's voice,
And if it came at last, hark, and rejoice!
There blush'd no summer eve but I would steer
My skiff along green shelving coasts, to hear
The shepherd's pipe come clear from aery steep,
Mingled with ceaseless bleatings of his sheep.

III, 318–360

But this idyl of wholesome, simple bliss that never cloys was suddenly shattered. Glaucus "began/ To feel distemper'd longings" (III, 374–375), which were increased by the coyness of Scylla, whom he loved "to the very white of truth." When his passion became unbearable, he sought out Circe, thinking she might find some relief for him, but instead she cunningly turned Glaucus' affections toward herself and displaced Scylla in his eyes (III, 460 ff.). In his infatuation with Circe, Glaucus had come under a daemonic enthrallment even more complete and engulfing than Endymion's with Cynthia. Glaucus now tells of it in lines and images which clearly point forward to *La Belle Dame sans Merci* and show that Keats had the core of that poem in mind as early as 1817 when he was writing *Endymion:*

With tears, and smiles, and honey-words she wove
A net whose thraldom was more bliss than all
The range of flower'd Elysium.

                .   .   .   .

    Who could resist? Who in this universe?
She did so breathe ambrosia; so immerse
My fine existence in a golden clime.
She took me like a child of suckling time,
And cradled me in roses. Thus condemn'd,

The current of my former life was stemm'd,
And to this arbitrary queen of sense
I bow'd a tranced vassal: nor would thence
Have mov'd, even though Amphion's harp had woo'd
Me back to Scylla o'er the billows rude.

III, 426–462

Glaucus is in exactly the condition of Endymion when he had said after his early enthralling experience with Cynthia, "I see nothing earthly worth my compassing," and in precisely the condition of the knight in *La Belle Dame* at the end of that poem, although the elfin lady therein is no Circe: after his enchantress is gone and even after he has seen the vision of her other victims, the "pale kings and princes" whose lips "with horrid warning gaped wide," this knight cannot but continue to search for her in vain, unable either to regain her or to resume the course of ordinary life, for its simple joys have paled into insignificance because of the greater ecstasies that he had known in his daemonic love:

And this is why I sojourn here,
   Alone and palely loitering,
Though the sedge has wither'd from the lake,
   And no birds sing.

Glaucus voices somewhat similar feelings when Circe deserts him:

'One morn she left me sleeping: half awake
I sought for her smooth arms and lips, to slake
My greedy thirst. . . .
But she was gone. Whereat the barbed shafts
Of disappointment stuck in me so sore,

That out I ran and search'd the forest o'er.
Wandering about in pine and cedar gloom
Damp awe assail'd me. . . .'

III, 477–484

One function of his encounter with Glaucus is to afford Endymion the rare opportunity to witness in another creature's life what is in process of befalling himself: the course and effects of a daemonic prepossession that threatens to carry him beyond the bounds which are safe for mortals, which Keats had mentioned before *Endymion* and will mention later. The Glaucus story also parallels another crucial strain in that of Endymion to some degree; in surmounting his fascination with Cynthia he grows toward reconciliation with actuality just as Glaucus does in surmounting his enthrallment to Circe—a significant aspect of the spiritualization through humanization[16] of both Glaucus and Endymion, although Cynthia is no Circe. At this point Glaucus tells of hearing a man who had been turned into an elephant begging Circe for death as a release from his terrible plight, and then continues the account of his initiation:

'That curst magician's name fell icy numb
Upon my wild conjecturing: truth had come
Naked and sabre-like against my heart.

. . . . .

Think, my deliverer, how desolate

[16] Jacob D. Wigod has aptly designated Keats's single "deep and abiding idealistic faith" to be "spiritualization-through-humanization," which neatly indicates the nature of Endymion's initiation in the course of the poem. "The Meaning of *Endymion*," *PMLA*, LXVIII (September, 1953), 790n. Cf. Thorpe, *The Mind of John Keats*, pp. 60, 62. Stuart Sperry also frequently voices essentially this view (see note 3 above).

My waking must have been! disgust, and hate,
And terrors manifold divided me.'

III, 555–562

Similarly desolate later is the condition of the knight in *La Belle Dame* when he finds himself on the cold hillside after the termination of his enthrallment. Further suggestions of this knight's condition appear in the curse which Circe now pronounces upon Glaucus:

'here I chase
'Eternally away from thee all bloom
'Of youth. . . .
'Thou shalt not go the way of aged men;
'But live and wither. . . .'

III, 590–597

Keats narrates the termination of Glaucus' adventure with Circe in terms which suggest the refreshing effect of actual experience to one just emerging from the aftermath of the daemonic:

In this guise
Enforced, at the last by ocean's foam
I found me; by my fresh, my native home.
Its tempering coolness, to my life akin,
Came salutary as I waded in;
And, with a blind voluptuous rage, I gave
Battle to the swollen billow-ridge. . . .

III, 606–612

Glaucus learns the full extent of the curse upon him when he finds a scroll in the hand of a drowned man shortly after a shipwreck. When Glaucus reads the scroll aloud to him, Endymion learns that his own fate is now inextricably bound up with that of Glaucus, here revealed as a seeker after essence like Endymion. In part the scroll reveals what Glaucus must do to escape death in the watery prison in which Circe's curse has lodged him:

> '*If he explores all forms and substances*
> *Straight homeward to their symbol-essences;*
> *He shall not die. Moreover, and in chief,*
>
> . . . . .
>
> *—all lovers tempest-tost,*
> *And in the savage overwhelming lost,*
> *He shall deposit side by side, until*
> *Time's creeping shall the dreary space fulfil:*
> *Which done, and all these labours ripened,*
> *A youth, by heavenly power lov'd and led,*
> *Shall stand before him; whom he shall direct*
> *How to consummate all. The youth elect*
> *Must do the thing, or both will be destroy'd.*'
>
> III, 699–711

Here the scroll ends, but the text of the poem continues:

> 'Then,' cried the young Endymion, overjoy'd,
> 'We are twin brothers in this destiny!
> Say, I intreat thee, what achievement high
> Is, in this restless world, for me reserv'd.
> What! if from thee my wandering feet had swerv'd,
> Had we both perish'd?'
>
> III, 712–717

In willingly accepting the role of deliverer of Glaucus and in thereby linking himself to Glaucus in active sympathy, Endymion feels a salutary return of joy in actions and feelings like those in the common human lot. His spontaneous elation stems from this wholehearted participation in these events rather than from daemonic transports of sequestered ecstasy. This is surely the major turning point in his conflict between the daemonic and the actual as well as in the more hidden conflict between the daemonic and the ideal. From this point on, the daemonic does not so fully override and superimpose itself upon the ideal, and Endymion is well on the way toward discovering the ideal emerging in the actual as his humanization continues. Although the daemonic is not yet completely eclipsed, from here on it gradually wanes.

For example, after Endymion performs the rites that free Glaucus from the curse[17] and the two of them together have then reanimated Scylla and the dead lovers gathered by Glaucus during his long bondage (III, 703–705, 721–723, 735–736, 780–786), again this new note of deep joy from selfless involvement in sympathetic action is stressed:

> The two deliverers tasted a pure wine
> Of happiness. . . .
> Speechless they eyed each other, and about
> The fair assembly wander'd to and fro,
> Distracted with the richest overflow
> Of joy. . . .
>
> III, 801–806

Since the outcome of the episode shows Glaucus and Endymion saved from destruction (and the dead lovers revived), the implication is strong that deep involvement in the dae-

---

[17] III, 747–797. Chanting, Glaucus tears the scroll into small pieces, binds his blue cloak round Endymion, and strikes his wand nine times against the empty air. Then at Glaucus' direction Endymion unravels a tangled thread, winds it to a clue, and scatters pieces of the scroll upon Glaucus, upon Scylla, and upon the dead lovers.

monic leads to death but that involvement in humanity, even to self-forgetfulness, leads to spiritual life and enduring joy and hence points out the secure road to the ideal—a road to the heart of human life, not a road out of it which can easily turn into the path of daemonic prepossession and isolation. The episode is a crucial part of the process of spiritualization through humanization which constitutes the major initiation in the poem; only when the daemonic that has been impeding it begins to be overcome can this spiritualizing process develop vitally, and then it emerges into sharper relief when seen against the daemonic which it supersedes.

Moreover, from this point of vantage the immediately following hymn to Neptune and the events that occur in his palace also take on sharper effect and deeper significance; for water, rivers, and streams are among the most ancient and powerful symbols of the spiritual and elemental in human life. Coming just after the significant developments at the close of the Glaucus episode, the mighty hymn[18] to Neptune in his watery palace serves to reinforce these developments and to imply symbolically that Endymion has at last found the true road to the ideal in the archetypal in humanity. This is the road that leads on to the final events in the poem and helps to indicate their meaning. Kindred strains of thought are also implied symbolically in some of the lines that conclude Book III as Endymion awakens:

> The youth at once arose: a placid lake
> Came quiet to his eyes; and forest green,
> Cooler than all the wonders he had seen.
>
> III, 1027–30

[18] It contains some of Keats's best verse up to this time—some of it worthy of Spenser, for example lines 949–959 and 969–977, which are suggestive of Spenser though not too derivative, I think.

IV

After these developments in Book III, the events that take place in Book IV can be seen to have greater pertinence, and the structure of the poem takes on a tighter narrative focus and unity than are usually credited to it. The more significant elements in the narrative can now be brought together and their interrelationship with each other and relevance to a central design clearly discerned.

Although in the previous Glaucus episode Endymion had passed a crucial turning point in his initiation—an initiation consisting chiefly of his growing away from preoccupation with the daemonic and toward full acceptance of the human world as it is—this initiation has not been completed. He is not yet willing to give up Cynthia. However, his humanization has progressed so far that he "cannot choose" but love the Indian maid, and obviously more strongly than Cynthia. Consequently, the main structural conflict between his daemonic proclivities, centering upon Cynthia, and his growing rapprochement with the actual world, now centering around the earthly Indian maid, continue to dominate the poem as its main action moves toward a denouement clearly in line with the direction apparent just after the major turning point in the Glaucus episode in Book III. Moreover, Endymion's irresistible love of the Indian maid subtly indicates that his eschewing the daemonic and embracing the actual is about to come full circle; for she is one who has *learned to live with sorrow and to welcome it*,[19] as her little song about it indicates immediately, and she is therefore a more fully adequate representa-

---

[19] Keats could have heard of Goethe's powerful treatment of this idea in *Wilhelm Meister*, but there is much of it in Wordsworth's *Peele Castle* and *The Excursion*, the latter of which Keats read and praised excessively.

tive in the poem of the world of humanity with its pain and imperfection than has been his sister Peona, who has never had the opportunity to deal with sorrow, since her even-tempered life has never encountered it.

After the inane reinvocation in the initial lines, Book IV gets under way with Endymion hearing the plaint of the lonely Indian maid calling for help in this foreign land. Before presenting Endymion's reaction, the poet, speaking in his own right to his protagonist, tips off the reader that Endymion's coming struggle to respond to the irresistible Indian maid and still love Cynthia will be a losing battle:

> Thou, Carian lord, hadst better have been tost
> Into a whirlpool. Vanish into air,
> Warm mountaineer. . . .
> Phoebe [i.e., Cynthia] is fairer far—O gaze no more:—
> Yet if thou wilt *behold all beauty's store*,
> Behold her [Indian maid] panting in the forest grass!
>
> IV, 52–59 (italics added)

So strongly designating the Indian maid the repository of "all beauty's store" surely indicates that the love of Cynthia is not the road to the ideal. In line with all this are Endymion's words shortly afterward as he feels his emotions torn between the goddess and the maid:

> 'Goddess! I love thee not the less: from thee
> By Juno's smile I turn not—no, no, no—
>
> .   .   .   .
>
> O fond pretence—
> For both, for both my love is so immense,
> I feel my heart is cut for them in twain.'
>
> IV, 92–97

His admitting to be "fond pretence" his anguished cry that he is not turning away from Cynthia indicates that he *is* doing so and that he now knows that he is doing so even though he still feels within him the basic conflict between the two claims. Daemonic pursuits do not die easily, and this new awareness of the direction in which he is now moving is hard for him to bear despite its inevitability. He cries out to the Indian maid:

> 'I am full of grief—
> Grief born of thee, young angel! fairest thief!
> Who stolen hast away the wings wherewith
> I was to top the heavens.'
>
> IV, 107–110

But shortly after, he implores her:

> 'Be thou my nurse; and let me understand
> How dying I shall kiss that lily hand.—'
>
> . . . .
>
> 'Dear lady,' . . . ' 'tis past:
> I love thee! and my days can never last.'
>
> IV, 117–138

This is a characteristic response of a person who has been under daemonic agency as he emerges from it; he thinks (for a time, or longer, or forever) that life for him cannot endure, because he cannot be content with the limitations of mortal life again even though he feels the mighty pull of actual life resuming its sway upon him and knows that he *should* be content, as Endymion admits. Considered without the definiteness and concreteness given by the daemonic, these heightened conflicting responses of Endymion seem merely confusing and contradictory; for a return from "the world of dreams" or from "visionary experience," as it has been called, does not throw a person into the turmoil that Endymion is in now and the knight is in at the end of *La Belle Dame sans Merci.*

As the poem continues, the Indian maid professes not to see cause for his grief but says that it would be a "guilt . . ./ Not to companion" him in it, and thus sings her much-admired song of sorrow, telling of her desolate aloneness after she was carried from her home in the train of Bacchus and later after she had parted from these revelers. The song has at least one stanza worthy of Spenser in his marriage hymns (lines 218–227). It ends with an admission of her previous long search for pleasure, like Endymion's, through "every clime" and then a strong acceptance of sorrow as a good, obviously a kind of choral commentary on the events taking place in Endymion's story at the moment, for he is learning to accept the limitations of mortality; and one of them is that mortal joy, unlike daemonic joy, is inseparable from sorrow, as Keats later set forth in *Ode on Melancholy:*

> 'Young stranger!
> I've been a ranger
> In search of pleasure throughout every clime:
> Alas, 'tis not for me!
> Bewitch'd I sure must be,
> To lose in grieving all my maiden prime.
>
> 'Come then, Sorrow!
> Sweetest Sorrow!
> Like an own babe I nurse thee on my breast:
> I thought to leave thee
> And deceive thee,
> But now of all the world I love thee best.

'There is not one,
No, no, not one
But thee to comfort a poor lonely maid;
Thou art her mother,
And her brother,
Her playmate, and her wooer in the shade.'

IV, 273–290

The last stanza indicates that sorrow is not only an insepa-rable part of human existence, but—strange as it may seem at first—a *desirable* part. What Keats means by this, I believe, is made clear by two passages in his letters and one in *Hyper-ion*, although facets of the idea appear elsewhere in his poetry, especially in the odes; for it is a cardinal principle of both his ontology and epistemology. It should be remembered that in the poem Endymion has represented himself as a seeker after essence and that up to this point he has been a bungling one indeed. Now he is about to learn.

First in a letter (November 22, 1817) to Benjamin Bailey, written when *Endymion* had been nearly completed, Keats included a copy of this "Song of Sorrow" from the poem and discussed the song and the core idea in it in part as follows:

I have the same Idea of *all* our Passions as of Love: they are all in their sublime, creative of essential Beauty—In a Word you may know my favourite Speculation by my first Book, and the little song I sent in my last—which is a representation from the fancy of the probable mode of operating in these Matters. . . . How-ever it may be, O for a Life of Sensations rather than of Thoughts! . . . Sure this cannot be exactly the case with a complex Mind— one that is imaginative and at the same time careful of its fruits— who would exist partly on sensation partly on thought—to whom it is necessary that years should bring the philosophic Mind. . . . If a Sparrow come before my Window I take part in its existence and pick about the Gravel. The first thing that strikes me on hea[r]ing a Misfortune having befalled another is this. 'Well it cannot be helped: he will *have the pleasure of trying the resources of his spirit*' [*Letters*, I, 184–186, italics added].

Keats means, first, that suffering and pain, which cause sorrow, are fundamental elements of universal reality and cannot be separated from it without distorting it, not even from "the principle of beauty in all things" (which he said he worshiped); and, second, that at the same time this sorrow is one of the human feelings ("Passions") which make accurate and reliable knowledge of this reality possible. Hence sorrow, along with the other emotions, *creates essential beauty for us as we are going through the process of knowing it*, somewhat in the manner which Coleridge designated "the common principle of being and knowing" (*principium commune essendi et cognoscendi*).[20] "Negative Capability," the capacity of the consciousness to be almost filled up by its object in a process of direct and intuitive knowing, begins in an emotion-charged sensory cognition and then moves progressively into the intuitive as the archetypal responses and capacities in the mind are activated by the object filling it up. Such is what Keats meant by stating above that the imaginative mind that is "careful of its fruits" exists "partly on sensation partly on thought." Thus the universals in the realm of the real, which include essential Beauty, are known more fully through the particulars by means of a medium partly constituted of the emotions,[21] including sorrow and grief.

[20] Coleridge, *Biographia Literaria*, ed. John Shawcross (London, 1954), I, 185. It had been published earlier in this year (1817), and evidently Keats had obtained a copy. See Robert Gittings, *John Keats* (Boston, 1968), pp. 174, 175, and various references in Keats's letters.
[21] In this view Keats has a strong and distinguished supporter in our century. The philosopher Elijah Jordon writes in *The Aesthetic Object* (Bloom-

The other passage from the letters, mentioned above, goes into the matter at great length; but a few sentences drawn together will put it succinctly. Two years later at the beginning of his great year he wrote in the same vein to George and Georgiana Keats (March 19–April 21, 1819):

> Nothing ever becomes real till it is experienced. . . . Look over the two last pages and ask yourselves whether I have not that in me which will bear the buffets of the world. It will be the best comment on my sonnet [*Why Did I Laugh To-night*]; it will show you that it was written with no Agony but that of ignorance; with no thirst of anything but knowledge when pushed to the point though the first steps to it were throug[h] my human passions—they went away, and I wrote with my Mind. . . . The common cognomen of this world among the misguided and superstitious is 'a vale of tears' from which we are to be redeemed by a certain arbitrary interposition of God and taken to Heaven— What a little circumscribe[d] straightened notion! Call the world if you Please "The vale of Soul-making" Then you will find out the use of the world. . . . Do you not see how necessary a World of Pains and troubles is to school an Intelligence and make it a soul? A Place where the heart must feel and suffer in a thousand diverse ways! Not merely is the Heart a Hornbook, It is the Minds Bible, it is the Minds experience [*Letters*, II, 81–103].

In his poetry the idea reaches its most concentrated expression in *Hyperion*, written in 1818 between the time of these two letters, where during his deification the young Apollo voices the part that sorrow plays in bringing him the "knowledge enormous" that is making a god of him:

---

ington, Ind., 1937), "Cognition itself can only be understood to approach the real when conceived as operating within the sustaining medium of feeling" (p. 72).

'Point me out the way
'To any one particular beauteous star,
'And I will flit into it with my lyre,
'And make its silvery splendour pant with bliss.

　　　　.　　　.　　　.　　　.

'Knowledge enormous makes a God of me.
'Names, deeds, *gray legends*, *dire events*, *rebellions*,
'Majesties, sovran voices, *agonies*,
'*Creations and destroyings*, all at once
'Pour into the wide hollows of my brain,
'And deify me, as if some blithe wine
'Or bright elixir peerless I had drunk,
'And so become immortal.'

　　　　　　　　　III, 99–120 (italics added)

Just as "agonies" along with ecstasies and instant responses to all kinds of experience are necessary to make possible the godlike knowing that befits the emerging Apollo in his deification, so are all those—sorrows as well as joys and the rest—necessary to facilitate the full, deep, sympathetic knowing that is requisite for Endymion in his humanization. Only thus can he approach the real, where the ideal resides. From the point of view of the anthropomorphic conception of deity applicable here, the two lines of growth in knowledge are parallel, although Apollo is moving up from mortality into godhead and Endymion is moving down from the neutral realm of the daemonic into full and rich humanity. Apollo is represented here simply as *man at the noblest and best* that it is possible to conceive. Hence this conception of Apollo is an ideal residing in the actual and derived from it, quite in line with then-current Aristotelian aesthetic theory inherited from the eighteenth century and refurbished by critics like William Hazlitt, whom Keats knew and whose lectures he attended.[22]

With all this in mind, one can see how significant it is that in the last stanza of her song the Indian maid maintains that sorrow is so inclusively meaningful to her as to fill the places of mother, brother, playmate, and lover. That is, sorrow is an avenue to wide, deep, and varied knowledge of our world and of its possibilities, the kind of knowledge toward which Endymion's initiation has been leading him.

After this point in the poem only a few highly pertinent developments leading to the denouement need to be drawn together and their interrelated significance pointed out. Endymion knows that he is in the process of giving up Cynthia but is in great conflict with himself about it, his feelings clearly divided between her and the Indian maid. However, he is soothed by the Indian maid's song and comforted by the thought of his impending future lot with her, which he accepts with mingled resignation and hope:

> I've no choice;
> I must be thy sad servant evermore:
> I cannot choose but kneel here and adore.
>
> .   .   .   .
>
> O thou could'st foster me beyond the brink
> Of recollection! make my watchful care
> Close up its bloodshot eyes, nor see despair!
> Do gently murder half my soul, and I
> Shall feel the other half so utterly!—
> I'm giddy at that cheek so fair and smooth;

[22] Keats owned a copy of Hazlitt's *On the Characters of Shakespeare's Plays* (London, 1818), now in the Keats Collection at Harvard University. He scored and freely annotated the chapter on *King Lear*. For Hazlitt's essays on the ideal, see P. P. Howe, ed., *Complete Works of William Hazlitt* (London, 1930–34), VIII, 317–321; XVIII, 77–84; XX, 302–306.

O let it blush so ever! let it soothe
My madness. . . .
And whisper one sweet word that I may know
This is the world. . . .

IV, 300–320

Her kisses and caresses, strikingly different from previous
such experiences, bring afterward neither the continued compulsive desire nor the cloying aftermath of daemonic sexual
experience. Once while with her, in spite of his divided heart,
he feels an awesome loss of self-identity as his soul seems to
be replaced by another that he cannot recognize or identify,
most likely a portent of things to come:

—her gentle soul
Hath no revenge in it: as it is whole
In tenderness, would I were whole in love!
Can I prize thee, fair maid, all price above,
Even when I feel as true as innocence?
I do, I do.—What is this soul then? Whence
Came it? It does not seem my own, and I
Have no self-passion or identity.

IV, 470–477

He has now reached the "Richer entanglements, enthralments
far/ More self-destroying" that lead to the "tip-top" of the
third and into the fourth stage in the scale of the "fellowship
with essence," where hangs the "orbed drop/ Of light" that is
love in its ideal reality (I, 798–805); and he has reached it
through aesthetic empathy in the actual world of men and
things, not in the neutral, daemonic realm between gods and
men.

As a result of all these developments, his voicing a final and unequivocal rejection of his daemonic pursuit of Cynthia is now made inevitable. This recantation, firm and resolute, comes significantly just after he has heard, during another journey through the sky, part of a beautiful choral wedding hymn being sung by "voices sweet" for the object of his daemonic love. The hymn (IV, 563–611) is subtly appropriate at this point in two ways, for his goddess is playing a dual role in the story now; she is in disguise the earthbound Indian maid, who is more like Diana, the major mode of her threefold self, than like Cynthia, one of her two lesser modes (the third being Hecate, of the underworld). Correspondingly, in the very first lines of the hymn she is pointedly identified as both Diana and Cynthia. Furthermore, the first part of the hymn is addressed to her as Diana, the more earthly side of her being, expressing joy at the presence at her feast chiefly of other earth-oriented deities—Hesperus, Zephyrus, Flora, and Aquarius; while the second part of the hymn is addressed to her as Cynthia, the celestial one, exhorting the other deities of the sky to make more bright her crescent on her wedding night and to join the throng of guests—the constellation of the Bear, Castor and Pollux, Centaur, Lion, and Andromeda. Thus the two parts of the hymn polarize the two extremes of Endymion's long, now-dying conflict and at the same time subtly hint at the nature and meaning of its impending resolution. Upon Endymion's return from the sky journey, after the shock of his first touch of earth, he begins his full recantation:

> to him
> Who lives beyond earth's boundary, grief is dim,
> Sorrow is but a shadow. . . .
>
> IV, 619–621

In view of what has been brought out previously in connection with the song of sorrow, this statement is highly pertinent: if grief is dim and sorrow but a shadow in regions beyond earth's boundary, so in final analysis must beauty be also; for grief and sorrow, which are not possible in the daemonic realm outside the human pale, are necessary for human beings in their world to apprehend the fullness of the real, where beauty resides, where lies the "principle of Beauty in all things" (*Letters*, I, 266, 403; II, 263).

Consequently, it is now understandable that Endymion immediately afterward voices a genuine happiness at having his feet firmly planted on the earth at last both literally and figuratively. How different from the time when he had exclaimed in daemonic rapture to Cynthia, "I do think the bars/ That kept my spirit in are burst" (II, 185–186) and had believed that "the stings/ Of human neighbourhood envenom all" (I, 621–622). Now his recantation continues in a distinct anti-daemonic mood, in which the ordinary world of men and things appears to have a doubly heightened sheen of beauty:

> now I see
> The grass; I feel the solid ground—Ah, me!
>
> .   .   .   .
>
> Behold upon this happy earth we are;
>
> .   .   .   .
>
> By thee [Indian maid] will I sit
> For ever: let our fate stop here—a kid
> I on this spot will offer: Pan will bid
> Us live in peace, in love and peace among
> His forest wildernesses. *I have clung*
> *To nothing, lov'd a nothing, nothing seen*

Or felt but a great dream! O I have been
Presumptuous against love, against the sky,
Against all elements, against the tie
Of mortals each to each, against the blooms
Of flowers, rush of rivers, and the tombs
Of heroes gone! Against his proper glory
Has my own soul conspired: so my story
Will I to children utter, and repent.
There never liv'd a mortal man, who bent
His appetite beyond his natural sphere,
But starv'd and died. My sweetest Indian, here,
Here will I kneel, for thou redeemed hast
My life from too thin breathing: gone and past
Are cloudy phantasms. . . .

                       No, never more
Shall airy voices cheat me to the shore
Of tangled wonder, breathless and aghast.

                IV, 621–655 (italics added)

Now an important part of his initiation has been completed. For the first time he realizes fully that his quest has been a mistaken one with pernicious effects upon him; and he clearly designates it such in terms which indicate that he knows he has emerged from a condition very much like that of the knight in *La Belle Dame* (who does not emerge from it), for this knight's appetite beyond the mortal sphere similarly had led him through suprahuman ecstasy to an aftermath in which he "starv'd." Endymion acknowledges here that in his "presumptuous" quest he had nearly lost belief in the value of human love, the natural order, the beauties of nature, and the fundamental human ties. He is drawing back just in time.

Seen in this light, as a recantation of a daemonic quest,

Endymion's giving up the pursuit of Cynthia ceases to be puzzling and falls into place as an understandable sequel to most of the incidents in the main action; for the pursuer of the neo-Platonic ideal Beauty does not draw back from it just as he is approaching it and then designate it an empty dream, or a region of "too thin breathing," where one "starv'd and died." He may designate it unattainable or beyond reach and he may give up the quest for it, but he does not deny its value, as Endymion does. But when viewed as a recantation of daemonic love, Endymion's giving up his quest seems an inevitable result of previous developments in the plot and an acceptable outcome of the two central conflicts in the over-all structure of the poem and in the mind of Endymion: (1) that between the daemonic and the actual, and (2) that between the daemonic and the ideal, the former having continually superimposed itself upon and usurped the latter. In fact, Endymion's daemonic proclivity has been steadily obscuring in his mind both the pursuit of the ideal and the value of the actual, separating the two from each other. Now that the daemonic is at last rejected, the actual rises into prominence, and the ideal within it can be known.

Paradoxical as it may seem at this point in Endymion's recantation, Cynthia is not to be excluded from what represents that ideal. In view of the force and vehemence of Endymion's statement, especially his saying that he had "lov'd a nothing," he may seem to be repudiating and rejecting Cynthia herself. But he is apparently not doing so; he is renouncing only his over-intense, daemonic pursuit of union with her, which Peona had repeatedly labeled impious and perilous. This had brought the ill effects upon him; they were not caused by anything that Cynthia had willed or had done. In his feverish, emotion-charged mind he had been turning her into a daemonic agent, which intrinsically she is not. Now, along with his better understanding of the actual world, he is also beginning to gain a clearer view of his relationship to her. In the same passage he says:

> Adieu, my daintiest Dream! although *so vast*
> *My love is still for thee.* The hour may come
> When we shall meet in pure elysium.
> On earth I may not love thee; and therefore
> Doves will I offer up, and sweetest store
> All through the teeming year: so thou wilt shine
> On me, and *on this damsel fair of mine,*
> *And bless our simple lives.*
>
> IV, 656–663 (italics added)

These disclosures are of the utmost importance. As has been said, Keats does not authenticate Cynthia satisfactorily as the representative of the ideal, but he nevertheless places her in that top position as a polar point; and he never in any way disparages her, or allows another character to disparage her, anywhere in the entire poem. Only Endymion unwittingly debases her in his frenzied daemonic excitement. But here the highly significant words "although so vast" placed just before "My love is still for thee" indicate not only that his love for her continues but that it is becoming vaster now, that he is beginning to envision her as a broader, more inclusive being than before. His allusion to a possible happy union with her in the hereafter ("pure elysium") may be more of an after-thought than evidence of a deliberate choice of heaven over earth, for he has just chosen earth quite emphatically for now and is about to enumerate its joys convincingly; and he says only that the hour of their meeting in elysium *may* come, not that it *will* come. Also, his asking Cynthia's blessing on both himself and his earthly bride in their life together suggests that he now acknowledges quite a different relationship between himself and the goddess; she is no longer the object of erotic desire and longing, but has become in proper perspective something greater than a rival to his earthly love. Therefore a possible meeting in elysium would be different from what he had long sought. There is no subsequent reference to such a meeting, and the final scene presents Endymion's happiness with Cynthia attained here on earth. In sum, there is insufficient evidence that the reference to elysium indicates a major line of development from here on. But whatever the purpose of the reference, Keats's retaining Cynthia in the scheme of things as a more inclusive entity points toward earlier and later developments which help to make sense of the termination of the poem, as does Endymion's simple statement, "On earth I may not love thee," which sounds the death knell of his daemonic proclivity.

After the high point of his recantation, when Endymion describes what he expects to be his future lot on earth with the Indian maid, he brings back into the poem the sustained beauty and mellow ripeness of ordinary things, which had predominated at the beginning, before Endymion appeared on the scene in rapt enthrallment. There is again a hint of *To Autumn* in it. After glorying in "one human kiss" and "one sigh of real breath" from the Indian maid, he continues:

> Where shall our dwelling be? Under the brow
> Of some steep mossy hill, where ivy dun
> Would hide us up, although spring leaves were none;
> And where dark yew trees, as we rustle through,
> Will drop their scarlet berry cups of dew?
>
> .   .   .   .   .

Honey from out the gnarled hive I'll bring,
And apples, wan with sweetness, gather thee,—
Cresses that grow where no man may them see,
And sorrel untorn by the dew-claw'd stag:
Pipes will I fashion of the syrinx flag,
That thou mayest always know whither I roam,
When it shall please thee in our quiet home
To listen and think of love. Still let me speak;
Still let me dive into the joy I seek,—
For yet the past doth prison me. The rill,
Thou haply mayst delight in, will I fill
With fairy fishes from the mountain tarn,
And thou shalt feed them from the squirrel's barn.

IV, 670–694

The image of "the squirrel's barn" is quite appropriately the same as the much-improved "squirrel's granary" in the anti-daemonic opening lines of *La Belle Dame sans Merci*, where all is well in the world of men and things, in contrast to that of the pale knight in his bewitched, feverish, hopeless plight. Endymion concludes, "Say, is not bliss within our perfect seisure?/ O that I could not doubt!"

However, instead of final proof of this earthly bliss, the central object and symbol of it is immediately and incongruously snatched away. The Indian maid unequivocally refuses to be his love, saying that it is forbidden and that she must become a vestal maiden of Diana. This sudden turn of events leaves Endymion stunned with astonishment; for his quest had seemed to be coming to a close with his willing acceptance of the aesthetic and spiritual experience to be found in the common sphere of mankind as constituting enough for mortal happiness. Nearly everything in the poem had pointed that way for a long time; now all is confusingly reversed seemingly without discernible reason.

Shortly thereafter, the very last scene presents the transfiguration of the dark Indian maid into the blonde Cynthia, who lovingly accepts Endymion and explains that the delay had been caused by her own foolish fear (see II, 781–794), by "decrees of fate," and by his need "from this mortal state/ . . . by some unlook'd for change" to "be spiritualiz'd" (IV, 989–993). These terminal events make the main action and denouement turn out in final analysis to be something like this: a young man, so fiercely in love with a supernatural maiden (who may embody the ideal) that all his values are overturned and himself starkly sequestered from the world, grows through a slow initiation to discern that she is unattainable and that the effects of his quest for her are pernicious; consequently finds a human maiden to love; gives up the supernatural one as intended mate; and adjusts manfully to the human sphere—only to be rewarded by seeing the supernatural powers snatch away his new-found earthly maiden and reward him with the very goddess whom he has just given up as unsuitable to his mortal condition! On the level of the action, the explanation is given that the new-found one was the old one in disguise all the time, which has sufficient bases in myth. But on the level of idea, the glaring defect in the matter is pointed out in many interpretations: that is, Endymion, having adjusted to the human world, is now given for his good conduct a suprahuman life in a "spiritual" realm above the human, where love for things earthly and love for things immortal are "fused." This explanation has always seemed lame, illogical, unsatisfying, and entirely too fanciful to fit the preceding developments in the plot. There is truly something of the discovery of the ideal in the actual in the poem; but left as it is, it is not at all satisfactory or convincing as story, as metaphysics, or as allegory.

But the bases of a more acceptable explanation of these final events in the action are at least partially built into the poem as it stands, although they are not fully articulated. Keats's imagination, though now immature, was potentially a very great one and, as Byron said, a very beautiful one; and it evidently had, even at this early time, too much of the synthesizing, modifying, and completing power to leave matters as incoherent as they may seem. Keats usually chose his Grecian goddesses with discrimination, as shown in his selection of Psyche for the great ode, and there are reasons to believe that he did so here.

From the point of view of the whole poem, Cynthia *alone* cannot be held to represent ideal beauty, although she is obviously the high sheen of it in its visible manifestations. She is an immortal, not a daemonic creature; but she has been the unwitting cause and agent of Endymion's continually making himself something worse than a daemonic creature: a human being in a daemonic state, sequestered from his world and out of contact with it. Cynthia is in truth only one aspect of the threefold deity Diana (or Artemis in Greek nomenclature). Diana appears in mythology as Cynthia (from Mount Cynthus) in her celestial mode when she is associated with the moon; as Diana (or Artemis) in her most frequent and prominent modes as goddess of poor folk, of earthly matters, of the hunt, and (very appropriately here) of young men in their growing pains; and as Hecate in her function as a goddess of the underworld with its sorrowful shades. She is therefore symbolic of a wide, deep, and inclusive reality of which her mode as moon goddess (Cynthia) is only a part. Keats knew this well from its prominence in his classical dictionary, and at just about this time or within a few months[23] he built his sonnet *To Homer* upon this idea. Having prepared the way soundly in the three quatrains, he concludes the sonnet by stating that Homer's vast insight into all life constituted a threefold, godlike knowledge like that of Diana and therefore sufficient to fill up his own "giant ignorance":

> Such seeing hadst thou, as it once befel
> To Dian, Queen of Earth, and Heaven, and Hell.

Something of this more inclusive and accurate perceiving, though indeed a lesser mode of it, is what Endymion has gained during his long initiation. That is, the *ideal that he has finally discovered* in his quest and its resulting effects upon him are more correctly indicated by what the triple goddess in her fullness represents than by what *that single part of her* known as Cynthia represents. The Cynthia-Diana-Hecate triplex represents quite well both the course of Endymion's initiation and the nature of the ideal to which he voices adherence when renouncing the pursuit of Cynthia and, therefore, when describing the life he hopes to lead with his Indian maid. In Michael Drayton's *Endimion and Phoebe* the goddess is designated once by her multiple names (lines 823–868) and again in his *The Man in the Moone*, which we know Keats read (lines 475–478). Keats's sonnet *To Homer*, quoted above, seems to owe something to this latter passage in Drayton concerning the goddess:

> For with long Titles doe we her invest,
> So these great three most powerful of the rest,
> PHOEBE, DIANA, HECATE, doe tell,
> Her Soveraigntie in Heaven, in Earth and Hell.

[23] W. J. Bate, *John Keats* (Cambridge, Mass., 1963), p. 298n.

But how much is there in Keats's poem to support the view that the threefold Diana represents the ideal that is achieved in the quest and how much of this evidence seems deliberate rather than accidental? There is a great deal to support the view, and there is evidence that Keats built much of it into the poem deliberately, although he did not emphasize and point up the idea fully. As has been shown, the chief incidents in the story—from Endymion's first experiencing the anti-dae-monic, in the underworld in the *presence of Diana's image* and *through her agency* (II, 284–322), until after his union with the sorrow-taught Indian maid and the giving up of Cynthia—have led him step by step to accept, as rich and satisfying, a way of life made up of what is represented by the triform Diana and not by Cynthia alone. Moreover, the three-fold realm of Diana coincides with the full setting of this main line of action in the poem, for some of its incidents occur in the heavens, some on the earth, and some in the underworld. Diana has a part in events that take place in all three of these regions, and at times seems to preside over what takes place there.

For example, in his first experience of the anti-daemonic, mentioned above, it is she whom he invokes for aid in her capacity as goddess of earthly things and human relationships (II, 313–322), for which he desperately longs, and she whom he implores to deliver him from that "rapacious deep" so completely cut off from them. Thus she early becomes the chief heavenly opposer of the daemonic in the poem just as Peona is the principal earthly opponent of it. Immediately after his plea, Diana makes flowers and grass grow up be-tween the paving stones at his feet (II, 341–347), as if sug-gesting that he will ultimately find his heart's desire in the earthly region of her chief influence and that she is providing ways to keep alive his interest in this realm of experience at a crucial time in his quest. Shortly afterward, when asking help and pity for Alpheus and Arethusa, Endymion addresses her as "gentle Goddess of my pilgrimage" (II, 1014), as if she were presiding over whatever values are to be found during this part of the quest.

Furthermore, the specific characteristics of the Indian maid reveal her to be far more truly the earthly Diana in disguise, with suggestions of her underworld role as Hecate, than celestial Cynthia alone in disguise, as is encouraged by uncritical acceptance of the last lines spoken at the end by the Indian maid-transfigured-into-Cynthia, explaining her long delay (IV, 988–993). That is, although goddesses in disguise may take whatever identity they please, it hardly seems accidental that the Indian maid as we see her in the poem is strikingly a mortal counterpart of Diana: she is from the humble and lowly ranks, of whom Diana was special patron; she is chiefly concerned with making the most of the earthly lot; and she places high value on chastity. In addition, her acceptance of sorrow and strong enunciation of its value give her some of the aura of Hecate, Diana's underworld self, and the mode of her being furthest removed from the bright Cynthia.

Further, it could hardly be accidental that several times in the poem Keats deliberately asserts the single identity of Cynthia and Diana.[24] Appropriately, the first instance occurs during Endymion's initial experience of the anti-daemonic, discussed above, as if Keats were preparing the way for his protagonist's initiation to involve a discovery of the broader and more inclusive aspects of the object of his pursuit (II,

[24] Douglas Bush alludes to the goddess as Diana in the poem without developing the implications. *Mythology and the Romantic Tradition* (Cambridge, Mass., 1937), pp. 92, 94, 100.

302–310). Another such indication of their single identity appears shortly after the Indian maid's song of sorrow (IV, 427–431). Very soon thereafter the most emphatic instance occurs in the celestial wedding hymn (IV, 563–611), where Keats refers to the *one* goddess by both names and treats them as one throughout the hymn, which continues to be heard until the end of the poem (IV, 875–876, 964–968), although it is once called a vesper hymn (IV, 834).

In view of these increasing efforts of Keats to affirm the oneness of the two goddesses, it is now less puzzling that the Indian maid before her transfiguration rejects Endymion. A permanent union with her now, with no more said about Cynthia, could give the aura of the plain and somber to what Endymion is attaining, especially in view of the previous strong emphasis on the Indian maid's full acceptance of sorrow. The result could be something of a "letdown," which would mar the satisfying beauty Endymion perceives in the Indian maid and foresees in his future life with her. Having structured an initiation into the full scale of what the triple goddess represents, Keats seemed no more willing for his protagonist to gain only the "middle third" of these values than he was willing for him to obtain only the "upper third" of them. Therefore, the bright sheen of beauty is added to the picture through the transfiguration, bringing the threefold Diana complex full circle. This increasing affirmation of the whole Diana myth in the poem makes some other things less puzzling also. As mentioned earlier, even after his emphatic recantation of his Cynthia quest, Endymion says, "although *so vast/* My love is still for thee" (IV, 656–657, italics added), a statement which strongly suggests that he is glimmeringly perceiving what is represented by the threefold goddess *in toto.*

Still more significant, the presence of the full Diana triplex in the poem offers a plausible explanation of the single most puzzling passage in it: Endymion's exclaiming that he has a "triple soul" when making his last effort to convince himself that his love for Cynthia has not lessened because of his irresistibly increasing love for the Indian maid:

> 'Goddess! I love thee not the less: from thee
> By Juno's smile I turn not—no, no, no—
> While the great waters are at ebb and flow.—
> I have a triple soul! O fond pretence—
> For both, for both my love is so immense,
> I feel my heart is cut for them in twain.'
>
> IV, 92–97

There are several reasons for believing that the exclamation "I have a triple soul" indicates that Endymion has a momentary awareness here that the being now beginning to fill his soul in an empathic union different from the daemonic is the threefold Hecate-Diana-Cynthia complex and not Cynthia alone as of old; but as yet he does not know the Indian maid's relationship to this triad and therefore now considers her an entirely separate entity in opposition to the goddess, drawing his love away from her and making his claim of undiminished affection for her a "fond pretence." The position of this exclamation in the passage clearly divides it into two distinctly separate parts: what precedes this phrase (i.e., that his love for Cynthia has not lessened) is what he is trying in vain to maintain and now finds to be a "fond pretence," and what follows it (i.e., that he loves both her and the Indian maid and is torn between them) is the true state of affairs. Therefore the words "fond pretence" constitute syntactically a dividing line that places the reference to his triple soul, since it precedes, clearly with what pertains to his goddess love alone and not with what pertains to his mortal love of the maid, which comes after. Hence a meaning for "triple soul" must be sought in relation to the goddess considered separately, and obviously not at all in relation to the maid or involving the maid at this time; therefore the term "triple" must of necessity refer to the triple goddess, while the maid remains a second entity apart. With this twofold division firmly established, the concluding lines of the passage, with their formerly puzzling sudden change from "I have a triple soul" to "for both my love is so immense," now become perfectly clear in meaning and at the same time corroborate the foregoing explanation; for they clearly show that Endymion is thinking of the Indian maid as one entity and the goddess as another, although in his initiation he glimmeringly apprehends a tripartite aspect of the latter at times. The words "triple soul" could hardly refer, as often maintained, to Endymion's three loves in the narrative —the unknown maiden in Book I, Cynthia, and the Indian maid in Book IV—because if that is the case the immediately following change to two in "for both my love is so immense" is left utterly inexplicable. That Keats could have overlooked so glaring an incongruity is hard to believe. Moreover, an acceptable explanation of the change from "triple" to "both" must have to do with the high excitement of the moment, and the inclusion of the unknown maiden, far back in Book I, does not fit this demand at all. That Endymion is having a momentary intuition of the triple identity of the goddess he loved is the best explanation I have found;[25] and the fact that this

[25] Another possibility is that Endymion is voicing a feeling of empathic union with the two (Cynthia and the maid) in which he feels their two souls and his own together, making up a threesome which he calls "a triple soul"; but this explanation leaves still inexplicable the reference to "both" in "for both my love is so immense" and also now the exclamation "O fond pretence." If Keats had

passage comes just before the Indian maid's song of sorrow makes this reference to the triple nature of the goddess an additional evidence that Diana's lower mode as Hecate, with her affirmation of the values of sorrow, is not left out of the representation, although hers receives the least articulation of the three. Last, the text of the passage in Keats's first draft of the poem (Woodhouse's collation) indicates more strongly yet that "triple soul" refers to the triform nature of the goddess; and, significantly, these indications are not refined away in revisions before printing. The text of the first draft reads as follows:

> Goddess! I love thee not the less: from thee
> By Juno's smile I turn not—no, no, no—
> While the fair moon gives light, or rivers flow
> My adoration of thee is yet pure
> As infants prattling. How is this—why sure
> I have a tripple [*sic*] soul! O fond pretence—
> For both, for both my love is so immense,
> I feel my heart is cut for them in twain.[26]

It seems quite possible that Endymion voices this shadowy intuition of the triple nature of the goddess as part of a greater

---

identified the unknown maiden in Book I as Diana in disguise, instead of Cynthia in disguise, we could then easily contend that the Indian maid is Hecate, and Cynthia in her own right would make up a threesome out of his three loves in the narrative that correspond with the triple goddess; but he distinctly identifies the unknown maiden as Cynthia, and there is no way to see it otherwise. Again, the best explanation seems to be that "triple soul" refers to the triform nature of the goddess, and this assumption in turn makes intelligible and meaningful the succeeding words "pretence" and "both."

[26] Garrod, *op. cit.*, p. 161n. The word "feel" in the last line of this quotation appears as "fell" in Garrod's 1958 edition, an obvious typographical error subsequently corrected in the last printing of the paperback edition (Oxford, 1966). The word appears as "feel" in all other important editions of the poem, including the first in 1818.

articulation of the element, once intended but never fully executed and pointed up in the poem, although a good many traces of it remain; for the full Diana triad well symbolizes the complex of ideas dramatized by the major incidents that constitute the plot.

In the very last lines, including the scene of the transfiguration itself, there are several elements that support this view. Just before the scene begins, the poet speaks a word of comfort to his protagonist:

> Endymion! unhappy! it nigh grieves
> Me to behold thee thus in last extreme:
> *Ensky'd ere this*, but truly that I deem
> *Truth the best music* in a first-born song.
> IV, 770–773 (italics added)

There are evidences that Endymion is never "ensky'd" and that truth prevails all the way in this "first-born song." At the end when the Indian maid-transfigured-into-Cynthia explains the long delay in their union and refers to his initiation, she pointedly avoids the word "ensky'd" or "immortalized" and says that " 'twas fit that from this mortal state/ Thou shouldst . . ./ Be *spiritualiz'd*" (IV, 991–993, italics added). According to the scale of essence in Book I, as has been pointed out, one can become spiritualized in this world by reaching the fourth stage, that in which he perceives the essence of earthly love, which Endymion achieved in his "self-destroying" love of the Indian maid (IV, 477). One does not have to be "ensky'd" or immortalized in order to be spiritualized. In setting forth this scale, it should now be remembered, Endymion had included a mortal's love of a goddess only as a hypothetical *fifth* stage put in the form of a question, largely to rationalize his forbidden goddess love to the apprehensive Peona; and this pursuit, as the poem increasingly deviated from neo-Platonic development, did not lead to a higher stage of essence but proved to be daemonic, and was at last given up—the expected culmination of the main line of action up to that time. Further, the next thing that is said continues the implications of the foregoing; instead of saying that she will forever take Endymion with her through the starry sky, as Endymion had frequently imagined in his daemonic dreams, she says rather "we shall range/ These forests, and . . ./ . . . hither shalt thou [Peona] flee/ To meet us many a time" (IV, 993–996). The skies were the haunts of Cynthia, but the forests of earth were the customary haunts of Diana; and as she says all this she is holding aloft her well-known bow (IV, 988), a sign and symbol of her earthly region of influence. Moreover, there is something in the way in which Keats states the transfiguration that is very much to the point: Cynthia does not supplant the Indian maid and take her place; the Indian maid simply takes on the radiant blue eyes and blonde hair of Cynthia right here on the earth. This way of handling the matter seems to imply that the maid retains within her being what she already represents and *adds to it* what Cynthia represents, the bright sheen of that which pleases and satisfies. Keats could just as easily have asserted here at the end that the maid *became* Cynthia and was wafted to the skies, and Endymion along with her. But he pointedly does not do so.

Evidently Keats continued to hold "truth the best music" right on to the end of the poem—truth to the basic lines of the myth in his narrative and truth to what is metaphysically possible in his allegory. On the mythological plane Endymion remains a mortal loved by a goddess who seems much more earth-oriented at the end; on the allegorical plane he emerges victorious from his battle with the daemonic and becomes a man of balance, sanity, and wisdom whose experience has made him by his own admission "More happy than betides mortality" (IV, 859). It seems an intricate irony that the object of his daemonic prepossession, which separated him from the human lot, contained within herself the means of his initiation into fuller and richer humanity; he needed only to discover the full range of values represented by the greater entity of which Cynthia was merely a part and to give up his frenzied, daemonic fixation on one part of the triad alone.

Looking back over the whole work, one can see that Keats has vitalized his protagonist quite beyond the passivity characteristic of him in previous accounts of the legend that served as sources, just as the conception and significance of the goddess whom he pursued were enlarged and expanded as the poem progressed. In Keats's handling, Endymion became something of the archetypal mythical hero and the goddess became very largely the Universal Mother, who encompasses "the whole round of existence" and represents within her feminine image "the totality of what can be known," as these two enduring conceptions have been traced out by Professor Joseph Campbell[27] without mentioning Keats's poem. Endymion's archetypal characteristics are easy to recognize: he undertakes an earthly and an unearthly quest, he exists apart from the world for a time but returns with greater knowledge, he pursues an inclusive feminine image that changes as he grows, and he undergoes a profound initiation during the process. At one point in his book Professor Campbell sounds as if he is summing up the conclusion of Keats's

[27] Joseph Campbell, *The Hero with a Thousand Faces* (New York, 1967), pp. 113–115 and *passim*.

poem while making not the slightest reference to it directly or indirectly:

> The mystical marriage with the queen goddess of the world represents the hero's total mastery of life; for the woman is life, the hero its knower and master. And the testings of the hero, which were preliminary to the ultimate experience and deed, were symbolical of those crises of realization by means of which his consciousness came to be amplified and made capable of enduring the full possession of the mother-destroyer, his inevitable bride [pp. 120–121].

At the very beginning of the poem Pan had been invoked as the "Dread opener of the mysterious doors/ Leading to universal knowledge" (I, 288–289). Through the agency of the marvelous triple goddess, the Universal Mother of all, these doors were gradually opened for Endymion during his quest.

But why, it may well be asked, did Keats not give a clear and emphatic enunciation here at the end that he intended the goddess now to be taken as embracing the full Diana complex if that really is what he meant? In addition to the known fact that he was quite tired from his long effort, there are several possible answers. The best is very likely that he thought that his having repeatedly asserted the single identity of Cynthia and Diana toward the end and his having dramatized the values of sorrow in Book IV constituted a sufficient indication that his goddess had become a more inclusive symbol, especially since Endymion's spiritualization involves the discovery of the full meaning of the values represented by Diana. How else could Keats have expressed this matter satisfactorily without raising quite troublesome problems? To have changed her name to Diana would simply have made the whole thing more confusing. To have brought her into the last scene clearly designated as a trinity would have raised the same difficult problems of expression as are raised in Christian poems by poets who introduce the Holy Trinity. Only Dante among them has managed it well and briefly (near the end of the *Paradiso* in the *Commedia*), and Keats was no Dante. Even if he had been, Dante's brilliant image of the three concentric circles of different colored light occupying the same space (or anything similar) would have been utterly unsuitable to the anthropomorphic deities with which Keats was working in his quite different subject matter.

V

As a result of this long examination of the function of the daemonic element in the poem, some particular conclusions seem to be indicated.

Of first importance, this element identified and delineated the nature of a third realm of experience in addition to those of the actual and the ideal. The sustained presence of this third realm of the consciousness served to dramatize vividly that not all experience outside the customary area of the actual is ideal experience or the search for the ideal; for Endymion's quest beyond the actual nearly always took on daemonic characteristics and led nowhere. Therefore, the presence of this element largely explains why the quest for the ideal in the poem is blurred and clouded until the daemonic is dramatically renounced. The daemonic quest superimposes itself upon the ideal up to that point. The consequent revelation that the major conflict in the action is therefore between the actual and the daemonic rather than between the actual and the ideal strengthens the relationship between the ideal and the actual, as does the recurring anti-daemonic strain, and therefore helps to prepare for the all-important discovery near the end that the ideal lies embedded in the actual rather than apart from it. The daemonic element thus contributes to the cohesion of the structure of ideas expressed and helps to clarify them. Tracing the daemonic quest to its emphatic rejection reveals the considerable function in the poem of other aspects of the triple goddess than that of Cynthia alone and casts such doubts upon the presence of abstract idealism in the poem that sustained neo-Platonic interpretations, already on the wane, appear now to be even less tenable. For it is more than ever apparent that Keats did not carry through to the ultimate stage the full neo-Platonic framework of escalation which he had sketched out in the passage on "fellowship with essence" (I, 777 ff.). Rather, he progressively expanded the significance of the triple goddess into something of the Universal Mother, a vast symbol of all being. The main line of action in the poem is therefore symbolic of a young man's growing into knowledge of fundamental realities of earth as well as of heaven.

Moreover, the conflict between the daemonic and the actual, sustained in the poem from beginning to end, richly enhances the pervading beauty of the actual world through contrast, especially by giving it a sharply heightened value from anti-daemonic revulsion. This richer aura of beauty given to the phenomenal world balances off the magical quality of the high sheen of daemonic beauty in Keats's art; and both reappear handled with greater skill in the odes, sonnets, *The Eve of St. Agnes*, and *Lamia* throughout Keats's subsequent poetic life. Here in *Endymion* he worked out the specific nature of each of these two elements and the interplay of the two in the consciousness, and he began to acquire the ability to integrate and express them vividly. Consequently, the often-asserted importance of the poem to his development appears to have been even greater than supposed, and this development can now be charted more accurately and specifically in relation to his later and finer poems. For example, it has surely become apparent that in *Endymion* can be found the major elements and much of the imagery of *La Belle Dame sans Merci* and also many of the elements of that quite different poem, *To Autumn*. In fact, *Endymion* now suggests that much of his future poetic life would probably be a battle between the daemonic and the actual rather than between the actual and the ideal—as subsequent events proved true.

One of the most interesting aspects of the daemonic element in the poem is that in a sense it may be used critically as something of a catalyst to bring out more specifically the value in each of the three most prevalent types of interpretations and at the same time to unify these separate interpretations into a single more comprehensive one. First, interpretations like that of Newell Ford[28] which designate the quest chiefly a search for erotic experience are surely upheld in large part, for the quest nearly always becomes an erotic one intensified beyond the human and into the daemonic. Recognition of the nature of this quest leads to a better understanding of the crucial function of the recantation, which otherwise appears to be simply the giving up of the erotic quest, but which is considerably more than that; for the recantation, seen in part as a revulsion from the daemonic erotic, involves an immediately succeeding commitment to ordinary earthly experience and its sufficiency, including the sexual. Second, careful readings like that of Stuart Sperry,[29] which as-

[28] See note 2 above.
[29] See note 3 above.

sert that the poem presents a quest for visionary experience against the claims of humanity, become more fruitful when the specific nature of that experience is revealed to be daemonic, which makes more understandable the powerful challenge to human joy and beauty. Last, the many interpretations of the poem as a search for the ideal are clarified and corrected when the sustained juxtaposition of daemonic and anti-daemonic reveals why and how this quest is long blurred and submerged and consequently also reveals that the out-of-this-world element in the poem is predominantly daemonic rather than neo-Platonic. The centrality of the all-embracing conflict between daemonic and anti-daemonic is thus made evident by its catalytic power to elucidate and bring closer together these three different prevailing views. All three of them do indeed reveal something of what is in the total structure of the poem.

Finally, through the powerful tension created by this sustained central conflict, the whole poem is pulled together and given more unity than is usually acknowledged.[30] Incidents in the plot are revealed to have greater relevance to the total design, and many seemingly aimless passages are shown to be functional and organic. Nothing will ever elevate *Endymion* into the ranks of great and successful narrative poetry: there are still too much unrestrained and mawkish exuberance of expression and too much unevenness of texture. But it seems evident that the function of the daemonic element in the poem raises it a few degrees in the scale of narrative literature and shows it to be not nearly so loose and rambling and aimless as it is frequently described. In addition, certain passages of

[30] Well indeed has Earl R. Wasserman stated that *Endymion* has greater unity than is usually attributed to it. *The Finer Tone: Keats' Major Poems* (Baltimore, 1953), p. 10.

beautiful and effective verse are brought to the fore which otherwise remain unnoticed, for instance, the chastened, straightforward simplicity of Glaucus' narrative of his earlier life (III, 318–326) and Endymion's description of his anticipated earthly joys with the Indian maid (IV, 670–694). Surely it can no longer be maintained that the defects of the poem were beyond the power of revision to remedy. I believe that careful revision during 1819, when Keats's manuscripts reveal him to have been at the height of his powers of discrimination in diction and in architectonics, could have made this a poem of real beauty and power.

Keats was destined to batter longer at the limits of mortal experience before making his final proclamation of the rich fulfillment to be found in the common lot. Daemonic experience is firmly and completely rejected here in *Endymion*, but it is not so fully rejected in most of the greater poems of Keats's mature years. There it is repeatedly used with the same ambivalence as in *Endymion* to give unearthly beauty and structural tension to poems that would have been far less appealing without these elements. The most important single justification of his long treatment of the daemonic in *Endymion* is that later it gave another dimension to his major poems. Without this additional dimension they would have lacked the complexity and depth which have helped to win for them their high position in the poetry of the age.

CHAPTER THREE   FROM *ENDYMION* TO
*LA BELLE DAME
SANS MERCI*

The short poems which Keats wrote just after *Endymion* reveal him continuing his attempts to formulate a satisfactory view of life, which he had begun to work out in that long poem. These poems reflect a concern with gaining wider knowledge and with exploring the relationship, especially the conflict that he felt, between thought and sensation. He was almost entirely preoccupied at this time with that conflict rather than with the daemonic. However, the rejection of the daemonic at the end of *Endymion* had appeared more complete and final than subsequent events bore out. He had not given it up for good. He needed to discover its proper place in poetry and to evolve more subtle and controlled ways of utilizing it. Thrown back partly upon the sphere of rational thought and partly upon the realm of phenomena and sensation by his rejection of the daemonic, Keats consequently became engrossed in something of a sharp critical examination of both thought and sensation. In sum, he eventually found systematized and analytical thought too abstract and sequestered from vibrant, pulsing life; and he found sensation and phenomena too brief and transitory. Brevity and transience had not been squarely confronted at the time of Endymion's full acceptance of the actual world and vigorous assertion of its value. Keats had not yet realized (for *Hyperion* was not yet written) that "Negative Capability" resolves the dichotomy between sensation and thought by bridging the gap between the two and uniting them within the consciousness in a way that brings immediate, concrete, vivid knowing of the archetypal and timeless as well as of the present and particular. Probably because this solution to the problem of sensation versus thought was late in coming, Keats was subsequently impelled to undertake a reconsideration of the aesthetic value of the daemonic. His renewed interest in it was fortunate; for it gave to his later poetry the appeal of mystery and provided contrast with the actual and earthly.

But now, just after completing *Endymion*, he understandably takes up the problems of transience in relation to human happiness. In a simple lyric entitled *In a Drear-Nighted December* (1817), he laments that after their joy is gone "many a gentle girl and boy" cannot, like the bare tree and frozen brook, be unaware of their previous spring felicity, but must "writhe" at their "passed joy" because they are conscious beings and remember that departed happiness. He admits that poetry has never yet given a satisfactory anodyne for the pain of transience, such as is given in nature for the lower forms of life; and he does so in terms which suggest that he longs for poetry to attempt that difficult feat, as his own poetry did later and with considerable success, for his best poems do achieve something of what he says here that poetry has not yet given for the pain of transience:

> The feel of *not* to feel it[1]
> When there is none to heal it,
> Nor numbed sense to steel it,
> Was never said in rhyme.
>
> 21–24

Not complete obliviousness to the evanescence of beauty, as is ascribed to the tree and the brook, but lessened sensitivity to it for the moment ("the feel of *not* to feel it") is surely what is given in part as an anodyne to the sting of transience in poems like *To Autumn*, the fragment *Ode to May*, *Ode on a Grecian Urn*, and *Hyperion*.

But several short poems written in January, 1818, seem to reveal that he had put the daemonic aside only until he could acquire the wider and deeper knowledge to use it properly. In *Lines on Seeing a Lock of Milton's Hair*, he wrote:

> But vain is now the burning and the strife,
> Pangs are in vain, until I grow high-rife
> With old Philosophy.
>
> 29–31

Similarly, during the same month or shortly after, he wrote in *God of the Meridian:*

> God of Song,
>
> .   .   .   .
>
> O let me, let me share

[1] Various editors and critics have preferred this version of line 21, which is based on an autograph fair copy of the poem discussed by Alvin Whitley in *Harvard Library Bulletin*, V (1951), 116–122. Among those favoring it are J. M. Murry in *Poems* (New York, 1930), and in *Studies in Keats* (London, 1930), pp. 62–70; Amy Lowell in *John Keats* (Boston, 1925), I, 531–536; Sidney Colvin in *John Keats* (New York, 1925), pp. 158–160; and C. D. Thorpe in *Complete Poems and Selected Letters of John Keats* (New York, 1935), p. 206n. Garrod himself used this reading of the line in the last print-

> With the hot lyre and thee,
> The staid Philosophy.
> Temper my lonely hours,
> And let me see thy bowers
> More unalarm'd!
>
> 17–25

Still reaching out for vaster knowledge, though not for the "staid" philosophy (or any systematized knowledge), in the beautiful sonnet *When I Have Fears*, his first in Shakespearean form, he achieves prolonged serenity with the massed harvest imagery denoting what he yearns to "glean" from his teeming brain before death and to store in "high-piled books" that "hold like rich garners the full-ripen'd grain." When to this fame he adds love as the other major experience he wishes to enjoy before death, he significantly describes it "*unreflecting* love," not the self-conscious realization of it or an abstract conception of it. And when he concludes, it is his thinking of all the vast potential experiences in the "wide world" beyond both love and fame that submerges these two to "nothingness" in his thoughts:

> When I have fears that I may cease to be
>> Before my pen has glean'd my teeming brain,
> Before high-piled books, in charact'ry,
>> Hold like rich garners the full-ripen'd grain;
> When I behold, upon the night's starr'd face,
>> Huge cloudy symbols of a high romance,
> And think that I may never live to trace
>> Their shadows, with the magic hand of chance;

---

ing (1966) of his paperback edition (Oxford Standard Authors Series, 1956) and proclaims that the line was certainly written by Keats (p. 470n). It surely makes a stronger poem of the whole than the other frequent reading, "To know the change and feel it."

And when I feel, fair creature of an hour!
　　That I shall never look upon thee more,
Never have relish in the faery power
　　Of unreflecting love!—then on the shore
Of the wide world I stand alone, and think
　　Till love and face to nothingness do sink.

One of these experiences in the "wide world" beyond love and fame is his ability to "burn through," not merely to read, "the fierce dispute/ Betwixt damnation and impassion'd clay" that is Shakespeare's *King Lear*, which he celebrated in another fine sonnet, *On Sitting down to Read King Lear Once Again*, also written during January, 1818. These two sonnets seem to point toward his fourteen-line blank verse poem, *O Thou Whose Face Hath Felt* ("What the Thrush Said"), written on February 19, which pointedly reveals a change of direction in his quest for the knowledge befitting a poet:

O fret not after knowledge—I have none,
　　And yet my song comes native with the warmth.
O fret not after knowledge—I have none,
　　And yet the Evening listens.

9–12

That is, the poet is able to voice important things that he apprehends intuitively and directly (though not completely and perfectly) without the aid of systematized and abstract knowledge and at times is able to express them better without it. Appealingly enunciated here, this strain continues to recur in his poems of the time and leads on to the consummate statement of it in the deification of Apollo in *Hyperion*, which he began several months later in the year.

On March 25 in his verse epistle to J. H. Reynolds we can

clearly see that Keats's dissatisfaction with systematic knowledge, or with his inability to master it, not only throws him back momentarily upon a reliance on the sensory and intuitive but also impels him to realize that his mind spontaneously and irrepressibly seeks another dimension beyond the single plane of the actual, even though he is troubled by the lack of any "standard law" of knowing when imagination is projected beyond "its proper bound":

> Oh never will the prize,
> High reason, and the lore of good and ill
> Be my award. Things cannot to the will
> Be settled, but they tease us out of thought.
> *Or is it that Imagination brought*
> *Beyond its proper bound*, yet still confined,—
> Lost in a sort of Purgatory blind,
> *Cannot refer to any standard law*
> *Of either earth or heaven?*
>
> 74–82 (italics added)

When things that cannot be settled to the satisfaction of the will "tease us out of thought," that is, beyond the sphere where systematic thought is fruitful, these things if still held in the mind tease us either into the direct, empathic knowing made possible by what Keats called "Negative Capability," in which much pleasure is received and no harm is done since we are still in the world of men and minds, or into the remote and sequestered daemonic sphere, which is undoubtedly what he means above by "Imagination brought/ Beyond its proper bound," that is, brought where it cannot long sustain itself for lack of the concrete phenomena which it must have as its basic materials. For imagination feeds on the concretenesses of both minds and objects, reconciling opposites (such as form and particulars), unifying the diverse, and supplying the processive and organic vitalism in our knowing. But the sphere of "too thin breathing," as he had called the daemonic in *Endymion* (IV, 650), lacks both these concretenesses and therefore becomes indeed a "Purgatory blind," a neutral place that is neither earth nor heaven and therefore with no constants, no "standard law" of knowing or seeing. And it is strikingly apparent that where the daemonic is employed by Keats as a major element, except in *Lamia*, it is represented in part as a kind of purgatory, but an aesthetic rather than a religious one, from which the protagonist cannot emerge, as in *La Belle Dame sans Merci*, or succeeds in doing so, as in *Endymion*. However, Keats achieved a brief respite from these conflicting and troublesome gropings by May Day of this year, for in his fragment *Ode to May* he wrote with calm serenity of unknown rural Greek poets who made "great verse" for "a little clan," and he asked only a similar achievement for himself:

> Mother of Hermes! and still youthful Maia!
> May I sing to thee
> As thou wast hymned on the shores of Baiæ?
> Or may I woo thee
> In earlier Sicilian? or thy smiles
> Seek as they once were sought, in Grecian isles,
> By bards who died content on pleasant sward,
> Leaving great verse unto a little clan?
> O, give me their old vigour, and unheard
> Save of the quiet Primrose, and the span
> Of heaven and few ears,
> Rounded by thee, my song should die away

Content as theirs,
Rich in the simple worship of a day.

This is a beautiful statement of a fundamental and pervasive element of Keats's theory of poetry which he enunciates repeatedly: that poetry should help us to know the splendor of the moment as it passes, the abiding satisfaction that lies in "the simple worship of a day." In so doing it can at least lessen the pain of transience to some degree.

But there is evidence shortly afterward that he was still reaching beyond the actual for another dimension of experience that poetry could express. In one of the poems written in July, 1818, during his tour of the Burns country, Keats shows that he is thinking again of the daemonic as an area of experience with which poetry may deal if it can do so cautiously and guardedly. He has learned that incursions into this realm must of necessity be brief, but he has not yet determined fully and specifically the artistic purposes which the daemonic will best serve. But this poem reveals a highly significant turning point in the development of this element in his poetry between the time of *Endymion* and the time of *La Belle Dame sans Merci:* for, although severely skeptical of its value as extended experience, he does not reject it entirely, as at the end of *Endymion:*

Scanty the hour and few the steps beyond the bourn of care,
Beyond the sweet and bitter world,—beyond it unaware!
Scanty the hour and few the steps, *because a longer stay*
Would bar return, and make a man forget his mortal way:
O horrible! to lose the sight of well remember'd face,
Of Brother's eyes, of Sister's brow—constant to every place;

.   .   .   .

No, no, that horror cannot be, for at the cable's length

Man feels the gentle anchor pull and gladdens in its strength:—

. . . .

Yet be his anchor e'er so fast, room is there for a prayer
That man may never lose his mind on mountains black and bare;
That he may stray league after league some great birthplace to find
And keep his vision clear from speck, his inward sight unblind.

Lines Written in the Highlands after a Visit

to Burns's Country, 29–48 (italics added)

Keats is unmistakably referring to the daemonic here; for neither the analyses that can be made by what he called "consequitive reasoning," nor intuitive philosophical cognitions, nor mystical contemplation of a universal spirit can so completely separate man from the major joys of ordinary experience as to blot out their meaningfulness and make impossible a return to the satisfactions which they afford. Only the all-absorbing power of daemonic ecstasy could do so through rendering the customary joys of life pale and insignificant by comparison. And this result is emphatically designated undesirable by the statement, "at the cable's length/ Man feels the gentle anchor pull and gladdens in its strength." That is, at the utmost limits of desirable daemonic experience man feels the gentle but firm pull of the actual and ordinary, in which his life must be based if it is to continue. This gentle "pull" acts upon him beneficently just as the anchor cable of a properly moored ship prevents it from being lost or destroyed in a storm. Most important of all, man genuinely welcomes this "anchor pull" and "gladdens" in its power to link him to something fundamental and enduring, to that ocean bottom of reality comprised of the age-old human responses, emotions, and situations in the world of men and things; for it and not the daemonic is the residing place at least of universals, while the daemonic with its intensity and ephemeralness is the realm neither of absolutes nor of universals. The implications of the anchor image in the passage are far-reaching.

However, despite this ringing reassertion of the value of the anti-daemonic, carrying it a step beyond similar passages previously seen in *Endymion*, the passage clearly suggests that there is a legitimate place for the daemonic in poetry and experience, and that within safe bounds the daemonic is not pernicious: Keats does not say that there are *no* steps "beyond the bourn of care,/ Beyond the sweet and bitter world" and into some other; he says that these steps are few and the duration of that journey brief, therefore affirming both the existence of another realm and also a certain limited value of it. Only the "too long" sojourn there which "would bar return" is denigrated as a "horror," not the limited and controlled experiencing of it. Keats has found that the mind usually has an inherent safeguard against a deeper immersion that "would bar return" to the actual and fundamental, where man's spirit must be anchored, and that therefore few men will venture beyond the point of no return. Consequently, we do not find here the complete rejection of the daemonic and all its effects, as voiced near the end of *Endymion*, but a significant development beyond that point in two ways. First, having less fear of the daemonic because of this insight into it, he is in effect building up its importance again in his thought, and the artistically fruitful tension between it and the actual is on the way to resuscitation. Second and more important, this lessening fear and greater insight have put him on the way to acquiring suitable artistic control of the daemonic and suitable poetic purposes for which it could be used. These developments point toward *La Belle Dame sans Merci* and the great odes, where the daemonic is used with best effectiveness.

Evidence of this growing control and subtle purposiveness can be seen in minor vein in *The Eve of Saint Agnes*, which is not primarily a daemonic poem in main essentials, but one in which the finely subdued use of the element adds markedly to its great beauty and distinctive artistry. Although this is a story of mortal lovers in the phenomenal world, the events supposedly occur in a Gothic castle in the distant past; and this remote time and setting allowed Keats to give the story a coloring of his own choosing, for its plot is a stock item in narrative literature. In his rendering of it, Keats threw over the central scene in the bedroom, especially Madeline's observance of the rites of Saint Agnes' Eve and Porphyro's part in them, a sustained daemonic atmosphere that adds subtly to the charm of the principals shut away from the world and wholly preoccupied with each other, for this atmosphere is made to blend with the concrete description of the bitter cold outside contrasted against the warmth and security within. The daemonic atmosphere naturally harmonizes with the Gothic setting, and with the decay and death in the background. From this remote enchanted room, dimly glimmering with daemonic beauty, these mortal lovers flee away into a life in the actual world that we find no reason in the poem to consider other than a happy one "o'er the southern moors" and hence out of reach of "dwarfish Hildebrand" and Porphyro's other feuding enemies[2]—that is, for the brief time during

[2] I cannot agree with Earl R. Wasserman's view that the lovers are progressively "refined out of existence" into a better world, for the evidence seems not at all convincing; and the over-all movement of the action and the main line of the poetic treatment of it are in just the opposite direction—into more normal and ordinary life rather than away from it. See *The Finer Tone: Keats' Major Poems* (Baltimore, 1953), pp. 123–125.

which such love can give happiness in the mortal world. Keats shows in unobtrusive ways his full awareness that he is giving the optimistic view of the matter.

The aura of daemonic enchantment is rendered in smoothly modulated phrases which recur frequently enough to sustain the mood without dominating the whole poem. First, what "old dames" had told Madeline about the rites of this night is here summarized in terms which foretell for the performer of these ceremonies a dream vision of a rendezvous with her lover decidedly above the ordinary in pleasure:

> They told her how, upon St. Agnes' Eve,
> Young virgins might have visions of delight,
> And soft adorings from their loves receive
> Upon the honey'd middle of the night.
>
> 46–49

Then, Madeline is first presented in a state approaching daemonic preoccupation with her thoughts of this witching time now very near:

> She danc'd along with vague, regardless eyes,
> Anxious her lips, her breathing quick and short:
> The hallow'd hour was near at hand: she sighs
>
> .   .   .   .
>
> Hoodwink'd with faery fancy; all amort,
> Save to St. Agnes and her lambs unshorn,
> And all the bliss to be before to-morrow morn.
>
> 64–72

When Porphyro learns from Angela that Madeline is observing the rites, his reactions harmonize with the foregoing insofar as the texture and atmosphere go, although he doubts her success unaided by him in the flesh; and this skepticism of

Porphyro concerning the efficacy of the rites to bring the promised bliss is evidence that Keats is deliberately keeping the daemonic element in the poem to the minimum necessary to give a magical atmosphere to an otherwise ordinary stock story:

> But soon his eyes grew brilliant, when she told
> His lady's purpose; and he scarce could brook
> Tears, at the thought of those enchantments cold
> And Madeline asleep in lap of legends old.
>
> .   .   .   .
>
> While legion'd fairies pac'd the coverlet,
> And pale enchantment held her sleepy-eyed.
>
> 132–169

Then come two lines which heighten the daemonic atmosphere thrown over the two mortal lovers, without suggesting that they represent anything supramortal:

> Never on such a night have lovers met,
> Since Merlin paid his Demon all the monstrous debt.
>
> 170–171

Some of the most skillful blending of this eerie atmosphere with the vivid, concrete imagery of the setting and background of the story occurs in the presentation of Madeline's entry into the bedroom (where Porphyro is in hiding) and the subsequent events there; for she is conceived as a vibrant maiden of real flesh and blood, and at first the daemonic overtones are quite unobtrusively suggested. As she entered and closed the door, "she panted, all akin/ To spirits of the air, and visions wide" (201–202); shut away from the world there, she is "Blissfully haven'd both from joy and pain" (240), an echo of daemonic apartness from human agitation, subtly modified to suit the temporary purpose here; and the sequestered room is termed a "paradise" "In the retired quiet of the night" (244, 274), obviously an aesthetic paradise. Madeline now in bed, enfolded in the bedclothes, is described as "Clasp'd like a missal where swart Paynims pray" (241), an allusion which recalls the romances of chivalry, with their frequent adventures in Moslem lands, from which Keats obtained much of his knowledge of the daemonic in narrative literature. Porphyro repeatedly represents himself as an "eremite" and her as his "heaven," a typical situation in these romances where knights errant often undergo daemonic enthrallment to a nonmortal female, which Madeline distinctly is not, but references in the poem to such a relationship help to sustain the atmosphere and mood. The apex of this daemonic coloring is reached as Porphyro leans over her bed attempting to wake her:

> 'twas a midnight charm
> Impossible to melt as iced stream:
>
> .   .   .   .
>
> It seem'd he never, never could redeem
> From such a stedfast spell his lady's eyes.
>
> 282–287

Her awakening and the following events are also given a daemonic aura. Porphyro succeeds in rousing her by playing on her lute "an ancient ditty, long since mute,/ In Provence call'd, 'La belle dame sans mercy' " (291–292), a title which of itself recalls the daemonic relationship of knight and elf queen, although Keats had not yet written his poem so entitled. Just as a person under daemonic agency is at times startled and displeased by the subsequent return of the actual, so Madeline upon awakening experiences "a painful change, that nigh expell'd/ The blisses of her dream" (300–301); for she finds not the Porphyro of the dream, invested with daemonic splendor, but a youth with "sad eyes," "pallid, chill, and drear." The difference between dream and actuality in her mind is not the only reason for Porphyro's paleness; he is pale with fear that his sudden presence in the flesh in her bedroom will offend and frighten her, resulting in his losing her. Since Madeline and Porphyro are both mortals, though projected in a daemonic setting, a dramatic recantation and difficult readjustment to the actual world, as in *Endymion*, are not necessary here for either of these lovers. Madeline implores Porphyro to be again the glowing youth of her dream:

> 'Give me that voice again, my Porphyro,
> 'Those looks immortal, those complainings dear!
> 'Oh leave me not in this eternal woe,
> 'For if thou diest, my Love, I know not where to go.'
>
> 312–315

The "eternal woe" from which she begs deliverance is a typically daemonic element neatly modulated to suit the context here. It is not the "woe" of being left in the earthly world of transient phenomena, as one interpretation asserts;[3] for Porphyro, being a mortal, has no power to take her into any other world, and the last line above implies that she does not want any other. This "eternal woe" consists of being left immobilized in daemonic enthrallment without being able either to possess the enthralling object on the one hand or on the other hand to cease wanting it so much that nothing else is meaningful—an eternal woe indeed! What she is asking is that Porphyro bring her out of the spell now continuing into her

[3] Wasserman, *The Finer Tone*, pp. 105–107.

waking life, for only he can do so, and he can do so only by being in the flesh something like what he had been in her dream and by taking her away to a safe place where their mortal love can flourish. Were it otherwise, she could feel happiness at the thought of dying with him and leaving this sorry world, but there is no reliable evidence in the entire poem that this is her desire;[4] from the first she undertakes the rites of Saint Agnes' Eve in the hope of having a dream experience with her earthly lover, not with a nonmortal lover. Keats managed to project her sexuality without the least hint of grossness as it progresses from innocent dream-desire to full consummation.

Porphyro proves equal to the demands of the occasion. When he sees that his presence in the flesh in her bedroom does not offend her or lessen her ardor, he rises to what is expected:

> Beyond a mortal man impassion'd far
> At these voluptuous accents, he arose,
> Ethereal, flush'd, and like a throbbing star
> Seen mid the sapphire heaven's deep repose

[4] Surely it would be pressing out of context such images as the following to interpret them as indicating such a desire:

> And on her hair a glory, like a saint:
> She seem'd a splendid angel, newly drest,
> Save wings, for heaven. . . .
> 222–224

These and the few others somewhat similar merely convey her delicacy, purity, and chastity in her earthly state *up to this time;* these things are said *about* her from the outside by the narrator, not *by* her concerning her inner thoughts from the inside. They perform that function well and should not be pressed further. She does not desire heaven; she desires sexual-spiritual union with the man in this world whom she is destined to marry, preferably with benefit of clergy, but she shows no aversion to the fact that the union takes place shortly before a marriage ceremony which is clearly implied after their escape from the castle (lines 334–351).

Into her dream he melted, as the rose
Blendeth its odour with the violet.

316–321

In short, he consummated the love relation with her then and there,[5] vowed eternal fidelity, promised immediate marriage, and led her away through the storm to a home "o'er the southern moors" (351) and therefore safe from his enemies within the castle. There is no reliable evidence anywhere in the poem to impel readers to believe otherwise, although many have done so.[6]

In the few remaining stanzas, after the high point of the sexual-spiritual consummation and vows, the daemonic atmosphere is sustained to the very end, but in subsiding tone, for the lovers are emerging into the world of common day. The physical details of their escape are put in a daemonic way, but in subdued and dying cadence. Outside the castle "the iced gusts still rave and beat" (327), suggesting the eerie voices of daemonic creatures that cannot reach them now and disturb their new-found human love. The storm is termed "an elfin-storm from faery land,/ . . . but a boon indeed" (343–344), for it facilitates their flight by impeding pursuit.

[5] This we know for certain from the canceled passages and from what Keats said about the matter to his friends who objected: John Taylor (his publisher), Richard Woodhouse, and Charles Brown. See their comments about Keats's attitude in *Letters*, II, 163–182.

[6] Jack Stillinger has strongly opposed allegorizing the poem in "The Hoodwinking of Madeline: Scepticism in 'The Eve of St. Agnes,'" *Studies in Philology*, LVIII (1961), 535–555, and has summarized the differing interpretations of the conclusion of the story: (1) the lovers depart from the world of mortality entirely and enter another world of eternal felicity; (2) they face reality and possibly perish in the storm; (3) they undergo penance in "that second circle of sad hell," the place of carnal sinners in the Fifth Canto of the *Inferno*, as Keats describes it in his sonnet *On a Dream;* (4) they find a happy life in the human world (p. 550n). The preponderance of evidence and suggestion in the poem surely supports this last view.

Nor can the "sleeping dragons all around"—that is, the drunken enemy guests—now do them harm as "they glide, like phantoms, into the wide hall" (361) and flee away to safety. The death-knell of the daemonic mood is appropriately sounded in the last stanza:

> That night the Baron dreamt of many a woe,
> And all his warrior-guests, with shade and form
> Of witch, and demon, and large coffin-worm,
> Were long be-nightmar'd.
>
> 372–375

That is, the lovers have left the daemonic world behind at the castle and have gone to fulfill their existence in the world of ordinary humanity. The living Porphyro had indeed melted into Madeline's dream.

A clear recognition that the finely controlled daemonic element merely serves to give mood and atmosphere in the poem renders untenable an allegorical interpretation, for nearly all the evidence usually adduced to support an allegorical reading is embedded within this daemonic element. Viewed within this context and this function, the evidence is not at all convincing as support for allegory; taken out of this context it appears distinctly warped and strained. I believe that Keats neither intended the poem as allegory nor that its total structure supports an allegorical interpretation. Seen as part of the full setting, the daemonic element harmonizes unobtrusively with the mouldering Gothic scene of the action and with the old age, feud, sin, death, and decay which surround the lovers and set off in powerful contrast their youth, vigor, beauty, and bloom. Without the effect of this contrast they lose much of their luster and appeal.

Having learned thus to control, modify, and direct the daemonic element to specific artistic purposes and to sustain it at just the proper level for the effect desired, Keats was very nearly ready to make greater use of it as a primary element, one which would occupy a more central and dominating position in a poem. No longer would *it* overpower *him*, as had been the case with *Endymion; he* could now be the master of *it*. He has recovered an interest in its artistic possibilities after his nearly complete rejection of it altogether at the end of *Endymion* and thereafter, but he has not yet discerned how deeply based it is in the human mind or how large a part it could play in a poem of great beauty and yet one in which he does not make the mistake of advocating it as a complete way of life. What was needed was for Keats to experience the daemonic himself and to experience it directly, not vicariously through one of his narrative protagonists, in order for him to savor deeply its compelling appeal and to know its full power. He would now be able to master and control the poetic representation of it after moving it to the center of the stage. Something was needed to impel him to give it a more central position in order to draw out its full potential.

The needed motivation in this direction came to him just after reading an episode in Dante a few weeks later, shortly before April 16, 1819, when he had a genuine and direct daemonic experience in a vivid dream in which he felt strongly and joyously its unusual features and strong appeal. He wrote a little-known sonnet about it and, more important, discussed the experience on April 16 in part of a journal letter to George and Georgiana Keats (*Letters*, II, 91) in terms which clearly reveal that he was captivated by the rare and strange beauty of it, just as were nearly all his narrative protagonists. This incident occurred only a few days—possibly no more than five days—before he wrote *La Belle Dame* sans *Merci;* and both the sonnet and the passage in the letter point in the direction of the central portion of that poem, the section in which the knight tells of his encounter with the elfin lady in the meads. If Keats had not had the experience that resulted from his reading Dante, it is quite possible that the magical poem of *La Belle Dame sans Merci* would never have come into existence. An early version of this poem is also included, without comment, in the same journal letter on April 21, five days later (*Letters*, II, 95–96).

Since Keats's discussion of his experience helps to bring out what he attempted to express in the sonnet, the pertinent portion of the letter should be examined first:

> The fifth canto of Dante pleases me more and more—it is that one in which he meets Paulo and Francesca—I had passed many days in rather a low state of mind and in the midst of them I dreamt of being in that region of Hell. The dream was one of the most delightful enjoyments I ever had in my life—I floated about the whirling atmosphere as it is described with a beautiful figure to whose lips mine were joined, at [as] it seem'd for an age—and in the midst of all this cold and darkness I was warm—even flowery tree tops sprung up and we rested on them sometimes with the lightness of a cloud till the wind blew us away again—I tried a Sonnet upon it—there are fourteen lines but nothing of what I felt in it—O that I could dream it every night [*Letters*, II, 91].

The sonnet, of rather mediocre quality, is included without title[7] at this point in the letter:

[7] Garrod (1958 ed., p. 471) prints the title as *On a Dream*, but Charles Brown seems to have been the originator of it, for various other titles appear in early versions and manuscripts. The sonnet should probably be designated *As Hermes Once*. Hunt, who published it in *The Indicator* on June 28, 1820, appended to it the signature *Caviare*, which he had also appended to a version of *La Belle Dame sans Merci* which he had published in *The Indicator* on May 10, 1820. See Garrod, 1958 ed., pp. 441n, 471n.

As Hermes once took to his feathers light
When lulled Argus, baffled, swoon'd and slept
So on a delphic reed my idle spright
So play'd, so charm'd so conquer'd, so bereft
The dragon world of all its hundred eyes
And seeing it asleep so fled away:—
Not to pure Ida with its snow[clad] cold skies,
Nor unto Tempe where Jove grieved that day,
But to that second circle of sad hell,
Where in the gust, the whirlwind and the flaw
Of Rain and hailstones lovers need not tell
Their sorrows—Pale were the sweet lips I saw
Pale were the lips I kiss'd and fair the fo[r]m
I floated with about that melancholy storm.

In the sonnet the experience does not come through so vividly and strikingly as in the letter, as Keats admitted; but the daemonic element is evidenced in the sonnet by the central idea: just as his "spright" by playing on the Delphic reed charmed, conquered, and "bereft" the "dragon world" of its ever-watchful "hundred eyes" that deter escape from the conventional, so his spright also bereft the second circle of Hell of its manifold horrors through his all-engulfing concentration upon the beautiful female with the pale lips. The result was an uninhibited enjoyment of his feeling of being joined to her and an enjoyment of it that is *amoral*, characterized by complete neutrality as to the relation of her and her situation to good and evil—highly typical of daemonic experience. Dante's guilty lovers eternally linked together in punishment have been transformed into John Keats and a strangely beautiful female linked together in ecstasy for what "seemed an age." Keats's wholehearted, incautious, uninhibited enjoyment of it and his extreme fascination with it even after awakening are revealed in the letter by his designating the experience "one of the most delightful enjoyments" he had ever had, his saying that "in the midst of all this cold and darkness I was warm," and his frank desire to experience it every night.

One may well ask *why* this experience affected Keats so strongly. The best answer is probably that the Jungian archetype called the *anima* image, one of the archetypes in the collective unconscious, was beginning to emerge into his consciousness and to become attached to forms suitable for projection outward in an art structure. Jung conceived archetypes as deep patterns of cognition original in the lower subconscious, not put into it from the outside. The *anima* is a potential for knowing the feminine in all its power, both positive and negative; and its counterpart is the *animus*, woman's similar potential for knowing the masculine. These elements of the structure of mind make daemonic experience possible; and they explain the profound depth of the human capability for it. In his discussion of man's potential for knowing the feminine, Carl Jung states in part:

> The anima image, which lends the mother such superhuman glamour in the eyes of the son, gradually becomes tarnished by commonplace reality and sinks back into the unconscious, but without in any way losing its original tension and instinctivity. It is ready to spring out and project itself at the first opportunity, the moment a woman makes an impression that is out of the ordinary. . . . The love life of a man reveals the psychology of this archetype in the form either of boundless fascination, overvaluation, and infatuation, or of misogyny in all its gradations and variants, none of which can be explained by the real nature of the "object". . . .
>
> When projected, the anima always has a feminine form with

definite characteristics. This empirical finding does not mean that the archetype is constituted like that *in itself.* . . .

Empirically speaking, we are dealing all the time with "types," definite forms that can be named and distinguished. But as soon as you divest these types of the phenomenology presented by the case material, and try to examine them in relation to other archetypal forms, they branch out into such far-reaching ramifications in the history of symbols that one comes to the conclusion that the basic psychic elements are infinitely varied and ever changing, so as utterly to defy our powers of imagination.[8]

If something like this is what had been transpiring in Keats's subconscious, as surely seems likely, it helps to explain the *why* of his extreme fascination with the feminine creature in his daemonic dream. And this emerging archetype from the depths immediately found much with which it could coalesce in the conscious levels of his mind derived from his long reading of mythology, romances of chivalry, and fairy lore, and from his previous uses of daemonic elements in his poems. But, as he had said, knowledge means little until it has been proved upon the pulses. Now its compelling appeal has been proved to him experientially and has become linked with archetypal elements in the depths of his being. His writing the mediocre little sonnet, its ineptness notwithstanding, was highly significant; for it shows his reviving tendency in early 1819, at the threshold of his greatest year, to consider the daemonic suitable material for poetry—as if with his remarkable artistic instinct he sensed that his poetry needed another dimension of some kind beyond the plane of the actual even though he had not developed real skills in the handling of

[8] Herbert Read, ed., *The Collected Works of Carl G. Jung*, tr. R. F. C. Hull, IX, Part I (New York, 1959), 69–70.

allegory or in depicting anything "other worldly," such as Christian or Platonic idealism.

Apparently the stages of development through which Keats came to produce *La Belle Dame sans Merci* embraced events in his life and in his career that extended throughout his productive period. In *Endymion* he had set forth in uneven and often uncontrolled verse a long quest for daemonic beauty, and in that poem he had worked out what proved to be his basic skeptical attitude toward it and its relationship to the actualities of man's lot; but he had not given it up entirely, for some of the short poems of 1818 show his revival of interest in it and his acceptance of man's limited capacity for it, especially *Lines Written in the Highlands after a Visit to Burns's Country*. Then, soon after he had learned in early 1819 to control and sustain the daemonic in the atmosphere and mood of *The Eve of St. Agnes*, he experienced its full power and beauty upon his own pulses in his daemonic dream of the pale maiden transposed from Dante, as given in his sonnet and the passage in the journal letter about it. In view of what he stressed in both of these, one can easily understand why he wrote *La Belle Dame sans Merci* within a period of no more than the five days from April 16 to 21 that separate the texts of the sonnet and the poem in the letter; he could have written the poem the very next day or even on the same day, for it is inserted in the portion of the letter dated April 21 without comment as to the particular day on which he composed it. Obviously the magic poem of *La Belle Dame sans Merci* brings to full flower something that has roots both far and deep in the basic elements that constituted the mind and art of its author.

CHAPTER FOUR

LA BELLE DAME
SANS MERCI:
THE HIGH POINT

Because of its great beauty and appeal, Keats's *La Belle Dame sans Merci* has been widely discussed, although few who have written about it have attempted a full and detailed exegesis. Most interpreters have sidestepped the heart of the poem, and many have widely missed its central currents; for it is a poem which will not yield its richness to any single approach or accepted critical "method," especially a rigid one. Among critics farthest off course, it seems, are those who attempt to explain the poem simply in terms of autobiographical externals. For example, Edward Bostetter states that the poem resulted from Keats's love for Fanny Brawne, which had turned out "to be no spiritualization, but an enslavement; and Fanny a Circe instead of a Cynthia." [1] Similarly, Claude Finney considers the poem "a rebellion against the trammels of love" expressed in an objective form rather than in the personal mode which Keats used in the second of his odes to

[1] Edward Bostetter, *The Romantic Ventriloquists: Wordsworth, Coleridge, Keats, Shelley, Byron* (Seattle, 1963), p. 160.

Fanny.[2] John Middleton Murry in a kindred view maintains that the poem delineates "the beauty of life itself which is claiming, through Fanny, Keats for its sacrifice and victim." [3] Keats's falling in love with Fanny Brawne about the first of the year was perhaps among the various experiences that had something to do with his writing the poem; but such readings as these make this one possible autobiographical influence too direct and too large, they ignore the fact that Keats's love affair was going quite well at the time, and they ignore much deeper autobiographical influences, such as his having created similar protagonists in earlier narrative poems and his strong proclivity for highly imaginative experience generally. Worse still, such readings reduce this finely wrought poem, with its highly complex artistry and strange beauty, to a poem presenting a simple wail for a single disappointment, which would hardly capture the admiration of so many sophisticated readers and critics. Perhaps the nadir of autobiographical interpretations is reached in Aileen Ward's offering the explanation that the poem was inspired largely by a cruel joke played upon the desperately ill Tom Keats by Charles Wells, who, by writing letters to him under the guise of a French girl named "Amena," beguiled him into believing himself loved and into journeying to France[4]—a reading which gives the poem a touch of sardonic humor which is out of harmony with every other element in it.

Although many have muddied the waters, some of the

[2] Claude L. Finney, *The Evolution of Keats' Poetry* (Cambridge, Mass., 1936), II, 593.

[3] J. M. Murry, *Keats and Shakespeare: A Study of Keats' Poetical Life from 1816 to 1820* (London, 1935), p. 124.

[4] Aileen Ward, *John Keats: The Making of a Poet* (New York, 1963), pp. 272–274.

source hunters have at times succeeded in throwing some light on the nature of the poem. For example, Amy Lowell convincingly demonstrates that the mood and atmosphere were taken from the frequent episodes of knights enchanted by females in *Palmerin of England* and that more of the details came from this prose romance than from the Phædria-Acrasia episode in Spenser's *Faerie Queene* (II, Canto VI).[5] The large number of possible sources that have been mentioned shows that in his poem Keats was treating a widely used theme, that of mortal man's love experience with a supramortal female.

Earl Wasserman, in the most extensive and only really thorough study of the poem, points out subtle aspects of its structure and offers markedly helpful insights into various elements of its complexity.[6] However, pressing for an allegorical interpretation, he contends that Keats used the knight's journey with the nonmortal lady to her "elfin grot" to set forth his own progress heavenward toward spiritualization: through a rising series of intensities in the poem that constitute another "pleasure thermometer"[7]—nature, song, and love —the knight ascends into essence in her elfin grot, which symbolizes his proper spiritual home; but there he is tormented by his dream of pale kings, princes, and warriors who are "men of power" in the mortal world and who have been starved by its inadequacy. Realizing his kinship with their mortality, he expels himself from this paradise and quickly

[5] Amy Lowell, *John Keats* (Boston, 1925), II, 220–224.
[6] Earl R. Wasserman, *The Finer Tone: Keats' Major Poems* (Baltimore, 1953), pp. 63–83.
[7] Keats had discussed this in the letter (January 30, 1818) in which he sent to Taylor the lines on "fellowship with essence" to be inserted in *Endymion* while it was going through the press. Keats termed the "gradations of Happiness" in the passage "a kind of Pleasure Thermometer" (*Letters*, I, 218–219).

finds himself on the cold hillside of the fading, transient world of death and decay.

Francis Utley, while finding Wasserman's interpretation helpful, disagrees strongly, and on very good grounds, with his conception of the poem as depicting a spiritual quest: "The knight's weakness is anything but normal—it is the weakness of one from the blasted heath, the Hell of love, for the knight is no man but a pale revenant. Nor is 'honey wild' and 'manna dew' Wasserman's 'heaven-sent food which is life's proper pith'; it is a fraudulent facsimile of that food eaten in the other world and dooming the knight to destruction. The story, whatever its metaphysical implications, is a ballad about a ghost who loved an otherworldly creature, a fairy mistress from hell." [8] There is indeed nothing at all spiritual about the knight's encounter with the elfin lady, but there is nothing intrinsically evil about it either. As Bernard Breyer has pointed out earlier in an insight close to the heart of the poem, the quest therein is a search for the beautiful without the moral.[9] The poem does suggest meanings beyond itself, although it most certainly should not be "didacticized"; but the knight's encounter with the elfin lady, in my opinion, cannot be validly interpreted within the totality of the poem as a structured allegory with a set of direct equivalences which together unfold a religious or spiritual meaning.

As has surely become apparent earlier, I believe that *La Belle Dame sans Merci* is a poem presenting a daemonic experience beyond and divorced from the ordinary human world of actuality. It is narrated by the experiencer, the en-

[8] Francis Utley, "The Infernos of Lucretius and Keats's *La Belle Dame sans Merci*," *ELH*, XXV (June, 1958), 121.
[9] Bernard Breyer, "La Belle Dame sans Merci," *Explicator*, VI (December, 1947), Article 18.

thralled knight, to a listener from that human world who is thoroughly imbued with its values and contented with them. Thereby the two widely differing attitudes and sets of values, the daemonic on the one hand and the universally human on the other, are set off in stark and vivid juxtaposition without moral judgments of any kind. When it is viewed as a poem of this sort, all its manifold parts fall into place organically, and the various elements of its artistry unite into a totality that strikes the reader with a powerful impact. Its concentrated and evenly sustained texture is very nearly without flaw. It is Keats's consummate achievement with the daemonic, and stands at the apex of the poems in which he uses that element. Some aspects of the techniques and artistry that he worked out here reappear in the "great odes" and in *Lamia*, quite different though these later works are in basic form.

Even a cursory reading reveals significant matters of over-all structure and arrangement within the poem. Keats has moved the daemonic element to the center of the stage, just as in the undistinguished sonnet on his dream of the pale maiden (*As Hermes Once*), but has developed it more fully and worked out its potentialities. He has wisely not attempted to present the daemonic experience directly; direct presentation would have rendered it difficult to control and conducive to emotional extremes, as in *Endymion*. Also, he has moved himself out of the picture and has given it over entirely to the knight and his questioner, who together constitute the complete *dramatis personae* of what amounts to a stark, powerful, brief little one-act drama. Neither can be equated with John Keats or can be designated Keats's spokesman, but each polarizes one of the two cardinal strains of Keats's poetic mind: first, his keen ability to feel the ordinary joys of existence on the plane of the actual, with which the questioner is in harmony; and second, his irrepressive drive to pierce beyond, to "burst our mortal bars" into more intense joys, here ascribed to the knight. Each speaks just one time, the questioner first and then the knight, who in the longer portion of the poem is replying to the other's query ("what can ail thee") by narrating his encounter with the elfin lady as the cause of his "woe-begone" condition. His journey and union with her have already transpired, and we obtain all our knowledge of her and of his experience with her only from his report; but the full effects of these wonders upon the knight are still evident, and it is these effects that are rendered directly in the immediate scene taking place before the reader. They increasingly become apparent in a cumulative way partly from the questioner's comments upon the knight's behavior and appearance, partly through the compulsive, intent manner in which the knight recounts the adventure, and partly through his highly revealing statement at the end (*"this* is why I sojourn here"), the inclusive meaning of which adds much to the full import of the poem. By thus placing the daemonic encounter in the just-expired past, Keats avoided the difficulty of rendering it directly without undergoing consequent loss of immediacy and vividness, for there is still transpiring in the foreground an exciting scene presenting a dramatic contrast of two distinctly opposite human attitudes in confrontation, the elfin lady having been from the first just off stage. More important, by means of this arrangement Keats shifted much of the emphasis upon the knight's present condition rather than loading it all upon his already concluded adventure, and thereby subtly established the continuing aspect of the knight's ordeal. This shift of emphasis to the present scene also places the knight's state of mind right up against that of his questioner, who reveals more of himself than is immediately apparent. The bare, terse ballad form made possible the brevity and compression of these revelations of the first speaker, so as to lead quickly to the knight's narrative of his adventure, and also heightened the stark contrast between the mental states of the two in direct confrontation.

The significance of the first speaker and his function have not been pointed out fully. The basic fundamental of his mind —his habitual orientation to the plane of ordinary human life and marked contentment with it—becomes apparent at the very beginning and continues to unfold cumulatively throughout what he utters, as if Keats wished to center attention upon only that one facet of this questioner's identity. The absence of any direct evidence of his sex and age helps to throw emphasis upon this one element of his nature most important to the total design of the poem. The lone situation by the lake amidst the autumnal bleakness suggests that he may be male rather than female, possibly a youth in his early teens, although we cannot be sure. His knowledge and experience apparently have not extended beyond the customary plane of human activity, which he clearly finds sufficient for human happiness. I am discussing the earlier text throughout rather than the so-called revised version, which is much inferior to the former.

As the poem begins, the questioner, evidently passing by the bleak shore of the lake, comes upon the pale knight suddenly and asks him in surprise:

> O what can ail thee, knight-at-arms,
> Alone and palely loitering?

To the initial question ("what can ail thee?") the second line in effect adds another query: why do you linger here? Also, the line implies something that is later developed more fully:

that the knight normally would not be lingering here in this bleak place in late autumn and that his lingering, as well as his wasted appearance, has something to do with what ails him. Also, this second line hints that under the circumstances there is a better and more understandable place to be. These implications are strengthened and extended by the next two lines, which point toward the emerging structural framework of the poem:

> The sedge has wither'd from the lake,
>   And no birds sing.

That is, now in late autumn, when the sedge bordering the lake is withered and sere, and birds are mute, no sane man lingers in this bleak place; he goes home to the warmth of the fireside and the security of human companionship, which have always been the recourse to which man turns when the natural world is inclement or unpropitious. These lines further suggest that the initial inquiry ("what can ail thee?") does not necessarily refer to physical illness alone, for if that were the case we would expect the questioner to help the sufferer rather than to discuss the scenery. But he does not give the details of the knight's condition until stanza III. His lingering there at such a time is of sufficient import for half the stanza, even in this spare and terse poem, to be expended upon the bleakness of the place. In sum, the first stanza stresses one major point: the knight seems to need the ministrations of the world of human beings while being cut off from it by something operating within his own mind which makes him unable to turn toward humanity in his need.

This stark picture of the wasted knight beside the bleak lake now serves to set off sharply the full import of the last two lines of the second stanza. After repeating the initial question and indicating that the knight appears "haggard" and "woe-begone," the speaker adds something that clarifies what has been hinted in stanza I and reveals the balanced, twofold base on which the poem is shaping up:

> O what can ail thee, knight-at-arms,
>   So haggard and so woe-begone?
> The squirrel's granary is full,
>   And the harvest's done.

These last two lines contrast sharply against the first two lines of this second stanza and also against the last two lines of the first stanza and, in a dual antithetical relationship, do much to make clear the diverging mental and emotional states of the questioner and the bewitched knight, who now seem to inhabit totally different worlds. For these two simple lines, well prepared for earlier, elevate two yearly events of the season into highly expressive symbols. Together they serenely proclaim that all is well in the normal world of sentient life, that the bleak and silent lake shore, so engrossing the knight's attention, does not matter to human kind because the harvest is now gathered, its substance stored up to fill human needs, and because in the forest "the squirrel's granary is full," suggesting that even in the sphere of animal life there is sufficiency for all. The rich connotations of the words "granary" and "full" help to particularize "harvest." The three words together call up a picture of grain bins filled with wheat for the winter's bread, which in turn suggests that the storehouse of man's spirit may also be full, for now in November men draw closer to each other, relishing the fireside and human cheer. The withered sedge and absence of bird songs in stanza I are indicative of the immediate bleak aspects of nature in that particular place and time, not the aspects of *all* nature at *all* times and places; for here in the corresponding lines of stanza II are equally compelling evidences of the fruitful and productive aspects of nature that have filled the granaries both of men and animals and will do so year after year. Just as the bleakness and silence thus cannot be extended to symbolize the total natural world represented in the poem, they cannot validly be extended (as Professor Wasserman thinks) to symbolize the character of the entire world of human beings, with which all is well except for the knight cut off from humanity by his daemonic preoccupation. To represent nature as withered, eerie, and tainted is characteristic of daemonic narratives, for nature in such works is often considered the home of witch, demon, elf, and night hag. This aspect of nature as modified in the present poem well befits the knight searching for his supramortal lady, and he is fully in harmony with it; but it does not at all fit the mood of his questioner, whose affinity is decidedly with the other nature, the fruitful and propitious nature that recurringly fulfills man's needs. Keats managed to have both the bleak and the fruitful aspects of nature functioning simultaneously in the poem without disturbing its oneness of texture.

Thus the questioner is not simply a foil to set the knight to talking; he is a highly significant commentator upon the knight's appearance and behavior and upon the state of things in the world of common humanity. His comments establish a framework within which the story of the knight is to be viewed and comprehended; they also set up a few norms against which the effects of the knight's adventure can be interpreted and evaluated by the reader, for Keats himself does not do so. This questioner-commentator, with this set of ideas concerning the human lot on earth, remains prominently on the scene as listener, as the consciousness upon which the knight's hapless tale registers, until the very end of the little drama. And there at the end the knight, by repeating the first lines of the commentator's speech, re-emphasizes the other's continuing presence throughout and brings his views back into position as the framework within which we are receiving the knight's account of his adventure and its effects upon him.

In his third and last stanza the first speaker drops the role of questioner and becomes entirely commentator. Now he eschews the scenery and focuses all his attention upon the knight, thereby preparing for the impending central event in the poem, for the knight is about to narrate his adventure. However, by this time the first speaker has quietly revealed his own sharply different attitude toward the world, bringing quickly into play the conflict between the two polar points of the poem, and now the graphic details of the knight's wasted appearance simultaneously recall the contrasting ripeness and serenity in the first speaker's picture of man and nature at harvest time. Therefore, both of the diverging lines of development in the poem are still being rapidly brought forward in this third stanza, dealing ostensibly only with the knight, as he is revealed to be more and more isolated from the sphere of normal humanity and its satisfactions:

> I see a lilly on thy brow,
>> With anguish moist and fever dew,
> And on thy cheeks a fading rose
>> Fast withereth too.

Now it becomes apparent that his wasted condition has not brought apathy; on the contrary, he is still anguished and feverish from the intense preoccupation which now he can neither give up nor renew. He is pitiably suspended between two worlds. The "fever dew," beads of perspiration from his emotional rather than physical exertion, cover over and partly obscure the image of a lily, symbol of resurrection and continuing life, on his brow. On his cheeks the "fading rose" that "fast withereth," with dual emphasis on its decay, suggests at once two meanings of the rose that are applicable here; for, though different from each other, both express a part of the complex drama going on within the knight: first, the expiring of the sexual joy he had experienced with his elfin mistress, from the classical tradition of the rose as symbol of sexual desire; and second, the diminishing within him of the beauty springing from spiritual love, from the medieval and Romantic tradition of the rose as symbol of spirituality.[10] Both the indistinct lily and the fading rose enhance the pallor of his face and imply that his participation in the fullness of life and enduring beauty has been almost extinguished—not at all because he is now cut off from the elfin lady and her grot, as he surely is, but because his complete enthrallment with her and the grot had cut him off from the world of humanity in the first place, and because the continuing aftereffects of his enthrallment now preclude his finding joy or satisfaction in the human lot again. His paleness, exhaustion, fixed intentness, and haggard look all come from his having been consumed by the intense experience in the grot and by the continued obsession with her after she is gone; and the indistinct lily and fading rose point with profound irony toward the deeper effects of his isolation from the fullness and spirituality residing in the world of human beings. For if we take the disappearing lily and the fading rose to symbolize only his

[10] Without mentioning this poem Barbara Seward cogently discusses these differing meanings of the rose symbol in *The Symbolic Rose* (New York, 1960), pp. 55–66.

isolation from her and the grot, we must then take her and the grot to symbolize the sources of immortality and spiritual beauty.[11] And this we cannot at all do validly—not only because of differing long-established meanings of the symbols of lily and rose themselves, not only because of the widely differing basic image of the lady in several centuries of previous narrative (for she is essentially either the mischievous elf queen remolded and modified or else the nonmalicious fairy wife of the romances and folk tales), but more especially because there is nothing in the poem anywhere to indicate that Keats has transformed her established modes into one that suggests anything spiritual or good. Neither has he made her into a sinister evil creature of the Circe type,[12] for she is never cunning, wicked, deceitful, consciously and intentionally cruel, or haughty, insofar as we ever learn from the poem, and the knight takes the lead in bringing on his enthrallment with her. In creating her Keats either refined away from one traditional image all traits of deceit, sorcery, and trickery, which sometimes in the romances and folk tales she possessed, or else he shaped her from the other mode of the traditional figure that had none of these traits but only beneficent and positive qualities, for example Dame Tryamour (daughter of the king of fairies) in Thomas Chestre's fourteenth-century verse romance *Sir Launfal*, who loved that

[11] I disagree with Professor Wasserman, who does so take them: "Earthly life, then, is a spiritual solitude overcast with the pallor of death, and a denial of the 'honey wild, and manna dew,' the heaven-sent food which is life's proper pith. . . . Man is only a temporary resident in this world. The elfin grot being truly his home ethereal, mortal man, in the solitude of his self, can only 'sojourn here, . . . palely loitering' on the cold hill side of the world" (*The Finer Tone*, p. 78). I believe that just the converse is true in the poem. And the knight is not at all typical of mortal man, but distinctly atypical, since under daemonic agency.

[12] Francis Utley and Edward Bostetter have thus designated her. See notes 1 and 8 above.

knight with steady devotion and no trickery, taking him happily with her "ynto Fayrye" at the end in spite of his having broken her injunction to tell no man of her,[13] a frequent tabu in stories of a nonmortal female and a mortal lover (which Keats's knight is also breaking in relating his adventure to the listener). In reshaping one or the other or both of these traditional females for the purposes of his poem, Keats endowed his "Belle Dame" with mystery, glamour, delicacy, femininity, high sexuality, and haunting appeal; but not the good, spiritual, or evil. She is a nonmortal, daemonic creature of Celtic origins, and she is neutral as to good and evil because she is outside the human pale and all its restrictions. There is no context of good and evil in the particular daemonic matrix of the poem; to represent her as an evil being necessitates warping the poem into something which intrinsically it is not. And it is noteworthy that Keats did not give his poem a "happy" ending like that in *Sir Launfal*, for then it would have become a simple "replay" of medieval story rather than the powerful little psychological drama that it turned out to be.

An important clue to a valid interpretation is given by a change in the diction which Keats made in revising this third stanza. He first wrote "death's lilly" and "death's rose" and then changed to the present reading, omitting "death's" in both places, which in addition to making better rhythm indicates that he did not wish the knight to be considered as nearing *certain* death, which would have taken away much of

---

[13] Thomas Chestre, *Sir Launfal*, ed. A. J. Bliss (London, 1960), pp. 63–82. Its major source was *Sir Landevale*, a Middle English adaptation of the twelfth-century Breton lay, *Sir Lanval*, by Marie de France. For a list of other versions of the basic theme, see Gerald Bordman, *Motif-Index of the English Metrical Romances*, Folklore Fellows Communications No. 190 (Helsinki, 1963), p. 34. See also G. V. Smithers, "Story-Patterns in Some Breton Lays," *Medium Aevum*, XXII, No. 2 (1953), 61–92.

the organic fluidity and suspense of the poem. To be sure, the knight may die if he does not find egress from the terrible stasis between two planes of being in which he is left when the poem ends; but he may in time come out of it and regain an appetite for the joys and satisfactions of the common lot, as is the case at times in the romances of chivalry and in the ballads based on them.[14] If such should be the outcome here, then the knight has managed to experience joys beyond the customary without having to pay the piper. Meanwhile, his sustained, balanced suspension between two planes of being, with no sign of impending reconciliation of the two, or of final outcome, endows the poem with compelling suspense and appeal.

The situation having been quickly set up to frame the account of his adventure, the knight begins his narrative in an anguished, compulsive rush, as if the act of telling it re-creates all the wonder of it and accentuates his terrible longing for the elfin lady. The movement of the verse speeds up accordingly, with a wealth of short quantities in the syllables accelerating the tempo—quite in contrast to the recent slow-paced, musing question and comment of the first speaker standing before him:

[14] For example, see *Palmerin of England* (London, 1807), *passim*, which we know that Keats read and scored; the medieval romance, *Thomas of Erceldoune*, and the ballad on the same legend, "Thomas Rhymer," as well as "The Elfin Bride, a Fairy Ballad," based on this romance and written in 1818 by F. M. Dovaston, a friend of J. H. Reynolds, who was close to Keats, as Professor Wasserman points out (*The Finer Tone*, pp. 71–72) and observes, "Dovaston, unlike Keats, drew from his narrative the conclusion that man should be content with his mortal lot." I believe that, although Keats wisely inserts no didactic comment (or any other comment), the totality of the poem leads to the conclusion that it is best for man to be content with his mortal lot unless his imagination can unite his suprahuman experiences into his whole life without such disorientation to the normal plane as befell the knight in the poem; and I believe that this conclusion is supported by elements in the odes, in his letters, and in *Lamia*.

I met a lady in the meads,
    Full beautiful—a faery's child,
Her hair was long, her foot was light,
    And her eyes were wild.

I made a garland for her head,
    And bracelets too, and fragrant zone;
She look'd at me as she did love,
    And made sweet moan.

I set her on my pacing steed,
    And nothing else saw all day long,
For sidelong would she bend, and sing
    A faery's song.

She found me roots of relish sweet,
    And honey wild, and manna dew,
And sure in language strange she said—
    'I love thee true'.

She took me to her elfin grot,
    And there she wept, and sigh'd full sore,
And there I shut her wild wild eyes
    With kisses four.

And there she lulled me asleep,
    And there I dream'd—Ah! woe betide!
The latest dream I ever dream'd
    On the cold hill side.

The lady's identity as a nonmortal, daemonic creature outside the human realm and its limitations is suggested at the outset by the knight's calling her "a faery's child," a spelling which Keats customarily used instead of *fairy* when referring to chivalric romance; and this general identification of her is built up and particularized by corroborating details that recur all the way through: "her foot was light"; "her eyes were wild," repeated again with increment; she sang "a faery's song"; she found the knight "honey wild, and manna dew," no ordinary food; she spoke "in language strange"; and she lived in an "elfin grot" beneath a "cold hill side," the usual home of such creatures. She is "full beautiful," and there is nothing to suggest that she is by nature sinister or has a sinister intent, although the engulfing preoccupation she can inspire in a mortal with his tacit assistance can be destructive if prolonged. This was true of Cynthia in *Endymion* earlier and will also be the case with *Lamia* later. The fact that she is called "The Beautiful Lady without Kindness" does not change this identification of her at all; this appellation does not mean that instead of kindness she has unkindness in her heart. She has neither kindness nor unkindness; for, since she is outside the pale of human limitations, she is neutral as to good and evil and knows nothing of either. She can experience joy, ecstasy, attachment, sorrow—even constancy as *inclination*, but not constancy as *obligation*, for obligation is a matter of human morality. But her lack of it is no more evil than the wren's lack of it. However, it is not necessarily her inconstancy that brings the termination of the love union in the poem; the knight's normally mortal inability to sustain the intensity of daemonic ecstasy is a sufficient cause of its sudden end whether or not she remained constant; and it is noteworthy that the knight nowhere charges her with inconstancy or deception, or hints at either. We cannot at all be sure that her affection changed before he in his mortal limitations failed the demands of the occasion, and the fact that she "wept, and sigh'd full sore" and had to be comforted by him suggests both that she had not changed and that she knew that he in his mortality inevitably would soon fall away. There are two compelling reasons for doubting that her tears are part of a planned deception: first, there is no reliable evidence whatever in the poem that she plans or deals in willful deceit, and her prototypes in previous literature do not, as has been pointed out; second, since willful deceit is a mode of human evil and she is conceived as a suprahuman daemonic creature beyond both good and evil, then deceit cannot accurately be attributed to her within the matrix of ideas and conceptions upon which the poem rests. The use of the word "as" in the knight's statement "She look'd at me as she did love" is dictated by the compression of the ballad form and does not necessarily indicate deception; and when he reports that she said "I love thee true," there is not the slightest evidence that *he* doubted it or that we are to do so. She acts according to the law of her neutral daemonic nature and does nothing that is evil, deceitful, or malicious; and she cannot rightly be designated "a fairy mistress from hell." [15] The knight's involvement with her, especially the initiation of it, is very much his own doing, as Professor Wasserman has pointed out.[16]

Chiefly through suggestion, symbol, and innuendo she is endowed with the aura of high sexuality which yet never violates delicacy, and the mutual involvement of the two is rendered with increasingly sexual overtones of rare charm.

[15] Utley, "The Infernos of Lucretius and Keats's *La Belle Dame sans Merci*," p. 121.
[16] *The Finer Tone*, pp. 78–81.

The knight, taking the lead, made a "garland for her head," "bracelets," and "fragrant zone," which together constitute a thrice-reiterated feminine sex symbol; and she, responding, "look'd . . . love" with her "wild wild eyes" and "made sweet moan." Then the knight, still directing events, set her on his "pacing steed," an image replete with sexual suggestion, and began during the journey to move into full enthrallment with her, in which he "nothing else saw all day long" as she bent "sidelong" and sang "a faery's song."

In turn, her own involvement almost equals his as she responds further: she found for him "roots of relish sweet," "honey wild," and "manna dew"; she said, "in language strange," "I love thee true"; and she took him to her "elfin grot," [17] another obvious female sexual symbol, and there they evidently consummated ecstatic sexual union. But then she seemed suddenly to gain foreknowledge of their impending separation, for "she wept, and sigh'd full sore," and he had to soothe and comfort her and shut her "wild wild eyes" with kisses. And there in the grot, as would be quite natural under

[17] Professor Wasserman maintains that all these details indicate that she now takes the lead and directs events, as evidenced by the shift in pronoun from "I" predominantly in stanzas IV–VI to "she" in stanzas VII–IX; but this shift could have resulted simply from the technical exigencies of narration, since the knight in his account is following a usual plan of telling in alternation what one said and did and then what the other replied and did in response, as must be the case in any such narrative unless there is a conscious intention to make one of the two lovers in the affair entirely, unnaturally, and insipidly passive. The knight's narrative is an account of passionate sexual love lifted beyond the human sphere into the daemonic—into suprahuman intensity. With one partner entirely passive no instance of sexual love can be said to have reached even the limit of human intensity, much less of an intensity beyond that, which this is surely represented to be, whatever the name we give it; and it is not convincing as something symbolically spiritual. I do not believe that she so actively seizes the lead as simply responds in kind, for all the things she does are for him and not necessarily steps in a scheme of entrapment—things which she knew best how to do in that time and place, including leading him to the grot, for only she knew the way. Her lulling him to sleep later is perfectly natural under the circumstances—i.e., after consummation.

the circumstances, she finally lulls him to sleep. There is no reliable evidence of intended malice or fraud in this or in any other of her actions.

In his sleep he has a remarkable dream, one of the most captivating passages in the poem, in which the mingled beauty and terror of the daemonic is revealed in a simultaneous remoteness and immediacy that impel a reader to sense its potentiality in the depths of his own psyche. In this dream the true nature of the love experience with the elfin lady begins to become apparent, though far more fully to the reader than to the knight; and he begins the transition out of the realm into which he had followed her:

IX

And there she lulled me asleep,
   And there I dream'd—Ah, woe betide!
The latest dream I ever dream'd
   On the cold hill side.

X

I saw pale kings and princes too,
   Pale warriors, death-pale were they all;
They cried—'La Belle Dame sans Merci
   Hath thee in thrall!'

XI

I saw their starved lips in the gloam,
   With horrid warning gaped wide,
And I awoke and found me here,
   On the cold hill's side.

His seemingly weird dream is powerfully expressive and functional, and its meaning is strikingly clear; for it is a remarkable projection in visual images of what he was beginning to know as it welled up from the depths of his subconscious into his conscious mind: that in his daemonic love he had passed beyond his mortal limitations, that these limitations were now reasserting themselves and were either to separate him from the captivating creature forever or to allow him to become completely enslaved and be destroyed. Hence the aura of terror mingled with glimmering, haunting beauty. For whatever she was when he met her in the meads—mortal, nonmortal, or figment of the imagination—she had served as a "hook" for the *anima*,[18] as an instrument or agent for drawing up from the collective unconscious (not simply from the *personal* unconscious) the all-inclusive pattern for knowing the feminine in its positive, joy-giving aspects and also in its engulfing and destructive capacities. In the account of his journey and lovemaking in the grot he had set forth the joyous and positive side of the archetypal *anima;* now in the vision of the "pale kings and princes" who had preceded him there, with their "starved lips" gaping wide in "horrid warning," he is revealing with unparalleled visual power the very moment at which the destructive and engulfing element in this archetype emerges from the unconscious and begins to take on suitable images by means of which he apprehends it, as it must do in order for him to apprehend it. And how suitable the images indeed! Outwardly, in terms of their literary origins, they call to mind all the men who had gone before in pursuit of the ultimate feminine; inwardly they portray his not-yet-fully-conscious awareness that a daemonic hunger has been stirred which can never be satisfied, for it exists because of what has been activated in *him*, not simply because of what is in the elfin lady. For him to dream that the pale kings and

[18] See above, Chapter I, pp. 19–20 and note 17.

warriors tell him that the Beautiful Lady without Kindness
has him in thrall is the way in which his subconscious begins
to inform his conscious mind of that fact. But this hunger can
enslave, and he is still entirely receptive to that enslavement.[19]

Quite appropriately, it is during the course of this dream,
which renders forth the emerging discovery in the deepest
levels of his conscious life, that the knight completes his
transition out of the realm of ecstatic joy into which he had
been projected. He awakes and finds himself on the cold hillside, and the final stanza begins with what may seem an
incongruous assertion:

XII

And this is why I sojourn here,
　Alone and palely loitering,
Though the sedge has wither'd from the lake,
　And no birds sing.

If the pronoun "this" in the first line above is taken to refer
only to what immediately precedes, that is, to the dream vision of the pale kings and princes warning the knight back,
we may well feel that the ending does not make sense at all,
for we may legitimately ask why he does not gladly accept
their warning, break the spell he is under, and happily go
home to the warm fireside. But the pronoun "this" refers not
only to the dream warning alone but to the full revelation in

---

[19] I cannot agree with Professor Wasserman's assertion that the "pale kings
and princes" are "men of power" from the actual world who are "death-pale"
because they have lived out their lives on the mortal plane and have never been
able to enter the elfin grot and who intrude into the knight's dream to warn
him of his own mortality just when he is on the brink of bliss (*The Finer Tone*,
pp. 75–80). Just the converse seems more truly the case, for the young
questioner (the most authentic representative of life on the plane of mortality)
is not at all pale. The kings and princes are pale with exhaustion from their
own experience in the grot and hence are able to warn the knight of his danger.

his entire narrative; and consequently, the words "this is why I sojourn here" mean something like the following: My faery love has brought me such ecstatic joy that all normal, human pleasures have now become unpalatable, and neither the impossibility of its longer duration nor the possibility of my enslavement can impel me to do other than continually search for her in vain amidst the bleakness and silence here. By now it is apparent that in the poem all external statements, actions, responses, and elements from previous literature are but the materials with which Keats set forth a drama of a man's inner life; for the protagonist in *La Belle Dame*, through the results of a meeting or an imagined meeting with a nonmortal female, has experienced the full force of the *anima* archetype within him and has known both the suprahuman beauty and the terrible destructiveness of the ultrafeminine.

By repeating in his last three lines almost exactly the words of the questioner in the first stanza, the narrator not only brings the poem full circle structurally but also re-emphasizes the importance of the first speaker's advocacy of the ordinary human satisfactions, and reaffirms his conception of the sufficiency of the human world for human needs. Against this serenity and ripeness of the normal human realm, the wasted knight and his world of glimmering beauty and terror stand out in sharply defined contrast. By having the knight enter a neutral daemonic realm instead of a distinctly evil one, Keats threw over his poem the glamour of the forbidden without the stigma of the immoral. This master stroke is augmented by the withholding of the final outcome; we never learn whether the knight ever regained an appetite for the satisfactions of the common lot and reassumed his place in the human family or whether he lapsed back into complete enthrallment and eventual death. Now we can well understand why Keats underlined the words and scored the margins of the passage in *Palmerin of England* in which a knight under daemonic enthrallment before his enchanted lady, whom he is unable to rouse, becomes "so passionately afflicted that his judgment and reason clearly abandoned him, and he determined to remain in that strange dwelling place beside his lady, not remembering that he had no other food there than his own *imaginations, which would sooner destroy than support him.*" [20] Keats's fascination with the passage suggests that through it he was discovering something of the dual nature of the *anima* archetype within the male psyche, and the basic condition and situation of the knight in the passage are markedly similar to those of Keats's knight, though there are differences in details.

Since things are left in a fluid state at the end, we continue to wonder about the final outcome of the knight's psychic adventure and thus continue to be involved in the poem after completing the reading of it, as the last bleak scene lingers in the mind still unfolding anew. Indeed for this man the sedge has withered from the lake and no birds sing; if they did sing, he would not hear them, and if the sedge were green, he would not see it. His senses and consciousness are still attuned to the daemonic beauty of the elfin grot, and even in the satisfying world of the harvest and the squirrel's granary he is truly forlorn.

Although we are strongly dissuaded, happily, from indulging in simple didactic interpretations of the poem, some reflections concerning the import of what it presents are in order. The juxtaposition of the daemonic world and the world

[20] *Palmerin of England*, translated by Anthony Munday and corrected by Robert Southey (London, 1807), IV, 181. Leigh Hunt indicated that Keats underlined the last eight words as italicized here. See above, Chapter I, note 11.

of normal humanity is managed in such a way as to throw into very favorable light the richness of the human lot. Its joys are not inconsiderable, their cost is light, and they are ever-present and available. On the other hand, the remote, strange beauty and ecstasy of the daemonic world are invested with superior glamour and almost irresistible appeal. But these endure but briefly, and their cost may be high, in fact so high as to "make a man forget his mortal way" and "lose the sight of well remember'd face,/ Of Brother's eyes, of Sister's brow." [21] Keats's knight has gone beyond the point where he can feel "the gentle anchor pull" calling him back to humanity and beyond the point where he can "gladden in its strength," but perhaps he has not gone beyond the point that "would bar return." [22] For that we must wait for *Lamia*. By starkly juxtaposing the two realms of conscious life in *La Belle Dame* without judging them, Keats is in effect, intentionally or otherwise, inviting us to consider the cost and the gain, just as he had brought Endymion to do earlier. An excursion into daemonic ecstasy without permanent loss of the appeal of ever-present common joy is an extension of experience not to be missed and highly to be valued. But if the cost is too great in common currency the value of the experience diminishes in proportion, and it varies with each individual.

In addition to producing in *La Belle Dame sans Merci* one of his most distinctive poems, Keats managed for the first time to construct and to project his daemonic "other world" with compression, masterly control, skill, and power. Inevitably this world beyond the common consciousness was to play a part in the "great odes," for he composed *La Belle Dame sans Merci* at the very threshold of that time, the apex

---

[21] *Lines Written in the Highlands after a Visit to Burns's Country*, 32–34.
[22] *Ibid.*, 40, 32.

of his poetic career. Within a few days of completing this poem he was at work on the first of these, the *Ode to Psyche;* and he composed all the others except *To Autumn* within a month after that. What he had brought to full development in *La Belle Dame sans Merci* also played a crucial part, in one way or another and in varying degrees, in almost all of these later poems, which are universally recognized as his greatest achievements.

CHAPTER FIVE   A DIMENSION
OF THE GREAT ODES

By the time Keats's great year of 1819 arrived, it is apparent
that when his imagination pierced beyond the plane of the
actual it usually projected itself into an emotion-charged daemonic realm rather than into a region of ideal forms or mystical values. This pattern seems by now to have become habitual; we have seen it operating functionally in all his most
significant poems up to this time—*Endymion*, *The Eve of St.
Agnes*, and *La Belle Dame sans Merci*, in which it reached
full flower artistically—and we have seen it playing a significant part in less important poems such as the sonnet *As
Hermes Once*, closely related to *La Belle Dame* in theme, and
the verse epistle *To J. H. Reynolds, Esq.*, in which Keats had
proclaimed that "Imagination brought/ Beyond its proper
bound . . ./ Cannot refer to any standard law/ Of either
earth or heaven" (78–82). As a result of this now habitual
tendency to pierce irrepressibly beyond the actual but into
suprahuman ecstasy rather than into transcendent spiritual
values ordered and stabilized by some "standard law" of
thought, it is not surprising that this tendency and resulting
daemonic element also operate in a similar pattern in the great
odes of 1819, as they are now generally called. In view of his

wise theorizing about it as in the verse epistle above (wise for him though not for a Spenser, a Blake, or a Shelley) and in view of his judicious handling of it in previous poems, it is not surprising to find this daemonic element utilized in these odes with more finesse, control, and restraint than ever before. Keats's odes are firmly rooted in the actual, but the daemonic element provides a second dimension of poetic experience beyond the actual, which through sharp contrast accentuates the beauty of the phenomenal world just as it does in his narrative poems, and at the same time adds mystery, complexity, and depth to the total effect in the odes. Without these qualities the odes would present lyrical experience on one single plane and would then lack much of their unique power and appeal.[1]

Though seen more strikingly in later odes, after Keats had settled on an over-all structure and stanza form, this second dimension of experience provided by the daemonic element, I believe, is what gives to the earliest one, *Ode to Psyche*, the distinction and special charm that account for its success.[2]

[1] Since many fruitful explications have revealed the beauty and inner structure of most of the odes, I shall for the sake of brevity point out here the daemonic element in five of them briefly without undertaking full-length exegeses and without opposing differing views. Most often, attention to the daemonic element serves to augment, to support, and in part at times to correct responsible and careful interpretations already available. A collection reprinting significant studies of Keats's odes, with a selected bibliography, has been published recently: Jack Stillinger, ed., *Twentieth Century Interpretations of Keats's Odes* (Englewood Cliffs, N.J., 1968). More than half of a previous collection of Keats studies makes easily available other important interpretations of the odes: W. J. Bate, ed., *Twentieth Century Views of Keats* (Englewood Cliffs, N.J., 1964), also with a selected bibliography. Selective lists of studies of each ode (except *Ode on Indolence*) are given in R. H. Fogle, ed., *Romantic Poets and Prose Writers*, Goldentree Bibliographies (New York, 1967). Inclusive bibliographies may be found in *PMLA* (1922—), *ELH* (1937–49), *Philological Quarterly* (1950–64), *English Language Notes* (1965—), and *Keats-Shelley Journal* (1952—).

[2] For further treatment of *Ode to Psyche*, the reader should consult especially David Perkins, *The Quest for Permanence* (Cambridge, Mass., 1959), pp. 222–228; Charles W. Hagelman's informative and imaginative essay, "Keats's

This poem of praise is cast somewhat in the mode of a dream vision of Psyche, the Grecian goddess of the soul, that is so vivid as to seem an actual encounter with her:

> Surely I dreamt to-day, or did I see
>   The winged Psyche with awaken'd eyes?
>   5–6

With increasing intensity he soon begins to concentrate on the aspect of Psyche which most fascinates him and with which he is primarily concerned. Being the latest born of "Olympus' faded hierarchy," she came into godhead too late to receive a just share of worship from adoring mortals:

> Fairer than Pheobe's sapphire-region'd star,
>   Or Vesper, amorous glow-worm of the sky;
> Fairer than these, though temple thou hast none,
>   Nor altar heap'd with flowers;
> Nor virgin-choir to make delicious moan
>   Upon the midnight hours;
> No voice, no lute, no pipe, no incense sweet
>   From chain-swung censer teeming;
> No shrine, no grove, no oracle, no heat
>   Of pale-mouth'd prophet dreaming.
>
> O brightest! though too late for antique vows,
>   Too, too late for the fond believing lyre,
> When holy were the haunted forest boughs,
>   Holy the air, the water, and the fire;
> Yet even in these days so far retir'd
>   From happy pieties, thy lucent fans,

Medical Training and the Last Stanza of the 'Ode to Psyche,' " *Keats-Shelley Journal*, XI (1962), 73–82; and Harold Bloom, *The Visionary Company* (New York, 1961), pp. 389–397, reprinted in Bate, *Twentieth Century Views of Keats*, pp. 91–101.

Fluttering among the faint Olympians,
I see, and sing, by my own eyes inspired.

                                    26–43

He then enunciates the central aim of the poem: his determination to compensate for all this lack of attention to her by the
zeal and power of his own devotion alone and his priestly
offices for her. With considerable audacity he is setting up a
great vacuum which he intends later to fill, a structural device
that he had used successfully in his second sonnet on Homer.
Here in *Ode To Psyche* he indicates his major intention as
follows:

> So let me be thy choir, and make a moan
>   Upon the midnight hours;
> Thy voice, thy lute, thy pipe, thy incense sweet
>   From swinged censer teeming;
> Thy shrine, thy grove, thy oracle, thy heat
>   Of pale-mouth'd prophet dreaming.

                                    44–49

In his manner of declaring this intention Keats builds cohesion into the center of the poem, tying together the deficiency
of Psyche worship with his intended compensation for it, by
using the same key words in the same order in two pairs of
related lines. By simply removing the negative "no" before
each item in lines 32 and 34, and substituting "thy" in corresponding places, he neatly turns these lines into the parallel
lines 46 and 48, in which he vows that he will become all
these things to her:

> Thy voice, thy lute, thy pipe, thy incense sweet
>
>   .   .   .   .
>
> Thy shrine, thy grove, thy oracle, thy heat.

The repetition of the change from negative to positive in the parallel language emphasizes the central change in the structure of the poem from enunciation of the lack of Psyche worship to enunciation of the way to fulfill that need just before the accomplishing of that difficult task in the last section, his major aim in the poem.

With all these deliberately fostered expectations the final rendering of this compensatory worship in the form of a "fane" with proper rituals in progress, which the poet as self-appointed priest builds to Psyche with mere words, could easily be disappointing; but miraculously it is not, for it lives up to the speaker's promises remarkably. One of the main reasons for his success with it is that in deep truth it is, as he says, constructed in "some untrodden region" of his mind which no other impetus save this one had ever impelled him to enter; for when we examine the unearthly beauty of this "fane" in detail we find it to be a daemonic temple in a daemonic realm of his consciousness, where none of the customary limitations operate in the natural or in the human modes of being. "Branched thoughts, new grown" take the place of murmuring pines beside its porticoes; "wild-ridged mountains steep by steep" surround it; its "rosy sanctuary" is embellished "with buds, and bells, and stars" that have no name, because they are daemonic and hence neither of earth nor heaven; and, most significantly, its gardener will be forever breeding flowers, but "will never breed the same," for the progeny are not limited by natural law to the genus of their lineage in a daemonic realm. We are now at the heart of the poem and in its second dimension—the one beyond the actual plane of the sensory but in which the senses still operate in a suprahuman way. Keats has managed matters so as to have the concrete vividness of the senses and at the same time a dimension beyond them that is not abstract, although the use of this extra dimension brings some of the same advantages without the defects. By means of it he achieved range and depth in his lyricism in an unusual way and in a way that brought up no problems as to the credibility of what he is saying. It is entirely acceptable to the intellect when taken *in toto* as he renders it. In setting forth this final passage it seems that Keats simply relaxed and let the lyrical splendors flow in an uninhibited stream, now well prepared for, that held within itself its own order and control, just as in a passage long prepared for in a Mozart concerto:

> Yes, I will be thy priest, and build a fane
>   In some untrodden region of my mind,
> Where branched thoughts, new grown with pleasant pain,
>   Instead of pines shall murmur in the wind:
> Far, far around shall those dark-cluster'd trees
>   Fledge the wild-ridged mountains steep by steep;
> And there by zephyrs, streams, and birds, and bees,
>   The moss-lain Dryads shall be lull'd to sleep;
> And in the midst of this wide quietness
> A rosy sanctuary will I dress
> With the wreath'd trellis of a working brain,
>   With buds, and bells, and stars without a name,
> With all the gardener Fancy e'er could feign,
>   Who breeding flowers, will never breed the same:
> And there shall be for thee all soft delight
>   That shadowy thought can win,
> A bright torch, and a casement ope at night,
>   To let the warm Love in!

50–67

Even a goddess should be pleased with such adulation of such a unique kind. From the time of *I Stood Tip-toe*, back in 1816 before *Endymion*, Keats had been speaking of those who could "burst our mortal bars" and rise into "some wond'rous region" (190–191). In this hymn of praise to Psyche as goddess of the consciousness he demonstrates before our eyes how the consciousness can transcend itself and create beauties beyond its customary bounds and yet all the while never offend the intellectual faculties, never passing into mystical values of doubtful ontological status or into a pretense that the new dimension of beauty is other than what in truth it is: daemonic beauty constructed "in some untrodden region" of his mind, not meant to be long sustained though it may recur when he contemplates late-born Psyche again. Throughout the passage he continually indicates the truth of what it is during the very time that he is casting its spell upon the reader.

Unlike most of the other odes, *Psyche* terminates while still in the second dimension constituted by the daemonic, although there is a hint of return to the human realm in "the warm Love" mentioned in the final line. In the other odes which make use of daemonic elements the termination usually comes after a clear and deliberate rejection or breaking off of the sojourn beyond the actual, and this second shift from one plane to another in these odes serves to re-emphasize the difference between the daemonic and the actual. Since the structure of *Ode to Psyche* does not include this second major shift of plane, but ends while on the daemonic level, the function of the daemonic in the poem is not so readily discernible at first as it appears after several readings. But the poem gains markedly in depth, complexity, and appeal from Keats's effective use of this element structurally in the climactic position. His success with it in *Ode to Psyche* reveals that he has made the highly significant transition from using it predominantly in narrative poems to the more difficult employment of it in lyrical structures of an elevated and serious kind.

In the *Ode on Indolence*,[3] probably the least appreciated of the group, Keats makes quite a different use of the daemonic element that is again functional and fruitful. In this poem a structuring and unifying tension between the two planes of the daemonic and the actual, not evident in *To Psyche* as a conflict, is employed as an element in the central framework of the whole, though it is not so fully developed and exploited as in *Ode to a Nightingale* and *Ode on a Grecian Urn*. In *Ode on Indolence* the daemonic world beckons appealingly and hovers enticingly in the foreground throughout, but the speaker decides not to enter it, as he seems for a time about to

___

[3] Although there is no conclusive evidence of its exact date of composition during the spring of 1819, I believe that it was written next after *Ode to Psyche*, which was completed by April 30 (*Letters*, II, 106–108); for the *Ode on Indolence* lacks the well-defined structure, even texture, and sustained rich imagery of *Nightingale* and *Grecian Urn*, while revealing a structure that seems to point in the direction of that more fully developed in those greater poems, where the same stanza form as in *Indolence* is better handled also. Moreover, Keats had the actual experience which served as the basis of the poem back on March 19 (*Letters*, II, 78–79). Robert Gittings, in his new biography *John Keats* (Boston, 1968), p. 313, states that the poem was written early in the spring and names the exact day with "little doubt" as May 4, which seems about right, but his evidence is not conclusive though significant. Aileen Ward in *John Keats: The Making of a Poet* (New York, 1963), pp. 432–433, also gives a worthy argument that *Indolence* was written early though after *Psyche*. Many distinguished Keatsians have believed so, including Sidney Colvin, *John Keats*, 3rd ed. (London, 1920), pp. 352–353. W. J. Bate thinks that *Indolence* was written late in the spring and after *Nightingale* and *Grecian Urn*, but the phrases and images in *Indolence* which he considers possible echoes of *Nightingale* and *Grecian Urn* seem more like adumbrations in *Indolence* later perfected in these two odes: *John Keats* (Cambridge, Mass., 1963), p. 528. Professor Bate's discussion of *Ode on Indolence* is primarily biographical (*ibid.*, pp. 527–530). Apparently no full-scale explication or critical analysis of the poem exists, but in his brief treatment Professor Bloom, I think, points to the heart of the piece: "The mood is turned inward toward Keats himself" (*Visionary Company*, pp. 410–411).

do; and his refusal constitutes something of a dramatic reversal of what appears to be expected, a crucial change of direction which points toward what I believe to be the fundamental idea which the poem dramatizes. Essentially, this ode presents Keats in the very process of feeling the reality of his own being rather than uniting his consciousness with an aesthetic object apart from himself. This experience is heightened by being set off against the three shadowy figures continually passing before him. Since they represent love, ambition, and "my demon Poesy"—objectives that men frequently pursue with relentless intensity and engulfing zeal—they are potential daemonic agents capable of absorbing all his interest and luring him away from the "new-leav'd vine" and "throstle's lay" that made "ripe" the "drowsy hour" in which the sense of self-being became strong within him.

It is highly significant at the beginning that he inserted under the title a motto from the famous passage in the Sermon on the Mount (Matthew VI: 28–31) that begins, "Consider the lilies of the field, how they grow; they toil not, neither do they spin: And yet I say unto you, That even Solomon in all his glory was not arrayed like one of these." Just below his title Keats printed only the words "They toil not, neither do they spin." That is, they are not a means to a separate end or a cause of a resulting effect; they contain within themselves their own purpose and justification, for *being* is their only purpose. The motto provides a clue to the essential point in the poem, for Keats tries to convey that he had achieved something of a kindred state of pure being during that morning when he steadfastly warded off his "demon Poesy." Banishing his "demon" focuses the poem on the realm of the actual, but he subtly pierces beneath the sensory without going into the mystical or ideal, which would have brought on an "apartness" or retreat from actuality that he resolutely kept out of the poem. Instead, what he is doing is perceiving intuitively and immediately—that is, without the mediation of the senses—his own state of rich awareness while it is in process. Small wonder that he said of the experience, "This is the only happiness" (*Letters*, II, 79). He made being and knowing as nearly one as is possible, and he was able to do so because the particular nature of his cognitive indolence gave him a good look within. It is understandable that he liked writing this ode better than anything else he had done during this memorable spring and that he felt himself "a little more of a Philosopher" and a little less of "a versifying Pet-lamb" than he had been before (*Letters*, II, 116).

The poem begins[4] with the speaker stating that one morning three figures in sandals and white robes appeared and passed before him, "like figures on a marble urn" when it is turned to the other side. They passed by three times, the last time turning their faces toward him. At first he did not know their identity, but later he "burn'd" to follow them and "ached for wings" with which to do so when he recognized the three

---

[4] It is beyond question that H. W. Garrod in the standard edition of Keats's poems has arbitrarily rearranged the correct order of the stanzas of *Indolence* given in Charles Brown's transcript, the only manuscript text of the poem based on a Keats holograph, as Jack Stillinger has conclusively demonstrated in an article, "The Text of Keats's 'Ode on Indolence,'" *Studies in Bibliography*, XXII (1969), 255–258, and I acknowledge with thanks his allowing me to see galley proofs of the article before publication. Garrod moved stanza V to the position of stanza III, pushing III down to IV and IV to V—a serious injury to the movement and to the sense of the poem. For a correct order of the stanzas we must go back to Brown's manuscript or to the first printed text of the poem in R. M. Milnes's *Life, Letters, and Literary Remains of John Keats* (London, 1848), followed by some modern editors before Garrod, e.g., C. D. Thorpe, ed., *Complete Poems and Selected Letters of John Keats* (New York, 1935). I am using Garrod's text but with Milnes's order of stanzas, and I am numbering the lines of the poem according to Milnes's version, beyond doubt the correct order.

as the "fair Maid . . . Love," "Ambition, pale of cheek," and that "maiden most unmeek,—/ . . . my demon Poesy" (24–30). Thus an entirely different dimension of reality is suddenly opened up to view, a dimension in which the speaker could lose his new-found sense of self-identity; and the poem, taking on complexity now, seems about to be precipitated into it. The speaker is in the same position as Endymion (II, 212–213) when "a voice" urged him to fear not "to follow/ Where airy voices lead," or in that of the knight in *La Belle Dame sans Merci*, who obviously had not feared to follow the elfin lady. But here in the ode there is at this point a sudden reversal, for instead of following the figures before him the speaker declares, "They faded, and, forsooth! I wanted wings" (31). That is, he lacked wings to follow, although it soon appears that he is no longer regretful. However, this second dimension of experience, which the three figures represent, lingers throughout the piece as an ever-present possibility, for we cannot be sure that the speaker's refusal to follow them is permanent until near the end. Thereby, range and depth are given to the poem; for although the daemonic world is never entered, its continued presence as a possibility makes us continually aware that Keats is not dealing with a single plane of experience.

In truth, the dramatic reversal ushered in by the words "They faded" (31) has been prepared for quite fully in previous lines. Early in the poem (12–14) the speaker had asked whether the coming of the three figures before him in "so hush a masque" was a "deep-disguised plot/ To steal away, and *leave without a task/* My idle days?" The word "task" refers to such active work as writing a poem, as becomes apparent later when he banishes his "demon Poesy," for at the moment he juxtaposes to this task the importance of his rare mood, in which the "blissful cloud of summer-indolence" (16) blunted the sharpness of the individual senses but left receptive their capability to take in enough of his surroundings to keep his consciousness sufficiently in action for it to be an object of knowledge to itself as knower. It must be acting if it is to be known as a concrete object rather than as a shadowy abstraction. Hence it is quite understandable that at this point he wishes that the three figures would "melt, and leave my sense/ Unhaunted quite of all but—nothingness" (19–20); that is, leave his consciousness "unhaunted" by all but the cognition of itself, which is what "all but—nothingness" would have to be unless the passage means that he is longing for complete extinction, and nothing else in the entire poem indicates that desire, but all opposes it. The whole experience seems a lyrical counterpart to Shakespeare's dramatic "Ripeness is all" in *King Lear* (V, ii, 11); and Keats proclaims, "Ripe was the drowsy hour" (15), that is, ripe with cognizance of himself and his relationship to his world. He is knowing beyond the senses without entirely leaving them, knowing directly and concretely the splendor of *to be*. Keats supports this proclamation of the glory of the moment with effective detail: "Pain had no sting, and pleasure's wreath no flower" (18); his consciousness was "a lawn besprinkled o'er/ With flowers, and stirring shades"; "The morn was clouded" with the water of life, "but no shower fell,/ Tho' in her lids hung the sweet tears of May"; "The open casement press'd a new-leav'd vine" and "Let in the budding warmth and throstle's lay" (43–48). He can easily declare to the three figures:

> O shadows! 'twas a time to bid farewell!
> Upon your skirts had fallen no tears of mine.
> 49–50

Therefore, even after he had recognized their identity and momentarily "burn'd" to follow them, he understandably gives them up readily, takes up the main theme, and carries it to fruition. Like the lilies he neither toils nor spins during this drowsy hour, but he apprehends anew the wonder of existence and will not be lured beyond the affirmation of it. He quickly disposes of the blandishments of Love and Ambition, "a man's little heart's short fever-fit" (32–34), and briefly repudiates "the voice of busy common-sense" (40); but he gives particular attention and greater emphasis to denying the appeal of his "demon Poesy":

> For Poesy!—no,—she has not a joy,—
> At least for me,—so sweet as drowsy noons,
> And evenings steep'd in honied indolence.
> 35–37

In the terminal stanza he banishes the three with finality and continues his "simple worship of a day," as he had expressed it a year earlier in *Ode to May*. Now he concludes the present ode somewhat similarly:

> So, ye three Ghosts, adieu! Ye cannot raise
> My head cool-bedded in the flowery grass;
> For I would not be dieted with praise,
> A pet-lamb in a sentimental farce!
> Fade softly from my eyes, and be once more
> In masque-like figures on the dreamy urn,
> Farewell! I yet have visions for the night,
> And for the day faint visions there is store;
> Vanish, ye Phantoms! from my idle spright,
> Into the clouds, and never more return!
> 51–60

The "faint visions" are all he desires, for they are just enough to keep his consciousness in sufficient aliveness to be its own object. Together with the earlier assertions of preference for his mood of cognitive indolence, these lines drive home his main point. He is not at all thinking of giving up poetry forever, but at the moment he chooses not to make the effort to be "dieted with praise" for mediocre poetry in print, "A pet-lamb in a sentimental farce," when he can live such moments of glowing existence. He finds that there is a wealth of satisfaction in conscious life during moments like these. The fact that he never published the poem during his lifetime may be pertinent to the central idea which it proclaims. In such rare moments human beings, like the lilies, "toil not, neither do they spin" but in united introversion and extraversion feel the reality of their own selfhood and apprehend the splendor of the moment in a way that helps to obviate the pain of transience.

Thus the poem displays the same consciousness which *Ode to Psyche* celebrated, acting out here a distinctly different power: there the consciousness was turned outward in the act of deifying the late-born Psyche; here in *Indolence* the consciousness is turned inward in the act of apprehending its own self-identity. Hence Keats here rejects both the daemonic and "Negative Capability," for the latter must involve an external object which fills the mind and is united with it, but in this ode the object known is the same as the subject knowing it, ruling out "Negative Capability" in favor of a cognitive experience even more rare and unusual. Keats has begun to develop the thematic design of the odes as a group.

His eschewing the lure of the daemonic at the beginning of the *Ode on Indolence* and his continuing to reject it throughout enabled him to focus attention firmly upon the actual world of minds and objects while he probed beneath its surface without ever in truth leaving its concreteness and particularity; and the near presence of the daemonic as a possibility, represented by the three figures, continually set off by contrast his finding contentment in feeling the reality of his consciousness while it was in action. Without this extra dimension the poem would not have been endowed with its combined subtlety and force. One cannot rightly claim that it should be elevated to a top position among Keats's odes, for it lacks the firm structure, rich imagery, even texture, and magical passages of the others; but it deserves without apology a respectable place within the group when considered in its full significance.[5]

While the *Ode to Psyche* revealed that Keats had made the important transition from use of the daemonic element only in narrative verse to successful employment of it in lyrical poems, the *Ode on Indolence* shows him consolidating and extending that gain with increasing skill, using it structurally in a way that points toward the basic framework of the greater *Ode to a Nightingale* and *Ode on a Grecian Urn.*

In these two odes the daemonic element is put to its most consummate use in Keats's lyrical poetry, lending power and distinction to both through the additional dimension of the experience it gives and providing the pivotal middle section of a strong tripartite structure, implicit in *Psyche* and *Indolence*, but now developed and exploited fully in both of these greater odes. This threefold structure in both poems shapes up basically as follows: (1) his initial contemplation of the nightingale or urn as objects separate and apart from the conscious-

[5] I think that Professor Stillinger is a bit too severe in tending to deny it a place in the group (*Keats's Odes*, p. 5n).

ness of the speaker; (2) his growing involvement with the bird world and urn world until they almost fill up his consciousness and unite with it, impelling a progressively daemonic state of mind in which he views objects in the bird world and urn world without mortal limitations for a time; (3) sudden termination of the daemonic state, leading to renewed contemplation of bird and urn as objects apart from the consciousness, but this time with affirmations concerning the particular nature and import of the preceding ecstatic experience in the middle sections of the poems. Without the extra dimension provided by the daemonic element in these middle sections, a dimension beyond that of the common consciousness that is neither ideal nor mystical, these two poems would lack their unusual power to make the reader feel that he is looking not upon a flat surface but into the depths of a vista that is endless. Without this element the two poems would unfold entirely on the plane of the sensuous. They would then have become simply lyrical idyls, for the sensuous is well handled in both. But as they are, with the additional dimension provided by the daemonic and its interplay with the actual, the poems are much more than idyls; they are penetrating commentaries on the problems of man's relationship to the world as it is and on his adjustment to it. At one and the same time, they portray vividly how man can find beauty in the world of concrete phenomena; how through imagination he can remake it, transform it, and escape from its limitations momentarily; and also why the inevitable bounds of this transformation and escape must not be transgressed. These two odes and *To Autumn*, taken together, move progressively from probing the outer limits of experience, to noble resignation before its limitations, and finally to serene acceptance of man's lot; for these poems carry to completion the tremendous discovery that the limits upon human experience have been placed generously far. With his imagination as a constituent part of man's world, it is replete with manifold beauty that is richly rewarding in spite of limitations.

Thus, when considered from a point of view that includes the daemonic, these odes reveal that there is remarkable unity and homogeneity in the whole Keats canon, for we have seen this element impelling the narrative poems to a kindred position in outcome and import in their different mode.

Though *Ode to a Nightingale* and *Ode on a Grecian Urn* are strikingly similar in basic framework and over-all plan, they differ notably in important particulars and in their final affirmations concerning the experience each presents. The nightingale is a living creature that has acquired a special status and something like sanctity from ages of human interest in it, and it therefore has a part in the whole matter of the human relationship to beautiful objects in nature; but, on the other hand, the urn is a nonliving art object produced by human minds and hands, and therefore is a symbol and a part of the relationship of human minds to works of art. While the transition from the first to the second major part in *Nightingale* is clear and distinct, even a little awkwardly so ("Already with thee," in line 35), the transition into the second major section in *Grecian Urn* is so smoothly modulated that the precise point is not discernible, although by the time of stanza 4 the speaker is deep within his period of involvement with the urn figures. In neither poem is the identification of speaker and object complete to the point of delusion, for "Negative Capability" does not entail the entire loss of self-consciousness but only most of it, and here certain key assertions and intimations concerning the contrast between the bird-urn world and the ordinary human world would not be possible if complete delusion had occurred in the middle part, nor would the affirmations at the end concerning the whole experience, which do much to give the poems their unique stature in lyrical poetry; for complete delusion during the crucial middle part would have blotted out all memory of it and made impossible its serving as the basis of the reflections in the concluding part. Last, the final comment on the significance of the journey with the bird is chiefly negative in quality ("the fancy cannot cheat so well/ As she is fam'd to do"), while the final comment concerning the journey to the sacrifice with the urn figures is essentially positive and forward-looking ("Thou shalt remain, in midst of other woe/ Than ours, a friend to man"), embodying a distinct advance in the treatment of the deep underlying theme of all the odes as a group: man's relationship to his world and adjustment to it, in which art can serve as a mediator and reconciler.

Thus, while *Psyche* deals with the power of the human consciousness to carry worship into deification and *Indolence* with the power to feel the reality of one's own being, *Nightingale* and *Grecian Urn* extend this delineation to include the ability of the consciousness to grasp the deeper significance of objects in nature and objects in art. *Ode on Melancholy* further extends the range of the odes to include the power of the consciousness to accept the pain of transience embedded in the heart of joy and to subsume this pain under the larger matter of full, accurate knowledge of all aspects of reality. *To Autumn* still further extends the range of the odes to include the consummate statement of the human mind's power to attain deep fulfillment in the ever-ripening present. Each ode in the group thus deals with the human consciousness apprehending an essentially different object or group of objects, and all the odes together include most of the fundamentals of human experience. They therefore have cohesion and unity among themselves and with the other major poems in the Keats canon.

Much of the richness of the first thirty-five lines of *Ode to a Nightingale*[6] will have to be passed over briefly here, including the famous lines which by words alone virtually produce the taste, smell, and presence of red wine, "With beaded bubbles winking at the brim,/ And purple-stained mouth" (15–17). In sum, this first of the three parts of the poem establishes several important bases which are built upon later. First it presents the central situation of the speaker in a state of "drowsy numbness," resembling that in *Ode on Indolence*, listening to the bird at a distance in "some melodious plot/ Of beechen green" as it sings "of summer in full-throated ease" (1–10). Next, this first part enunciates the desire of the speaker to leave his customary surroundings and through the stimulus of wine to join the bird and with it "fade away into the forest dim" (20)—but the agency of the wine is later rejected in favor of imagination alone (32–33). And last, the first part of the poem presents vividly in stanza 3 how death, decay, and transience pervade the human world, "Where youth grows pale, and spectre-thin, and dies" and "Beauty cannot keep her lustrous eyes,/ . . . beyond to-morrow" (26–30), which contrasts sharply with the ensuing daemonic

---

[6] R. H. Fogle's brilliant, inclusive, and authoritative explication is probably the most useful yet to appear: "Keats's *Ode to a Nightingale*," *PMLA*, LXVIII (March, 1953), 211–222, reprinted in Stillinger, *Keats's Odes*, which also includes the brief but very helpful discussion by Cleanth Brooks and R. P. Warren from *Understanding Poetry*, 3rd ed. (New York, 1960), pp. 426–430. Also useful is the discussion in Bloom, *Visionary Company*, pp. 397–403.

world which the bird's song enables him to create in his imagination, which seems to have no death and decay since it is free of human limitations.

Looking to imaginative union with the nightingale as an anodyne for the pervading transience in the world of humanity (31–33), the speaker initiates his sojourn in the forest with the bird abruptly, "Already with thee!" (35). This exclamation signalizes the beginning of the second major part of the poem. At first his empathic union with the nightingale remains on the plane of the actual in the world of nature, in which he revels with a new freedom uninhibited by thoughts of mortality. Since here in the forest there is "no light" except that which filters down from the moon "Through verdurous glooms and winding mossy ways" (38–40), he cannot quite see what flowers are at his feet; but by their smell he can

> guess each sweet
> Wherewith the seasonable month endows
> The grass, the thicket, and the fruit-tree wild;
> White hawthorn, and the pastoral eglantine;
> Fast fading violets cover'd up in leaves;
> And mid-May's eldest child,
> The coming musk-rose, full of dewy wine,
> The murmurous haunt of flies on summer eves.
>
> 43–50

Even the act of dying now seems to have lost its terrors and to have become a rich fulfillment, for in his empathic union with the bird his consciousness is partly sharing the bird's inability to conceive death and to know its horrors as people do (implied later in "Thou wast not born for death, immortal Bird" [61]). The speaker enjoys a momentary triumph over the world of mortality already depicted in the third stanza, for he is progressing rapidly toward the neutral daemonic realm where human limitations fall away:

> Darkling I listen; and, for many a time
>   I have been half in love with easeful Death,
> Call'd him soft names in many a mused rhyme,
>   To take into the air my quiet breath;
> Now more than ever seems it rich to die,
>   To cease upon the midnight with no pain,
>   While thou art pouring forth thy soul abroad
>   In such an ecstasy!
> Still wouldst thou sing, and I have ears in vain—
>   To thy high requiem become a sod.
>
> 51–60

But he suddenly realizes here that the presumed high fulfillment of death would bring him only oblivion, for the daemonic frequently reveals itself in contradictions (as Goethe had said); and the half-wish for death is overcome by the realization that in death he would be to the bird's "high requiem" merely unfeeling clay, "a sod." [7] This perception of his own mortality impels him to an even greater effort to find immortality in the bird, and he realizes joyously that it cannot know death or the conditions that hasten it in the human world and that its species will continue its song in the future as it has in the ancient past:

> Thou wast not born for death, immortal Bird!
> No hungry generations tread thee down.
>
> 61–62

[7] Anyone considering it an unequivocal death wish should consult Fogle's masterly discussion of the passage ("Keats's *Ode to a Nightingale*," p. 216) and Brooks and Warren's similar handling of it (*Understanding Poetry*, p. 430).

In the speaker's daemonic preoccupation the bird's song is becoming detached from the bird itself. Thinking predominantly of its "voice," its music always the same, he endows the bird with immortality and envisions its song in distant times and places where it had had a profound effect, he thinks, upon human beings in their mortal condition then as now:

> The voice I hear this passing night was heard
> In ancient days by emperor and clown:
> Perhaps the self-same song that found a path
> Through the sad heart of Ruth, when, sick for home,
> She stood in tears amid the alien corn.
>
> 63–67

The bird's song is ceasing to be merely an object in the world of nature and man, and is becoming a powerful agent of projection out of it. Now, with startling suddenness, the speaker soars to remote and perilous regions sequestered and cut off from man, where he experiences unearthly beauty for a few brief moments. He is at the height of the second dimension of the poem, far in the outer reaches of the daemonic. And there his sojourn beyond "mortal bars" comes simultaneously to its apex and eclipse:

> The same [song] that oft-times hath
> Charm'd magic casements, opening on the foam
> Of perilous seas, in faery lands forlorn.
> Forlorn! the very word is like a bell
> To toll me back from thee to my sole self!
>
> 68–72

Coming just at this point, where the pivotal middle section dramatically ends, these "magic casements" that open on the "perilous seas, in faery lands forlorn" constitute a powerfully expressive image, and much of its power derives from the fact that "forlorn" relates at once both to the daemonic world he is in and to the actual world he has left but is now re-entering. The whole image unfolding in the mind brings the instant realization that the remote apartness which gives the high point of the experience its special beauty and splendor also gives it its inevitable defect—a brevity and insubstantiality parallel to the ever-fading transience of actuality and the "perilous," lost condition of him who would attempt to sustain the daemonic state. Well had Keats written nearly a year earlier,

> Scanty the hour and few the steps beyond the bourn of care,
> Beyond the sweet and bitter world—beyond it unaware!
> Scanty the hour and few the steps, because a longer stay
> Would bar return, and make a man forget his mortal way:
>
> .   .   .   .
>
> No, no, that horror cannot be, for at the cable's length
> Man feels the gentle anchor pull and gladdens in its strength.
>
> *Lines Written in the Highlands after a*
> *Visit to Burns's Country*, 29–40 (1818)

Obviously, much that he had worked out during the two years since the completing of *Endymion* is compressed into the powerful image with which stanza 7 of *Ode to a Nightingale* comes to a close.

The brief third section of the poem, consisting of the final eighth stanza alone, deliberately breaks up the spell which the potent second section had cast over the reader. It appropriately asserts that "the fancy cannot cheat so well/ As she is fam'd to do, deceiving elf" and stresses again with complete intellectual honesty that what has been presented is either "a vision, or a waking dream" inspired by a bird's song. The daemonic part of the poem is quite short in proportion to the whole, for it constitutes only a portion of the sojourn beyond the customary human realm; but this daemonic element is all-important to the whole structurally and artistically, for, just as in *Psyche* and *Indolence*, it gives complexity and depth to the total experience presented and extends the range of what the odes express concerning man's world to include the beauty which objects in nature can give when they almost fill the consciousness completely.

The *Ode on a Grecian Urn*[8] extends the range of experience covered by the group to include what human art can mean to man when deeply enjoyed and appreciated; and this poem, too, at the end shows the speaker impelled back within the bounds of the common consciousness when, "at the cable's length" of the daemonic, he "feels the gentle anchor pull" built into the structure of the mind which fortunately unites him to his world at the same time that it restricts him to its limits and the few steps that are possible beyond. Here in a remarkable instance of the synthesizing power of the creative imagination the poet has brought together the static and the dynamic: the carved figures from the south frieze of the Parthenon, there framed by cold and rigid rectilinear form, but now encompassed by a quite different framework—the curved,

[8] This ode has proved almost inexhaustible in power to evoke commentary, as shown in H. T. Lyon, *Keats' Well-Read Urn* (New York, 1958), a collection of comment upon it extending from the 1820's to 1958). Claude L. Finney's interpretation is still helpful: *The Evolution of Keats's Poetry* (Cambridge, Mass., 1936), II, 636–646; also the fine essay by R. H. Fogle, "Empathic Imagery in Keats and Shelley," *PMLA*, LXI (March, 1946), 163–191; and Cleanth Brooks's "History without Footnotes: An Account of Keats' Urn," *Sewanee Review*, LII (1944), 89–101, reprinted in his *The Well-Wrought Urn* (New York, 1947). Other useful discussions may be found in Bate, *John Keats*, pp. 510–520, and in my "Passion and Permanence in Keats's *Ode on a Grecian Urn*," *ELH*, XXI (September, 1954), 208–220—both of which are reprinted in Stillinger, *Keats's Odes*, as are especially helpful comments on special problems by Douglas Bush (pp. 108–109) and M. H. Abrams (pp. 110–111).

flowing lines of the urn, which suggest organic vitality and the eternal process of regeneration, for in nearly all life the seed and egg are curved forms. This fundamental opposition is suggested in the first line by the poet's addressing the urn as "unravisd'd bride of quietness," which suggests its inviolate, undisturbed descent through the ages and also hints at its opposite, the living bride who transmits herself only by reproducing herself through successive generations. This opposition is heightened by the fact that in the particular curve of its shape the urn resembles the womanly body, which is the receptacle for the seeds of human life, while the urn is either a receptacle for nonliving substance or a decorative object that is premanently empty. On the urn is carved, fixed forever in the cold marble, a procession of people following the priest and heifer to the sacrifice; but out of the body of woman unfolds a living human procession going also to its sacrifice, the eternal sacrifice of the older generation for the younger in the life process. Like all human beings, the speaker longs both for the permanence of the carvings and for the organic vitality of actual life suggested by the urn form that frames the carvings. Keats sustains this basic opposition throughout the poem to the very end.

Unlike the beginning of *Ode to a Nightingale*, the *Ode on a Grecian Urn* gets under way swiftly, when the speaker addresses the urn in the first line as "Thou still unravish'd bride of quietness." The potent ambivalent image, "unravish'd bride," contains within itself both sides of the dual, conflicting strain that runs throughout the whole and provides its central tension. From this nucleus, suddenly and dramatically introduced at the beginning, there unfolds in the speaker's mind a sustained series of contradictions between the desirability of the art objects, which are permanent because they are lifeless, and the desirability of living creatures, who are transient because they are alive: the unheard melodies are sweeter than actual music but lack any real substance; the maiden pursued by the "Bold Lover" cannot fade but he can never draw closer to the kiss; the "happy love" depicted on the urn seems to "breathe" far above transient human passion but it has no existence except in representation in the cold marble, which in reality does not breathe at all. Though seeming only to muse upon the carvings, the speaker is continually striving to resolve these contradictions; and they steadily lead him toward the daemonic. Well had Goethe said that it most often expresses itself through contradictions.

The culmination of the oppositions and the apex of the daemonic are reached in stanza 4 at the height of the speaker's empathic union with the carved figures in the procession and the height of his obliviousness to the vital shape of the urn form that frames them. Momentarily he feels that they are living people in a world of permanence and that he is in their midst, although they never move or speak:

> Who are these coming to the sacrifice?
>   To what green altar, O mysterious priest,
> Lead'st thou that heifer lowing at the skies,
>   And all her silken flanks with garlands drest?
> What little town by river or sea shore,
>   Or mountain-built with peaceful citadel
>   Is emptied of its folk, this pious morn?
> And, little town, thy streets for evermore
>   Will silent be; and not a soul to tell
>   Why thou art desolate, can e'er return.

In the earlier lines of the stanza, through his intense preoccupation with the carved figures he has lifted them from their places on the urn and endowed them with the warm glow of living flesh; he has almost resolved the contradiction they have engendered in his mind between the appeal of their permanence and the unacceptability of their lifelessness. He has been led into a neutral daemonic region of neither earth nor heaven, fixed by no "standard law" of knowing. But with the realization in the final lines that the people in the procession, when accepted as actuality, have left some little Grecian town "emptied of its folk this pious morn" comes also the inevitable realization that the town from which they have come forth is "desolate," devoid of life, and will forever remain so; for none of its "folk" can "e'er return" to its deserted streets. Nor can the people in the procession move forward to the consummation of the sacrifice. In the midst of the warmth and glow imparted to them by the speaker's imagination they recede and fade; they reassume their immobile, lifeless status on the urn, a "Cold Pastoral." The daemonic world into which the speaker has been led is found to be as empty of enduring and meaningful content as the desolate little town eternally bereft of its populace.

Having failed to resolve the contradictions with which he has been dealing, in the last stanza the speaker simply accepts them in serene resignation. Hence the poem concludes with a much more positive affirmation concerning the part that graphic art can play in man's acceptance of his world than the affirmation at the end of *Ode to a Nightingale* concerning the part that a bird's song can play. Here he is not content to say merely that "the fancy cannot cheat so well/ As she is fam'd to do, deceiving elf," as in the final lines of that poem; and he goes far beyond the proclamation near the end of *Ode on Melancholy* that "in the very temple of Delight/ Veil'd Melancholy has her sovran shrine," although the *Ode on a Grecian Urn* up to this point has in part dramatized a concrete instance of this "Delight" which has melancholy at the heart of it. Now at the end, as the speaker again contemplates the urn in detachment, he re-emphasizes its form and shape as he enunciates a few truths that should be of real comfort to man in his present plight, with his fierce desire to overcome the mortal limitations that restrict his experience; for in the poem the inevitable termination of the brief daemonic excursion does not merely leave the speaker back at the point where he had begun. He reveals that it is a genuine comfort to him to realize that the urn with its carvings will "remain, in midst of other woe" than that of the present generation, "a friend to man," as it has been to the speaker in the present instance in the specific ways which emerge clearly here at the end. First, it has afforded him a brief period of beautiful and salutary release from the transience of mortality through participation in the more enduring world of the carved figures that depict the vibrant life of ancient Greece. Second, the urn has driven him back upon the mortal world with a sharpened insight into its beauty, worth, and substantiality and with a more willing acceptance of his mortal lot. From the vantage ground of the extreme point in his daemonic excursion, the "desolate" little town with eternally silent streets, he had perceived as if anew that the world of phenomena has an indispensable element which neither the art world of the carvings nor the daemonic world which they inspired can ever possess—the concrete, vital, organic, flux and flow of being. The outcome of his involvement with the urn had proved upon his pulses that the real and living beauty lies embedded in phenomena, however transient its single individuations may be, rather than in pictorial art or in the remote corridors of the daemonic. To know beauty in its fullness one must penetrate into this organic, processive realm, as the urn has helped him to do; for here is the residing place of both the particular and the universal. Even in the matter of sexual love, the transient heat of desire, that "leaves a heart high-sorrowful and cloy'd," is only its immediate individuation, not its essential reality; in essence love is a mode of participation in the life force unfolding in and through humanity. This sense of vibrant participation in a reality both organic and universal is what he had dramatically failed to find in his empathic union with the marble representation of life depicted by the carvings on the urn. This too-little-stressed aspect of the internal action in the speaker's mind goes far to explain the presence of slumbering life and silent unmoving vitality in this poem, ostensibly about a "Cold Pastoral" of carved figures in marble, and also helps to explain the speaker's final rejection of the urn as a substitute for actual experience, though not as a commentary upon actual experience. For the very reason that his empathic union with the urn figures had led him so perilously close to proclaiming the superiority of art to life (as the "art-for-art's-sake" critics believed he had proclaimed), the speaker feels the need to stress emphatically at the end that living beauty lies in the actual, not in the representation of it in sculpture or painting, which is only a "shadow of a magnitude," caught and fixed forever in stone. But if he had not carried his preoccupation with it into daemonic intensity he would not have been so powerfully thrown back upon the actual realm at the end and would not have experienced and valued this truth as deeply as then emerges. What he meant by "Beauty is truth, truth beauty" is just that simple, I think; beauty is the concrete truth of things and the universals in which they inhere in the actual world rather than the counterfeit representation of them in art. This simple explanation of the pseudo-philo-sophic statement, as it has been called, is an explanation that logically and properly follows and grows out of the entire preceding experience which the whole poem presents—per-haps the only explanation of the line which makes the ending of the poem fit the main body of the whole. The function of the daemonic element prepares for this affirmation interpreted in this way, for the inevitable revulsion against the daemonic near the end throws the actual world, where beauty resides, into higher relief than would be the case otherwise and em-phasizes that it is the actual world of minds and objects that embraces the organic and universal.

In the light of this explanation of the "Beauty is truth" equation, the more puzzling statement that comes next and concludes the poem is now made meaningful and functional. After the double equating of beauty and truth, as a part of what the urn says to man[9] (that is, *conveys* when deeply ap-preciated in its full significance as in the preceding body of the poem), the following is added: "—that is all/ Ye know on earth, and all ye need to know." This statement could not pos-sibly be true outside the well-established context within which the poem is coming to a close—a context predominantly about the relation between art and life. Outside this sphere men need to know much more indeed; but coming at the end of this particular poem and taken within the particular matrix of the last stanza, the statement is acceptable as a poetically exaggerated, emphatic way of proclaiming that this point ("Beauty is truth") is the most important thing men need to

[9] I have long believed that the urn "speaks" only figuratively and to man, or to the reader, as stated in my previous article on the poem (1954) mentioned in the preceding note; and this view of the matter seems to be prevailing, as evidenced in the summary of various views in the Appendix to Stillinger, *Keats's Odes*, pp. 113–114.

know *concerning the subject at hand* (the relation of art to life). For the speaker had dramatically learned in the poem that, even when experienced to the extent of full empathic union, art objects cannot fill the place of the actual life which they only represent. They cannot be substitutes for direct experience. It is not surprising that Keats heavily scored a passage in Southey's translation of *Palmerin of England* (III, 298) which terminates an incident in which several knights had become so captivated by carved images of their ladies that they seemed unable to break the spell of enchantment which these carvings had cast over them.

> When they had long looked on, Daliarte at length said, Sirs, methinks if you be not interrupted, you will take up your perpetual abode here, and these lifeless images cause you to forget them whom your duty commandeth you to remember; I pray you yield not so absolutely to these, which are no other but shapes without substance, for in beholding these you do but mis-spend your time, looking for that recompense which they have not the power to give you. It is more necessary to go to them whom the pictures represent, who in time will more content your hearts than . . . these toys whose fantastic appearance you may at any time enjoy.[10]

Beauty is indeed truth; art only captures and fixes some elements of this truth in an enduring form that we can repeatedly contemplate at length and thus learn something about actual experience, as he has done in the poem. And one thing that he has learned is that the life process is as enduring as the art; for, while the procession of figures on the urn will always remain fixed in their stillness and immobility, the

[10] See above, Chapter I, note 11.

living procession that emerges from the body of woman will eternally re-create itself through "generation" and go on vibrant and alive forever.

The *Ode on a Grecian Urn*, when viewed in full perspective, is thus the most compelling statement of the anti-daemonic in all Keats's lyrical poetry before its consummate triumph a few months later in *To Autumn*, toward which this last stanza of *Grecian Urn* directly points. Keats is getting the better of the dilemma which he presented so powerfully in *Ode on Melancholy*, a poem replete with the contradictions which lead either to the daemonic or to acceptance and resignation, and the latter are clearly implied at the end of *Melancholy*. The *Ode on a Grecian Urn* sets forth the values and results of this resignation and acceptance in greater particularity and detail than the more limited scope of *Melancholy* allowed.

As mentioned earlier, each of Keats's odes deals with a particular capacity of the consciousness to apprehend deeply some element of the world in which man must live and to which he must be reconciled.[11] *Psyche* depicts powerfully the human mind's capacity to deify the goddess of the soul; *Indolence* the ability to grasp fully the reality of conscious selfhood; *Melancholy* the capacity to discern, embedded amidst the pain of transience, a remarkable completing power that brings experience full circle; *Nightingale* the ability to respond deeply to the beauty called up by a bird's song in the forest; *Grecian Urn* the power to grasp the significance and

[11] W. J. Bate sees the theme of all the odes except *Psyche* as "that of process, and either the acceptance of it, or the hope to escape from it, or both in dramatic interplay" (*John Keats*, p. 512). L. M. Jones sees the thematic design of the group very nearly as I do but is uncertain about the relationship of *Indolence* and excludes *To Autumn*: "The 'Ode to Psyche': An Allegorical Introduction to Keats's Great Odes," *Keats-Shelley Memorial Bulletin*, IX

human import of pictorial art; and *To Autumn* the power to feel the ripeness and richness of the great cycle of nature as it ministers to the needs of man. Most of these poems at the same time reveal a structural use of the daemonic realm beyond that of the common consciousness skillfully manipulated to set off and emphasize the beauty of the actual by contrast and to enhance the expressive power of the total effect in each ode, just as is the case in the narrative poems. The odes therefore have a cyclical relationship among themselves and constitute a coherent group of poems with discernible thematic unity. Moreover, in the group there is a progressively stronger tendency of the speakers in the later odes to batter more vigorously at the barriers that restrict human experience to the confines of mortality before achieving resignation and acceptance of the mortal lot. The speakers in *Nightingale* and *Grecian Urn* learn through their lyrical experience precisely what the protagonists had learned through the action in the previous narrative poems: that the daemonic is even more transient and short-lived than the actual world of phenomena.

These odes, his greatest lyrical poems, show him moving steadily toward affirming that the actual world of men and things is the residing place of the universal and of the most satisfying beauty that men can know. It cannot be supplanted by the daemonic, which at best merely extends the range of beauty a few steps beyond the actual and at worst "spoils the singing of the Nightingale." None of Keats's characters or

(1958), 22–26. Robert D. Wagner denies that there is thematic unity among the odes and professes to be unable to understand how the poet who wrote *Psyche* could have written *Nightingale:* "Keats: 'Ode to Psyche' and the Second 'Hyperion,'" *Keats-Shelley Journal*, XIII (1964), 29–41. Robert F. Gleckner sagely discusses the importance of our confronting the problem of the interrelationship of the odes and of Keats's poems generally: "Keats's Odes: The Problems of the Limited Canon," *Studies in English Literature*, V (1965), 577–585.

speakers up to this time have been irrecoverably injured by daemonic beauty, for the inherent safeguard in the structure of the mind has always come into play at the point of danger, with the possible exception of the knight in *La Belle Dame sans Merci*, in whose case we cannot be sure as to the ultimate outcome since the main purpose of that poem is to present his weird stasis between two worlds after the encounter with the nonmortal lady. At this point in Keats's career, such is the way his uses of the daemonic element in his poems sum up. But in nearly all the poems already discussed herein, Keats has steadily reflected an awareness that mortal man can be injured and even destroyed by too much of the daemonic for his present mental and psychological constitution. Before he composed his consummate rendering of the supreme beauty of the actual world in *To Autumn*, he presented the single instance of a mortal who pursued the daemonic beyond the point of no return. This, I think, is the central aim of *Lamia*, which stands at precisely the opposite extreme from the triumph of the anti-daemonic soon to follow in *To Autumn*.

CHAPTER SIX

LAMIA:
THE POINT
OF NO RETURN

Although other poems of Keats have been given widely diverging interpretations, none has evoked as many mutually contradictory views as has *Lamia*, Keats's retelling of the ancient tale of a youth who loves and marries a beautiful woman who turns out to be a serpent. Evidently it was first recorded in European literature in the third century by Philostratus[1] and later summarized briefly by Robert Burton in the seventeenth century in *The Anatomy of Melancholy*,[2] from which Keats took the bare outlines of the plot. The story undoubtedly originated in a folk tale of great antiquity.[3] As

[1] Philostratus, *Life of Apollonius of Tyana*, tr. F. C. Conybeare (Loeb Classics, Cambridge, Mass., 1948), I, 403–409.

[2] Part 3, Sec. 2, Mem 1 Subs 1 (London, 1924), pp. 494–495.

[3] See Nai-tung Ting, "The Holy Man and the Snake Woman," *Fabula*, VIII (1966), 145–191, for an interesting and exhaustive study of the possibility, long believed by oriental scholars, that the European lamia story and the Chinese story of the snake woman and the holy man, which have striking parallels, are based on a common source not yet identified in Asiatic folklore. Lamia may be a daemoness descended from the Babylonian goddess Ishtar, goddess of nature, life, sexual love, home, and fertility, who was both admired and feared; and she may have a connection with Lilith, Adam's first wife, who was identified as a serpent (p. 148).

W. J. Bate has stated, "The meaning of *Lamia*, which Keats began in July 1819, has perhaps elicited more controversy than any other single problem raised by his verse." [4] In fact, interpretations have been so divergent that each of its major characters has been seen as representing glaringly contradictory values. For example, Lamia herself is designated "illusion" [5] or "a dream," [6] or "an evil embodiment of the wasting power of love, a *belle dame sans merci*" [7] by some critics; but by others she is considered to be "the poetic imagination," [8] "emotion," [9] "feeling" and "sensuousness," [10] and "a lovely elemental creature of passion." [11] Two of the most prominent interpreters assert that "the truth about the Lamia is that Keats himself did not know whether she was a thing of beauty or a thing of bale. He only knew that if he were to be deprived of her, he would die, which he did, in the poem and in fact." [12] Apollonius has elicited similarly conflicting views.

[4] W. J. Bate, *The Stylistic Development of Keats* (New York, 1958), p. 142.

[5] Bernice Slote, *Keats and the Dramatic Principle* (Lincoln, Neb., 1958), pp. 146–147; W. J. Bate, *John Keats* (Cambridge, Mass., 1963), p. 554; and Georgia S. Dunbar, "The Significance of the Humor in 'Lamia,'" *Keats-Shelley Journal*, VIII (1959), 24.

[6] Miriam Allott, " 'Isabella,' 'The Eve of St. Agnes' and 'Lamia,' " in Kenneth Muir, ed., *John Keats: A Reassessment* (Liverpool, 1958), p. 59.

[7] Douglas Bush, *Mythology and the Romantic Tradition* (Cambridge, Mass., 1937), p. 111.

[8] Claude L. Finney, *The Evolution of Keats's Poetry* (Cambridge, Mass., 1936), II, 698.

[9] Ernest de Selincourt, *The Poems of John Keats* (London, 1951), p. xli. Professor de Selincourt penetratingly suggests that in the poem Lycius' emotional side upbraids the intellectual even while recognizing "the right of the intellectual to supremacy" (p. xlii).

[10] John H. Roberts, "The Significance of 'Lamia,'" *PMLA*, L (June, 1935), 554.

[11] Werner Beyer, *Keats and the Daemon King* (New York, 1947), p. 237. In an uncorrupted world the serpent does not symbolize evil, and there are European lamia stories (e.g., that of Melusine) in which the lamia has no evil designs but truly loves her man (Nai-tung Ting, "The Holy Man and the Snake Woman," pp. 163–164).

[12] J. M. Murry, *Keats and Shakespeare* (London and New York, 1925), p. 159, quoted in agreement by Douglas Bush, *Mythology and the Romantic*

By some critics he is said to represent "folly," "cold philosophy," and "ruthless intellectualism," or "the reviewers who judged Keats's poems by the standard of common sense and reason";[13] but by other critics Apollonius is designated the representative of a valid partial truth which "cannot be disregarded," or "the same kind of knowledge" as Apollo in *Hyperion*, or even "the ideal of humanitarian philosophy."[14] Thus, while revealing together a relentless predilection for taking the major characters as rigid allegorical representations of preconceived values, interpreters of the poem cannot at all agree as to the identity of the value or idea which each character represents.

Moreover, these critics differ just as widely about Keats's attitude toward particular characters. The majority contend that Lamia has most of Keats's sympathy. But Ernest de Selincourt believes that Keats has greatest sympathy for Lycius, the young Corinthian who falls in love with her; and Douglas Bush believes that Apollonius represents one side of Keats's mind and therefore must receive a considerable part of the poet's sympathy.[15] C. D. Thorpe thinks that in Keats's mind neither Lamia nor Lycius nor Apollonius is "in the right," that all three are "falsities," that no one in *Lamia* represents "truth."[16]

The same pattern of confusingly opposite views is revealed

Tradition, p. 112. But in his footnote Professor Bush objects to Murry's pressing the autobiographical element in *Lamia* too far and states that "to take Apollonius as representing anything but one side of Keats is to empty the poem of its significance."

[13] Beyer, *Keats and the Daemon King*, p. 238; Slote, *Keats and the Dramatic Principle*, p. 168; Finney, *The Evolution of Keats's Poetry*, I, 700.

[14] Bate, *John Keats*, p. 560; Roberts, "The Significance of 'Lamia,' " p. 553.

[15] De Selincourt, *The Poems of John Keats*, p. xlii; Bush, *Mythology and the Romantic Tradition*, p. 112.

[16] C. D. Thorpe, ed., *Complete Poems and Selected Letters of John Keats* (New York, 1935), p. xliii.

in the meanings ascribed to the whole poem and its main action. Douglas Bush, who thinks that "the fundamental defect is that the poem has no emotional and philosophical unity," neatly sums up the three major categories of these differing interpretations as follows:

> Whether or not it was his original intention, Keats gave the poem a meaning, so that it takes its place among the many poems which embody the claims of the self and the senses and the claims of the world and "philosophy." But here Keats does not seem to know which side he is on, and a plausible case can be, and has been, made out for *Lamia* as a condemnation of philosophy, as a condemnation of the senses, and as a condemnation of the divorce between the two. Each of these interpretations can be supported by chapter and verse from Keats' other poems and from his letters, yet each leaves difficulties in *Lamia* itself.[17]

Miriam Allott attempts to circumvent some of these difficulties by avoiding all three of the prevalent interpretations and asserting that *Lamia* "leaves us in perplexity . . . not because Keats has lost his poetic integrity . . . but because his insight had laid bare a series of paradoxes which it is beyond his power to resolve." [18] Similarly, Bernice Slote avoids the beaten paths of interpretation and sees in the poem a conflict that it "represents but does not answer. . . . [Lamia and Apollonius] are a mixture of bright and black. That neither side is wholly right or wholly wrong simply focuses on the devastating reality of the poem: that the enchantment, the conflict, and the destruction do exist. This is the way life is." [19] Clearly,

[17] Bush, *Mythology and the Romantic Tradition*, pp. 110–111.
[18] Allott, " 'Isabella,' 'The Eve of St. Agnes' and 'Lamia,' " p. 62.
[19] Slote, *Keats and the Dramatic Principle*, p. 187.

the widely diverging views of the poem invite a new approach to the meaning of *Lamia*.

Most of this confusing disagreement about the characters and about the meaning of the whole story can be cleared up, I believe, if the poem is seen as Keats's last treatment of the daemonic quest—the one rendering of it in which he presented essentially the same story as in *Endymion* and in *La Belle Dame sans Merci* but with a denouement and terminal action that he had never worked out before, although seeds of it were clearly apparent in those earlier narratives and were implicit in the great odes. For *Lamia* presents the story of a young man who deliberately pursued daemonic experience beyond the point of no return and tried to make it a continuing thing, an entire way of life. The characters should not be taken as rigid allegorical equivalents of ideas, although they polarize recognizable human attitudes and drives, just as the incidents in the plot suggest internal actions and decisions of the mind. Viewing it in this way, we most assuredly can tell which "side" Keats is on, and in just exactly what way and with what reservations, for we can ascertain more correctly what the "sides" are and what the basic conflict is. And we can discover a meaning that fits the whole structure, for Professor Bush is surely right in saying that the story was not told for the sake of the story alone, but has meanings beyond itself. In addition to throwing light on the all-important matter of interpretation, an examination of the daemonic aspects of the poem will provide answers to other pertinent and intriguing questions that have been raised: Why did Keats choose this subject for his poem in the first place? What is his attitude toward individual characters? What is the extent and particular nature of the autobiographical element? What is the function of the introductory episode of Hermes and the nymph? What is the relationship of the poem to Keats's other poems? It seems on the surface to be strikingly different from the others and yet it is in reality markedly similar to them.

It is important to remember at the outset that Keats took the main lines of the plot and the characters of the story from the brief account in Robert Burton's *Anatomy of Melancholy*, which Keats had been reading continually from February through September, 1819,[20] during the summer of which he composed *Lamia*, completing it on September 5. As pointed out in Chapter I (see above, pp. 6, 18), other parts of Burton's book were among the sources of Keats's information about the nature of daemonic creatures and their relationships with human beings, particularly that not all of these creatures were necessarily evil, and that at times they loved and mated with human beings and could die, just as human beings do. That is, Burton's book is one of the sources from which Keats learned anew, just before beginning *Lamia* and while writing it, that some daemonic creatures were considered suprahuman but not supramortal. Such in effect is what Lamia says of herself in Burton's account, which Keats reproduced at the end of his poem, as follows:

> Philostratus, in his fourth book *de Vita Apollonii*, hath a memorable instance in this kind, which I may not omit, of one Menippus Lycius, a young man twenty-five years of age, that going betwixt Cenchreas and Corinth, met such a phantasm in the habit of a fair gentlewoman, which taking him by the hand, carried him home to her house in the suburbs of Corinth, and told

[20] See the passages indexed in H. E. Rollins' edition of Keats's letters, which show Keats echoing terms and phrases from Burton's book continually in letters to friends.

him she was a Phoenician by birth, and if he would tarry with her, he should hear her sing and play, and drink such wine as never any drank, and no man should molest him; but she, being fair and lovely, would live and die with him, that was fair and lovely to behold. The young man, a philosopher, otherwise staid and discreet, able to moderate his passions, though not this of love, tarried with her a while to his great content, and at last married her, to whose wedding, amongst other guests, came Apollonius; who, by some probable conjectures, found her out to be a serpent, a lamia; and that all her furniture was, like Tantalus' gold, described by Homer, no substance but mere illusions. When she saw herself descried, she wept, and desired Apollonius to be silent, but he would not be moved, and thereupon she, plate, house, and all that was in it, vanished in an instant: many thousands took notice of this fact, for it was done in the midst of Greece.[21]

What Keats made of this bare outline of the narrative is considerably more—and significantly different. I do not believe that he would have made it exactly what he did make it if he had not already written *Endymion*, the sonnet *As Hermes Once*, and *La Belle Dame sans Merci*. Quite in contrast to his source in Burton, Keats allowed the protagonist, Lycius, to die immediately after Lamia vanishes at the end, a very significant change in the plot. Such had always been a possible denouement in his previous narratives of the daemonic quest, but he had never made one of them terminate in this way before. Moreover, in working up his version of the story, Keats begins at the outset to remove the aura of evil from his serpentine heroine insofar as was possible and to authenticate her as a neutral daemonic female with lovable qualities and no malicious intent, somewhat like his other heroines in the

[21] See note 2 above.

kindred poems. Keats's additions to her portrait, designed to fill out and vivify the meager sketch of her in Burton, cumulatively align her basically with his previous conceptions of Cynthia in *Endymion*, the pale maiden in *As Hermes Once*, and the elfin lady in *La Belle Dame*.

One of the major functions of Lamia's part in the initial episode of Hermes' search for the nymph,[22] which Keats introduced ahead of the main story, is to accomplish the first step in this accreditation of his heroine as a feminine creature of warmth and appeal, genuinely involved in her love for Lycius. She is obviously drawn from the prototype of the nonmalicious faery mistress of chivalric romance, which Keats knew thoroughly, or from her evil counterpart refined by Keats into the former type, as we have found in his poetry before. In either case the result is the same in the particular traits given the character. In the poem Keats wrote,

> She seem'd, at once, some penanced lady elf,
> Some demon's mistress, or the demon's self.
>
> I, 55–56

This statement does not mean that she was evil. His saying that she seemed "a penanced lady elf" or "some demon's mistress" simply indicates that in her feelings and attitudes Keats is putting her in something like the same category as the elfin lady, who is called "a faery's child," in *La Belle Dame*. But in the famous description of Lamia's appearance before her change there is a striking difference which is subtly in harmony with what I believe to be Keats's over-all purpose of

---

[22] Probably elaborated from the tale of Mercury, Herse, and Aglaures at the end of book II of Sandys' translation of Ovid's *Metamorphoses*, from which Keats had taken the Glaucus and Scylla story used in the third book of *Endymion* (Bush, *Mythology and the Romantic Tradition*, p. 114n).

dramatizing in this poem a man's complete immersion in the daemonic and the resulting disastrous effects upon him; for, while the elfin lady in *La Belle Dame* is described entirely in physical details that sum up into a purely human image of the feminine, Lamia is first described in a heterogeneous assortment of disparate details that belong to no one living thing that ever existed, which instead of summing up into a recognizable representation, make up an amorphous something that the human mind feels difficulty in apprehending, because the mind has no archetype or previous pattern for accepting such a collection of splendors in one creature. Lycius never sees her in this shape, but readers do; and the glittering, disjointed totality of this early description of her must have been intended to tip them off that this is an attempt at imaging the ultimate in daemonic beauty, utterly beyond any "standard law" of being or knowing, but still mysteriously captivating:

> She was a gordian shape of dazzling hue,
> Vermilion-spotted, golden, green, and blue;
> Striped like a zebra, freckled like a pard,
> Eyed like a peacock, and all crimson barr'd;
> And full of silver moons, that, as she breathed,
> Dissolv'd, or brighter shone, or interwreathed
> Their lustres with the gloomier tapestries—
>
> .   .   .   .
>
> Upon her crest she wore a wannish fire
> Sprinkled with stars, like Ariadne's tiar:
> Her head was serpent, but ah, bitter-sweet!
> She had a woman's mouth with all its pearls complete:
> As for her eyes: what could such eyes do there
> But weep, and weep, that they were born so fair?

· · · ·

Her throat was serpent, but the words she spake
Came, as through bubbling honey, for Love's sake.

I, 47–65

However, in this assortment of glittering though hardly united particulars the predominance is not only serpentine but strongly feminine in certain details (headdress, mouth, teeth, eyes, voice), a fact which becomes extremely important in her transformation into a woman soon to take place. Keats refers to her in this stage as "the brilliance feminine." Moreover, the description points both forward (toward the impending transformation) and also backward (toward a possible earlier stage of existence than the serpentine). The statement that she seemed a "penanced lady elf,/ Some demon's mistress, or the demon's self" (I, 55–56) may be intended to suggest, without allowing us to pin it down and thus destroy the illusion of reality, that she was once a woman but is now serving a period of penance in serpent form, possibly for having once accepted a daemon lover, as mortal women sometimes did in ballads and romances. The poet asks,

What could such eyes do *there*
But weep, and weep, that they were born so fair?
As Proserpine still weeps for her Sicilian air.

I, 61–63 (italics added)

That is, what could such beautifully womanly eyes do but weep that they are in a debased serpentine form? The comparison to Proserpine's metamorphosis from Sicilian maiden to queen of Hades pointedly supports this suggestion. Keats is evidently attempting to convey the aura of the feminine within the serpentine, and the notion that something of a real woman is embedded in the wondrous snake is borne out by much that follows. Consequently, while there is no conclusive evidence to disprove her own statement about the matter, there is no compelling evidence to corroborate it either. Hence the reader is led to hold the idea of her prior womanhood in mind in a "willing suspension of disbelief" for a time, and that is all Keats needed to do toward making it credible. In bargaining with Hermes—offering to produce the nymph he seeks if he will turn her into woman form—Lamia declares that she was once a woman and that she loves a youth of Corinth. Whatever she is, we never find any reliable reason in the poem to question the genuineness of that love:

> 'I was a woman, let me have once more
> 'A woman's shape, and charming as before.
> 'I love a youth of Corinth—O the bliss!'
>
> I, 117–120

Soon after this declaration by Lamia the poet himself asserts that it was "when in the *serpent prison-house*" (I, 203, italics added) that she had fallen into her "swooning love" of Lycius, again implying that she is being conceived as a real woman who has been turned into a serpentine creature for a time. Keats had stated in the opening lines of the poem that he was writing of a far-off time "before the faery broods" had driven away nymphs, satyrs, and dryads, that is, of a time when such metamorphoses as Lamia's were believed to happen.

Keats surely had good reasons for adding the Hermes-nymph episode at the beginning of the tale which he took from Burton, for he was now at the height of his powers; and implanting the idea that Lamia's womanhood antedated her serpentine stage was one of the foremost of these reasons. The resulting advantages begin to appear immediately and continue to unfold subsequently. For example, the possibility of her having been formerly a real woman removes most of the grounds for the ugly suspicion that Lamia is simply deceiving Lycius. As the poem progresses she is very largely accredited as a woman genuinely in love; and as a result the bases for the charge of deceit very nearly vanish from the poem. Second, the possibility of her prior womanhood helps to make credible her metamorphosis by making it seem a transformation *back* into her original woman form and, more significantly, provides a different framework and context for this change than otherwise would have been possible, a framework notably suitable to Keats's aims. That is, the notion that Lamia is being changed *back again* from serpent to woman prepared the way for his making this, her apparently second metamorphosis, a process of *exorcising the sinister*, and hence most of the suggestion of evil, in the serpentine without expelling all its mysterious glamour, power, and appeal. For just as the aura of her prior womanhood had lingered on into her serpentine period, so now after her second metamorphosis the aura of the serpentine *divested of the sinister* continues to hover round her, adding to her glamour, after her return to womanhood. That Keats is working in this direction is discernible in the way in which he describes the wondrous change in Lamia and is apparent in subsequent developments:

> Left to herself, the serpent now began
> To change; her elfin blood in madness ran,
> Her mouth foam'd, and the grass, therewith besprent,
> Wither'd at dew so sweet and virulent;
> Her eyes in torture fix'd, and anguish drear,
> Hot, glaz'd, and wide, with lid-lashes all sear,
> Flash'd phosphor and sharp sparks, without one cooling tear.

The colours all inflam'd throughout her train,
She writh'd about, convulsed with scarlet pain:
A deep volcanian yellow took the place
Of all her milder-mooned body's grace;
And, as the lava ravishes the mead,
Spoilt all her silver mail, and golden brede,
Made gloom of all her frecklings, streaks and bars,
Eclips'd her crescents, and lick'd up her stars:
So that, in moments few, she was undrest
Of all her sapphires, greens, and amethyst,
And rubious-argent: of all these bereft,
Nothing but pain and ugliness were left.
Still shone her crown; that vanish'd, also she
Melted and disappear'd as suddenly;
And in the air, her new voice luting soft,
Cried, 'Lycius! gentle Lycius!'

I, 146–168

"The serpent prison" having been thus painfully purged away, Lamia is immediately proclaimed to be "now a lady bright,/ A full-born beauty new and exquisite" (I, 171–172). However, Keats gives repeated indications that she has not been divested of all the aura of her past or of all suprahuman powers and qualities:

for she was a maid
More beautiful than ever twisted braid,
Or sigh'd, or blush'd. . . .
A virgin purest lipp'd, yet in the lore
Of love deep learned to the red heart's core.

I, 185–190

Like the elfin lady in *La Belle Dame*, she sang to Lycius "A song of love, too sweet for earthly lyres" (I, 299); and she had the magic power to make considerable distances decrease "to a few paces" unsuspected by her companion (I, 346). She participates in humanity, but possesses powers and qualities greater than human.

Whatever Keats's success with the final product, and opinions vary, his over-all aim in the creation of the character Lamia from Burton's bare suggestion is readily discernible: to unite the charm of the womanly and the mysterious glamour of the serpentine, divested of its evil, into his most irresistible heroine. For centuries a standard image of captivating feminine appeal has been termed "serpentine beauty," and Keats found a way to use it without the aura of the evil and sinister that usually accompanies it. There was need for Lamia to be the most irresistible of all his suprahuman heroines because she had the hardest task to perform, a task which none of the others had been assigned before—to "make a man forget his mortal way" completely, to inspire him "at the cable's length" to resist "the gentle anchor pull" that links him with his world and to refuse to "gladden in its strength." [23] In short, Keats was attempting to create in Lamia a heroine who could inspire a man to pursue daemonic experience beyond the point of no return. In terms of Jungian psychology, Keats was trying to remake Lamia into a "hook" for the *anima*,[24] that is, a stimulus to the archetypal pattern in Lycius for overvaluing the feminine which would be so powerful that Lycius would be completely overwhelmed by his own engulfing preoccupation with her. Again, there is no gross deceit on her part; she is as captivated by her love for him as he by his

---

[23] See *Lines Written in the Highlands after a Visit to Burns's Country*, 32–40.
[24] See above, Chapters I, III, and IV, pp. 20–21, 121–123, 145–148.

love for her. In fact, we may say in Jungian terms that her *animus*, her latent archetypal pattern for apprehending and overvaluing the masculine to the point of her own destruction, is just as strongly activated as is his *anima*, as the terminal events in the story show, for she too is annihilated as a result of her deep attachment to Lycius and is made by Apollonius to "melt into a shade" (II, 238). The narrator never disparages Lamia, but he severely derogates Lycius near the end.

The powerful combination of womanly and suprahuman qualities in Lamia now explains some puzzling matters in the early stages of her relationship with Lycius: his persistently considering her more than mortal and her responsively playing at the role of goddess for a time, which seem in conflict with her own and the poet's insistence that she won Lycius' love as a woman. In view of the way Keats himself conceived of her there is really no conflict; and her suprahuman qualities help to motivate and explain Lycius' excessive devotion and overevaluation of her. It is significant that just before Lycius first sees Lamia the poet remarks, "His phantasy was lost, where reason fades,/ In the calm'd twilight of Platonic shades" (I, 235–236). Whether or not this seemingly trivial remark indicates Keats's considered view of Platonic thought, it serves adequately here to forewarn the reader that Lycius is about to make the mistake of complete attachment to something that lacks the substantiality and concreteness necessary to make it suitable for the human consciousness as now constituted. And this initial suggestion as to Lycius' bent is subtly repeated with a hint of the possible destruction of Lamia in the poet's rendering of Lycius' reaction when he first looked upon her. She had been waiting for him, but he passed without noticing her, and she called to him:

> 'Ah, Lycius bright,
> 'And will you leave me on the hills alone?
> 'Lycius, look back! and be some pity shown.'
> He did; not with cold wonder fearingly,
> But Orpheus-like at an Eurydice.
>
> I, 244–248

That is, he looked upon her with complete and all-absorbing attention, as if nothing else in earth or heaven mattered, just as Orpheus had looked back at Eurydice in the fatal moment. The intense, engulfing, daemonic nature of Lycius' preoccupation with Lamia and also an indication that her beauty is beyond human limitation are reflected again in the ensuing lines:

> And soon his eyes had drunk her beauty up,
> Leaving no drop in the bewildering cup,
> And still the cup was full. . . .
> she saw his chain so sure.
>
> I, 251–256

He is completely absorbed and enchained by this inexhaustible fountain of femininity flowing from sources beyond humanity. The first time Lycius addressed her, he called her a goddess, just as Endymion had designated Cynthia; and Lycius never ceased to consider her more than human, although she is clearly not a goddess as Keats conceived her:

> 'Leave thee alone! Look back! Ah, Goddess, see
> 'Whether my eyes can ever turn from thee!
> 'For pity do not this sad heart belie—
> 'Even as thou vanishest so shall I die.
>
> .   .   .   .

if thou shouldst fade
'Thy memory will waste me to a shade.'
                                I, 257–270

These lines are even more prophetic of the end of the story than the reference to Orpheus, for they introduce the basic image of destruction used to depict Lamia's demise ("waste me to a shade"), and they shift the emphasis from the ultimate fate of the heroine to that of the protagonist, which is a more central matter in any interpretation. His taking her to be suprahuman brought on the fear that she might vanish, for goddesses who loved mortals frequently did so and had to hold their love trysts in secret. Not far from the end, when about to inquire about her friends and her name, Lycius declares,

'I have not ask'd it, ever thinking thee
'Not mortal, but of heavenly progeny,
'As still I do.'
                                II, 86–88

So firmly and steadily thinking her supramortal, and clearly perceiving the fierce intensity of his devotion to her, Lycius should have known and undoubtedly did know that his love was daemonic and hence fraught with peril, as Endymion had finally discovered and his sister Peona had frequently voiced in that earlier poem.

Since Lycius addresses her as one, Lamia at the outset briefly plays at being a goddess in a charming passage of lighthearted make-believe (I, 271–300) which might be mistaken for gross deceit if the total context is not taken into account. She is enjoying the fun of pretense in what appears to her a love game initiated by him. She asks him what he can offer "to dull the nice remembrance" of her finer-than-mortal home and "what taste of purer air" he can provide "to sooth" her "essence." She is called by the poet "The cruel lady, without any show/ Of sorrow," as many coy mistresses in poetry have been addressed; but in view of what follows, immediately and later, this tag must not be taken literally. She feigns departure, but when he swoons for fear that she will leave him she does not depart, like a goddess disdaining a mortal, but revives him with a kiss (I, 294–295) followed by much love talk. She is throwing off the assumed goddess role and wooing him as a woman, though one with supranormal powers. She is entangling him "in her mesh," but she is already entangled in her love for him, and that fact gives legitimacy to her wiles as she, "Happy in beauty, life, and love, and every thing," sings to him "A song of love, too sweet for earthly lyres," that is, a daemonic love song, suggestive of the "faery's song" of the elfin lady to the knight in *La Belle Dame sans Merci*. Admittedly Lamia does not confess to Lycius the flaw in her lineage; few lovers ever do so. Shortly afterward, the narrator discusses what has been going on in the scene in lines which show Keats waxing facetious about some contemporary poetry:

> Let the mad poets say whate'er they please
> Of the sweets of Fairies, Peris, Goddesses,
> There is not such a treat among them all,
> Haunters of cavern, lake, and waterfall,
> As a real woman, lineal indeed
> From Pyrrha's pebbles or old Adam's seed.
> Thus gentle Lamia judg'd, and judg'd aright,
> That Lycius could not love in half a fright,
> So *threw the goddess off*, and won his heart

More pleasantly by playing woman's part,
With no more awe than what her beauty gave,
That, while it smote, *still guaranteed to save.*

I, 328–339 (italics added)

The last two lines surely indicate Keats's belief that Lamia's love would have wrought no harm to Lycius had he not made certain grievous mistakes in his management of his side of the affair. The most grievous was his flat rejection of all Lamia's pleas against his later decision to celebrate their love in a public wedding, which meant that Lycius was attempting to carry his daemonic dream into actuality as a way of life, not as a brief and minor addition to actual life, as Hermes in the initial episode had conceived his love of the nymph to be. That such an action is not possible with impunity Keats had repeatedly asserted in his poetry and letters, and he wrote his most vigorous assertion of the idea just a few days before or after in *The Fall of Hyperion.* Now in *Lamia* he is dramatizing in a narrative fiction that the attempt is doomed to failure and death.

Some of the functions of the introductory episode of Hermes and his nymph, which Keats added to the story at the beginning, are to emphasize the sharp contrast between the psychological constitutions and attitudes of Hermes and Lycius as lovers, to contrast their different ontological status, to contrast their apparently similar yet vastly different actions, and to emphasize the completely opposite results of these actions. Keats's saying of the Hermes-nymph affair "Real are the dreams of Gods" (I, 127) could be taken as evidence simply that immortals may live dreams safely and mortals may not do so. But such an imprecise generalization and oversimplification obscure some very important particulars.

First, Hermes in his quest for the nymph is lighthearted, not too serious or intense, "bent warm on amorous theft" (I, 8); while he talked with Lamia he "on his pinions lay,/ Like a stoop'd falcon ere he takes his prey" (I, 66–67), and when he let her breathe upon his brow to bring the nymph before him he "on half-shut feathers sank serene" (I, 122). That is, Hermes is retaining his self-possession and taking the pursuit of his nymph lightly. In contrast, Lycius from his first glimpse of Lamia onward is intense, deadly serious, and wholly preoccupied with Lamia to the exclusion of all else; and this initial attitude well prepares for his becoming completely engulfed in his love experience, as Hermes distinctly is not. It has been almost overlooked that, just before proclaiming the reality of the dreams of gods, Keats had said of the Hermes-nymph affair, "*It was no dream*" (I, 126, italics added). This statement puts an entirely different coloring over the whole passage, which continues, "or say a dream it was,/ Real are the dreams of Gods." The implications of the passage are that gods, with their supramortal powers, can make *all* their dreams become realities; but, conversely, while mortals can make *some* of their dreams become real, mortals cannot make real those dreams that demand something of the structure of the mortal mind that is not now possible, that is, the all-consuming, completely engulfing, balance-destroying daemonic dream. Keats is here foreshadowing that Lycius, in contrast to the god Hermes, will attempt to do something that is impossible for mortals.

Though not a goddess and possibly once a normal woman, Lamia possesses capabilities beyond the human, and the experience which she brings to Lycius is a daemonic love that makes normal human love seem tame and unpalatable by comparison and makes him oblivious to practical matters necessary to the conduct of life. This aspect of the love affair between her and Lycius is repeatedly in evidence throughout the poem. For instance, in addition to decreasing the distance in their journey to Corinth, she arranged that "They pass'd the city gates, he knew not how,/ So noiseless, and he never thought to know" (I, 348–349). The house to which she was leading him in Corinth was a daemonic one, "a place unknown/ Some time to any, but those two alone,/ And a few Persian mutes" (I, 388–390), later called a "purple-lined palace of sweet sin" (II, 31). As if he knew full well that he was doing something not best for him, Lycius went along "muffling his face," fearful of encounter with "greeting friends" (I, 362). In this frame of mind Lycius, with Lamia by his side, came upon his teacher Apollonius and shrank even more into his mantle; and Lamia asked Lycius why he had blinded himself from the man's "quick eyes" (I, 366–374). Lycius' reply is one of the most important passages in the whole poem, for it shows that without fully realizing it at the time he had already undergone a radical transposition of values and that Apollonius is not at all the archvillain of the piece, as he is so often represented. We see him almost entirely from Lycius' point of view *after* this transposition of values, hardly at all *before*. But the initial lines of Lycius' reply to Lamia indicate positively that quite a different view of Apollonius is the correct one up to this very moment, when Lycius and Lamia together confront Apollonius for the first time:

> "Tis Apollonius sage, my trusty guide
> 'And good instructor; but to-night he seems
> 'The ghost of folly haunting my sweet dreams.'
> I, 375–377

It is important to note the way in which Lycius puts this matter. He unequivocally affirms that Apollonius is his "sage," "trusty guide," and "good instructor," but then pointedly uses the words "to-night" and "he seems" in designating him "the ghost of folly haunting my sweet dreams." Obviously the image of Apollonius as "sage" (later echoed by the narrator, II, 222, 227), "trusty guide," and "good instructor" is the correct view of him that had prevailed in the minds of Lycius and the other Corinthians up to this very moment and must still prevail in the minds of his fellow townsmen, who have not undergone the drastic change that has taken place in the mind of Lycius. Nowhere in the entire poem is there sufficient reliable evidence upon which to deny the truth of Apollonius' claim voiced directly to Lycius near the end: "From every ill/ Of life have I preserv'd thee to this day" (II, 296–297). But in the mass of explicatory writing about the poem and the many attempts to see the characters as rigid allegorical equivalents of abstract ideas, this view of Apollonius has become almost completely lost. There is a strong predilection in most interpreters to feel sympathy for the lovers and to find excuses for them. This is not to say that they do not deserve sympathy, but sympathy for them should not obscure the truth of what caused their plight, for they had been "getting by" with their love completely unscathed for a considerable time. But Lycius' daemonic preoccupation with it (II, 50–55) while knowing it to be fraught with peril and his willful determination to become more deeply immersed in it through marriage—these excesses of Lycius eventually force the calm "sage," "trusty guide," and "good instructor" to become obdurate, stern, and implacable in his opposition rather than continuing gently to admonish, guide, and instruct. But for Lycius' excesses there would have been no excesses on

Apollonius' part. He refrains from all active interference until the actual wedding day. And then what Lycius' unrestrained and imprudent conduct forces Apollonius to become gives a surface color of plausibility to the excessively harsh condemnation of his teacher which Lycius utters. But, again, all the unequivocally derogatory statements about Apollonius are voiced by Lycius *after* his mind-shattering transposition of values. Taken from that point of view, as in fairness they must be taken, nearly all the strongest derogations of Apollonius evaporate into nothingness, such as Lycius' in his emotional upheaval calling Apollonius "ruthless man" and "gray-beard wretch" who deals out "proud-heart sophistries" as "his lashless eyelids stretch/ Around his demon eyes!" [25] In this last epithet lies a striking irony, for it is Lycius himself, not Apollonius, who is far gone in the labyrinths of the daemonic.

Attention to this fundamental matter in the technique of narration—technical narrative point of view, or focus of narration—will absolve Apollonius from the charge of nearly all that is sinister, malicious, or willfully destructive of a beautiful love without cause. When the point of view of what is being said is shifted from Lycius to the narrator himself, or to John Keats in effect since he never establishes separate identity or position in the piece for the narrator, *very little if any unequivocal derogation* of Apollonius remains. Although shortly after Lycius' accusation of "proud-heart sophistries," the narrator twice refers to Apollonius as "the sophist" (II, 291, 299), the purpose of the word "sophist" here may well be that of echoing the earlier "sophistries" (II, 285), partly in order to sustain a oneness of texture and tone in the poem and

[25] II, 277, 287, 288–289. The phrase "gray-beard wretch" could have been suggested to Keats by Coleridge's "grey-beard loon" for the mariner narrator in *Rime of the Ancient Mariner*, I, 11.

partly to show that the narrator is taking account of the mind of Lycius while not necessarily agreeing with his views. The narrator's echoing the word in this context could not possibly mean that the "sage," "trusty guide," and "good instructor" has really been suddenly turned into a sophist. It is the mind of Lycius that has drastically changed, not that of his teacher. The worst that can be said truthfully of Apollonius is that he becomes uncompromising and unyielding when he has no other choice.

And what of the famous passage about "all charms" vanishing "At the mere touch of cold philosophy," usually considered a devastating indictment of Apollonius? It reads as follows:

> Do not all charms fly
> At the mere touch of cold philosophy?
> There was an awful rainbow once in heaven:
> We know her woof, her texture; she is given
> In the dull catalogue of common things.
> Philosophy will clip an Angel's wings,
> Conquer all mysteries by rule and line,
> Empty the haunted air, and gnomed mine—
> Unweave a rainbow, as it erewhile made
> The tender-person'd Lamia melt into a shade.
>
> II, 229–238

It is pointedly significant that the narrator does not here commit himself in any way to a direct judgment of Apollonius, but puts all this in an initial rhetorical question and subsequent generalizations, which the reader must answer and particularize for himself. Keats is maintaining impartiality, avoiding sentimentality, and leaving matters of interpretation to the reader while the characters work out their destiny in the mind of the writer. The answer to the rhetorical question at the beginning of the passage when viewed within the context of the entire poem, even without reference to the other daemonic poems, is distinctly *not* a resounding "yes" but is in fact a firm and emphatic "no!" All charms do *not* vanish at the touch of cold philosophy, only the extreme charm of attempting to make daemonic experience a complete way of life, which would disintegrate the intelligence and make a man "forget his mortal way," the way in which he can live his life here with most satisfaction. Lamia and Lycius were left to the charm of their daemonic union unmolested until it took the pernicious direction of Lycius' determination to make it completely engulfing (II, 50–51), as he told her while "mirror'd small in paradise" in her eyes (II, 47), quite symbolic of his predicament. There is really no valid reason anywhere to consider Apollonius as "cold philosophy"; Keats omitted "cold" (II, 234) before stating that philosophy caused Lamia to "melt." Apollonius never makes an abstract analysis and never utters a sophistical argument or presents an extended discourse. When seen in the light of his function in the poem and of his true character, as indicated *before* Lycius' transposition of values, Apollonius is merely the voice of good sense, of good human sense, insisting vehemently upon what in the nature of things a mortal must do when in Lycius' situation. When freed from the superimposed image of the sinister interferer and destroyer thrown over him by the distraught Lycius and sentimental readers, Apollonius emerges as the one character in the cast who most nearly represents what in a piece of prose fiction is called the "center of intelligence," the mind that maintains and enunciates the ideas and values in terms of which the story has meaning. Most of the incidents in the action point unmistakably in this direction, and no other character could possibly qualify for the designation. Well indeed has Professor Bush pointed out that Apollonius must be considered as representing something of Keats's mind if the poem is to have any meaning at all.[26] Apollonius, in real truth, represents that sanity and balance in Keats's mind that, from *Endymion* on through the odes, had consistently impelled him to draw back before going completely off the deep end in his drive toward the beauty beyond mortality. The name itself suggests calm Apollonian wisdom as opposed to the Dionysian frenzy of the daemonic.

The next lines about the "awful rainbow once in heaven" are markedly pertinent. This was undoubtedly the rainbow that signalized God's covenant with Noah and all living creatures that the flood had ended and would not return (Genesis IX: 9–17), and the rainbow has been a symbol of hope in our common lot ever since. The rainbow throws a kind of sanctity over the world of nature and humanity; its fresh vaporous arch after a rain suggests the sufficiency of this world for man's mortal needs. But this is the world that Lycius is forsaking completely, obliterating its meaningfulness to him in a flood of daemonic prepossession and violating spiritual laws of his being. This symbolic rainbow "is given/ In the dull catalogue of common things" (II, 232–233), that is, in the standard records of our culture. The word "dull" here should not be taken at surface value; it is a part of the irony and ambivalence that Keats is maintaining in his effort at detachment. Common things are not dull to a human being who is not immersed in the daemonic, as they certainly were not dull to the first speaker in *La Belle Dame* or to Peona in *Endymion*. As for the ensuing statement that "Philosophy

[26] Bush, *Mythology and the Romantic Tradition*, p. 112n.

will clip an Angel's wings," philosophy (whatever it precisely may mean here) is surely not doing so in this instance, for Lamia is no angel except in the view of Lycius. Whatever she is, she is not evil or malicious, and she is genuinely in love with Lycius; but she is the agent that is inspiring his daemonic pursuit, a "hook" for his *anima*, and is therefore unquestionably harmful to him (though not wishing to be), and she must be removed from her present relationship to him. Apollonius is the only character in the story with the power to accomplish this necessary task, and he does not flinch from the duty of it; but he waits until it is unequivocally necessary —until the day of the highly symbolic wedding. The subsequent statement that philosophy can "unweave a rainbow" (II, 237), recalling Keats's and Lamb's strictures on Newton at Haydon's "immortal dinner," is again part of the detachment and urbanity which Keats is maintaining. He left it for readers to decide whether Apollonius or Lycius did most to "unweave" Lycius' rainbow, and the weight of evidence points strongly toward Lycius himself. Keats was slow to determine the exact time at which a beautiful daemonic illusion must be given up; he knew only that it must be given up at some point before it alienates a man from the world in which he must live out his days.

It is true that Keats does bring into the wording of this passage some of the pet strictures against systematized knowledge (II, 234–237) that have frequently reappeared as one side of his long conflict between sensation and thought, but just a few months earlier he had pretty well settled that conflict in *Hyperion*, when, in the deification of Apollo at the end (III, 99–135), he dramatized and emphasized how sensation through the process of "Negative Capability" grows immediately into knowledge that is at once both universal and concrete, hence godlike knowledge. Therefore it should not be surprising that here in *Lamia* most of the apparent derogation of Apollonius as one who deals too strictly in "thought" evaporates upon closer examination, for the time is too late in Keats's development for these strictures to carry much weight, and interpreters who press them are very likely riding a worn-out hobby-horse. In contrast to Apollonius, Lycius is severely downgraded by the narrator in terms which cannot be explained away. He is called "blinded Lycius" (I, 347), and later "senseless Lycius," and "Madman!" by the narrator when he insists upon the marriage in spite of the strong opposition of Lamia herself as well as of Apollonius:

> O senseless Lycius! Madman! wherefore flout
> The silent-blessing fate, warm cloister'd hours,
> And show to common eyes these bowers?
>
> II, 147–149

In the original version of this passage, included in a letter to his publisher on the day Keats completed the poem, the narrator also designated Lycius "dolt," "fool," and "lout" along with the other derogatory terms above (*Letters*, II, 158). This overwhelming condemnation of Lycius by the narrator makes Apollonius' calling Lycius "fool" seem rather mild.

When the false stigma of the sinister meddler is thus removed from Apollonius, a remarkably kindred relationship can be seen between the three leading characters in *Lamia* and the corresponding three leading characters in both *Endymion* and *La Belle Dame sans Merci*. Peona in *Endymion*, who steadily voices the worth and beauty of the actual world and persistently warns Endymion of the dangers of his daemonic proclivities; the first speaker in *La Belle Dame sans Merci*, who emphasizes the pleasures and satisfactions of ordinary life; and Apollonius in *Lamia*, who had preserved Lycius "from every ill/ Of life" and made a last desperate effort to save him—all three are obviously modes of the same basic character, one who is attuned to the ordinary plane of human existence and has found it good. Although there are differences among the three, all urge the protagonists to accept the human condition, find contentedness within it, and eschew experience which is beyond it. Similarly, the heroines in these three poems are all modes of the same basic feminine image, the supramortal lady love who is not evil or sinister, who is sincerely involved in love for her mortal mate, but who without intending him harm still inspires in him a daemonic preoccupation that is unfortunate for him since it undermines his necessary adjustment to the actual plane of being, where mortal man must live. Although Cynthia in *Endymion* is a goddess and the other two are not, but are daemonic creatures of less stature than goddesses, all function in the poems in the same basic way despite the differences among them and the different endings of the stories. And last, the three protagonists are even more strikingly similar to each other, for all are chiefly characterized by a fierce desire for experience beyond the customary limits of the human lot, and all of them obtain just enough joys beyond the usual to impair their adjustment to mortality. If Endymion had not rejected his pursuit of Cynthia, as Peona repeatedly urged, and had not come to perceive that he had loved "a nothing," he could have come to the same end as Lycius. If the knight in *La Belle Dame* should continue locked in his stasis between two worlds, in which we last see him as the poem ends, he could meet a fate similar to that of Lycius, and will *certainly* do so if he should lapse back into his engrossing quest for the elfin lady again. Apollonius in *Lamia* is simply Peona in *Endymion* and the first speaker in *La Belle Dame* grown older, more learned, more self-assured, more resolute, and more committed to what he believes to be a satisfactory life. He is more stark and formidable because the situation that he faced was more deadly and his pupil more immersed in it. He could not have known beforehand that his efforts to save his protégé would contribute to his death, but that event was more nearly brought on by Lycius' own willful enthrallment than by his teacher's intercession. In view of Keats's established pattern of treating matters in his daemonic narratives and in his odes, we can hardly deny that the mission of Apollonius was a worthy one and that Keats was more nearly on his "side" than on any other in spite of his detachment; for we can now see clearly what the "sides" were—not the claims of "cold philosophy" on the one hand and the claims of the "self," "senses," or "emotion" on the other, but the claims of the substantial and reliable beauty that is possible to man in the actual conditions of his existence as opposed to the lure of the ephemeral, delusive excitement of daemonic experience beyond. By this time in his development we can clearly see that Keats could not be on the "side" of the latter as a complete way of life, although in this poem he is trying to withhold his own views and to mask them at times with facetiousness. The conflict in the poem is not simply one between reality and illusion but a conflict between a certain kind of reality and a certain kind of illusion—a conflict between the reality made up of the common consciousness and phenomena as opposed to the illusion of the high worth of daemonic experience, from whose effects it is difficult to free the mind so that it can again deal satisfactorily with the common lot of all, as is necessary most of the time. Again, Keats is more nearly on Apollonius' side than on any other, and the supposed paradoxes and divided emphases in the poem vanish in the face of that fact, which is well supported by the basic structure of the poem as well as by fundamental elements in his other major poems.

Why Keats became sufficiently interested in the Lamia story in Burton to feel a desire to use it as the basis of a narrative should now be apparent. The autobiographical element in the poem is not so much personal as it is professional, not so much a veiled rendering of his fascination with Fanny Brawne as the completing and bringing to finality of a long-continued effort in his literary life and in his speculations concerning the nature of that beauty which can be a "sage" and "Physician to all men," as he said in *The Fall of Hyperion* (I, 189–190) that poetry should be. The Lamia story was simply another version of the story he liked most to tell while exploring this question of the nature of beauty that is of most worth to man. The three major characters of the Lamia story are but modes of the three leading characters in his two previous daemonic narratives; and, like the speakers in the odes and the protagonists in these narratives, the protagonist in the Lamia story was a human being striving to "burst our mortal bars" and test the quality and extent of experience that lies beyond. This ready version of his twice-used plot provided an opportunity for Keats to add to Burton's account a final scene involving the sudden death of the protagonist after Lamia is destroyed, for Burton's brief sketch has no hint of the demise of Lycius. Keats's changing the final ending of the tale in this way is highly indicative of what he was trying to express in his retelling of it; for this strikingly different denouement, along with his complex redevelopment of the major characters, enabled him to bring the various renderings of his favorite story full circle by presenting in this final narrative the one instance of a human being who pursued daemonic excitement beyond the point of no return and thus lost his mortal way irrevocably. No previous protagonist or ode speaker had ever done so, although some had approached this point. Hence Keats brought the story rapidly to a close when the steady gaze of Apollonius disintegrated the beauty that once was Lamia before Lycius' terrified eyes, and the youth dies, finding that he cannot live without the daemonic joy that she had brought him; for it had already usurped the place of all earthly joys in his life and had caused them to "melt into a shade" long before that fate befell the gentle Lamia, as it inevitably had to do.

The only major task now left to Keats in his long and recurrent treatment of this whole theme was to devote a poem entirely to a full presentation of the other extreme of it: the anti-daemonic, the apex of the "material sublime," that stands at the opposite pole from *Lamia*. This Keats accomplished consummately in his most nearly perfect major poem, the last of the great odes, *To Autumn*, which brought to a fitting close this long-continued theme in his poetry.

CHAPTER SEVEN

TO AUTUMN:
THE TRIUMPH OF THE
ANTI-DAEMONIC

In order to grasp the full relevance of Keats's last great poem to his previous daemonic narratives, which constitute an inter-related group within themselves and which also have striking thematic links with the great odes, it is necessary to observe some of the time relationships among his labors of the summer and autumn of 1819, his last productive period. He composed the first part of *Lamia* during the twelve or thirteen days between the last of June and July 11.[1] He then laid the poem aside unfinished for six weeks, during which he worked at times on the composition of the play *Otho the Great* with Charles Brown and, more important, on the revision of his epic fragment *Hyperion* into *The Fall of Hyperion*, with its vehement condemnation of the poetry of fanatical and obsessive dreams woven into the action and pointedly emphasized in the authorial comment within the poem. In fact, the opening lines of *The Fall of Hyperion* read like a direct castigation of Lycius "mirror'd small in paradise" in the pupils of Lamia's eyes in the sequestered, daemonic world which she had led him into; and these lines go on to sound again the anti-dae-

[1] W. J. Bate, *John Keats* (Cambridge, Mass., 1963), p. 537.

monic theme and to speak of a "proper bound" for the imagination that had been voiced more than a year before in the verse epistle *To J. H. Reynolds, Esq.*:

> O that our dreamings all of sleep or wake,
> Would all their colours from the Sunset take:
> From something of material sublime.
>
> 67–69

The opening lines of *The Fall of Hyperion* read as follows:

> Fanatics have their dreams, wherewith they weave
> A paradise for a sect. . . .
> For Poesy alone can tell her dreams,
> With the fine spell of words alone *can save*
> *Imagination from the sable charm*
> And dumb enchantment. . . .
> Whether the dream now purposed to rehearse
> Be Poet's or Fanatic's will be known
> When this warm scribe my hand is in the grave.
>
> I, 1–18 (italics added)

This prominent strain in *The Fall of Hyperion* comes to a head in the well-known passage that includes the narrator's following query to Moneta, the teacher of poets, just after she has linked together visionary poets and dreamers (I, 161–162) and is continuing to castigate them severely:

> 'Majestic shadow, tell me: sure not all
> Those melodies sung into the world's ear
> Are useless: sure a poet is a sage;
> A humanist, Physician to all men.
>
> .   .   .   .
>
> —The tall shade veil'd in drooping white

Then spake, so much more earnest. . . .
'The poet and the dreamer are distinct,
Diverse, sheer opposite, antipodes.
The one pours out a balm upon the world,
The other vexes it.'

I, 187–202

These lines were written shortly before or shortly after Keats completed writing *Lamia*, for he had accomplished this task by September 5, and he gave up working on *The Fall of Hyperion* by September 22.[2] The passage expresses strong aversion to the kind of thing that is dramatized in *Lamia;* and, originating after he had begun *Lamia* and so close upon his completing the poem, they must of necessity indicate something of his own judgment upon its main action—a judgment that militates strongly against our interpreting the poem from Lycius' and Lamia's point of view. This judgment does not contradict his well-known liking for the poem, evidenced by his stating that it had "that sort of fire in it which would take hold of people in some way—give them either a pleasant or unpleasant sensation,"[3] a statement written on the day before he wrote *To Autumn*, and also evidenced by his listing *Lamia* first in the title of the 1820 volume: *Lamia, Isabella, The Eve of St. Agnes, and Other Poems*, published in July. Rather, these comments in *The Fall of Hyperion* indicate the particular nature of his liking for *Lamia*. They indicate that he liked it because it powerfully dramatized the consequences of a false view of happiness for man and poet, not because he shared and approved of Lycius' destructive fascination with

[2] Bate, *John Keats*, pp. 580–585.
[3] Letter to George and Georgiana Keats, September 18, 1819 (*Letters*, II, 189).

daemonic beauty carried so far beyond what is possible for mortals; for the totality of his poems and letters, taken together, clearly shows that he could not have approved it even though he understood and pitied it.

It is highly significant that Keats completed Part II of *Lamia*, which concluded the poem, on September 5, 1819, just two weeks before the memorable day on which he wrote the whole of *To Autumn*, September 19. It is also significant that *Lamia* was continually on his mind during this two-week interval; he read the whole poem to Richard Woodhouse on September 11 and read through a part of it on September 18, the very day before he composed *To Autumn*.[4] These two facts help to account for what is strikingly apparent when the full implications of *Lamia* and *To Autumn* are considered side by side. For *To Autumn*, his last truly great poem, has a strong connection with *Lamia* in the way of antithesis; *To Autumn* powerfully expresses the direct opposite of what is expressed in *Lamia*, and this antithetical relationship is not too much obscured by the differences in structure between a lyrical poem and a narrative when the two are read together. *To Autumn* presents the final, consummate embodiment of the anti-daemonic strain that Keats had been juxtaposing against the daemonic element in the narrative poems and in the odes ever since the early lines of *Endymion*. Here in *To Autumn* there is a startling change from the other great odes in what the consciousness of the speaker centers upon and sustains in the foreground throughout. In the earlier odes there had been two dimensions of reality: the area of the senses and the common consciousness on the one hand, and on the other, the region of daemonic beauty just outside the

[4] *Letters*, II, 164, 189.

common consciousness, with the latter sharply set off against the former. But in *To Autumn* all is centered on one plane of being and knowing, that of the common consciousness sensitive to its surroundings in the phenomenal world and aware of the full beauty and meaningfulness of that world to humanity. This is not to say that the poem is a merely sensuous one, for it is far more indeed. There is not a trace of the continually recurring tendency in the previous odes and narratives to pierce beyond the plane of our common lot into what may lie beyond. Yet there are manifold varieties of richness, ripeness, and fulfillment in its flawless modulations, but all are within the reach of every sensitive and feeling man who has not become immune to their appeal. Here, at last, the promise implicit in the final lines of *Ode on a Grecian Urn* has been fulfilled, for here is quietly but conclusively demonstrated that "Beauty is truth," that is, beauty is actuality, and that is all that Keats ever meant by the statement. Here is expressed, unbroken and complete, the utmost contentment with man's position in the great cycle of birth, death, and rebirth and with his relationship to that cycle as it ministers to his needs and as he feels the full significance of that fact. There is here no need to attempt to "burst our mortal bars" and to soar into "some wondrous region" beyond; throughout the poem the poet keeps to the firm ground of nature and the common consciousness, the realm of what he had called the "material sublime," a term which largely designates the substance of the poem.

Surely Keats's having so recently set forth the ultimate in daemonic experience and its consequences in *Lamia*, and his rereading that poem entire a week before and in part the day before writing *To Autumn* had much to do with his serene glorification of the direct antithesis of *Lamia* in *To Autumn*, which presents the ripeness, richness, and satisfactions of the common lot with an emphasis upon them, a concentration of them, and an artistic shaping and molding of them never before so massed and interwoven by him in a single poem. Yet this skillfully modulated accumulation of the sights, activities, sounds, and atmosphere of early autumn as images of fulfillment is a continuation of a pattern of image and idea recurringly apparent in his poetry from the first, and this strain in his previous poetry had been frequently juxtaposed against the wild ecstasies of the daemonic as its direct opposite, as we have seen. His completing *Lamia* on September 5 and rereading it on September 11 and 18 evidently served as an immediate antithetical stimulus which accentuated his response to the beauty of the ripeness all about him on that mellow September 19, 1819, and at the same time moved the shaping power of his imagination to construct an entire poem of these beauties alone and of this one plane of being and knowing. Moreover, Keats's letters to J. H. Reynolds and to Richard Woodhouse written on September 21–22, in the latter of which Keats copied out the entire text of the poem, show that the mood and mental temper reflected in *To Autumn* were not temporary but remained with him for days afterward. To Reynolds he wrote in part as follows:

> How beautiful the season is now—How fine the air. A temperate sharpness about it. Really, without joking, chaste weather—Dian skies—I never lik'd stubble fields so much as now—Aye better than the chilly green of the spring. Somehow a stubble plain looks warm—in the same way that some pictures look warm—this struck me so much in my Sunday's walk that I composed upon it [i.e., the poem *To Autumn*]. I hope you are better employed than in gaping

after weather. I have been at different times so happy as not to know what weather it was [*Letters*, II, 167].

To find such beauty in stubble fields, which he made so much of also in the poem, is indeed the opposite extreme of the remote and sequestered beauty of daemonic experience. In the letter to Woodhouse, which included the text of the poem, Keats wrote: "O that I could [write] something . . . rural, pleasant, fountain-voiced—not plague you with unconnected nonsense" (*Letters*, II, 174).

But more than two years before, in the introductory lines of *Endymion*, Keats had written, "let Autumn bold,/ With universal tinge of sober gold,/ Be all about me when I make an end" (I, 55–57); and shortly afterward in the hymn to Pan he had proclaimed, "Broad leaved fig trees even now foredoom/ Their ripen'd fruitage; yellow girted bees/ Their golden honeycombs; our village leas/ Their fairest blossom'd beans and poppied corn;/ . . . yea, the fresh budding year/ All its completions" (I, 252–260). *To Autumn* is a poem concentrated upon all these "completions," and there is much "universal tinge of sober gold" within it. In *Endymion* Keats had set off the fruitfulness of the actual world, frequently in harvest imagery, against the wild ravings of Endymion for union with his out-of-this-world mistress, Cynthia, until the satisfactions of actuality come to a head and triumph in his rejection of the quest for Cynthia and acceptance of the humble and earthly Indian maid:

> Where shall our dwelling be? Under the brow
> Of some steep mossy hill, where ivy dun
> Would hide us up, although spring leaves were none;
> And where dark yew trees, as we rustle through,
> Will drop their scarlet berry cups of dew?

Honey from out the gnarled hive I'll bring,
And apples, wan with sweetness, gather thee.

IV, 670–683

Further, harvest imagery of fulfillment frequently appears in the shorter poems, as for example in the sonnet *When I Have Fears*, in which he wishes not to die before his pen has "glean'd" his "teeming brain" and "high-piled books, in charact'ry,/ Hold like rich garners the full-ripen'd grain" of his poetic harvest. The function of similar imagery to suggest satisfying earthly fulfillment in *La Belle Dame sans Merci* as set off against the daemonic longings of the knight has been traced out in detail in Chapter IV above. In sum, therefore, the cumulative presentation of such an array of harvest imagery symbolic of the earthly satisfactions available to man in *To Autumn* is a culmination of a pervasive strain already continually set off and contrasted against the daemonic in Keats's previous poetry. Consequently, it should not be difficult to believe that in *To Autumn* he shaped up his consummate statement of the joys of actuality partly to set them off against the ephemeral, dangerous joys of the daemonic and that he did so at least to some degree consciously and deliberately rather than by chance alone; for the full beauty and significance of *To Autumn* come out more clearly and sharply when seen against the backdrop of its direct opposite as set forth in *Lamia*. For all these reasons, therefore, it is fitting and proper to designate *To Autumn* the high point or triumph of the anti-daemonic in Keats's poetry, the fullest development of that fresh grasp of the beauty of actuality that is derived expressly from a revulsion against its antithesis in moments of daemonic ecstasy beyond the common weal recorded in previous poems.

Almost entirely superseded now are older interpretations of *To Autumn* as a somber death-song of the transience and ephemerality of all things earthly.[5] Now it seems difficult to understand how such interpretations of the poem ever came into existence unless through stock response to the title; there is nothing at all somber in it, and both its imagery and total effect work in the opposite direction from transience and decay. In truth, all the details, overtones, and structure of the poem conjoin to sustain an impression of the satisfaction and fulfillment which human beings can find in things earthly. Yet in some of the most highly respected treatments of the poem, I think, too much is still made of the degree to which it includes elements of transience, process, and death.[6] In a penetrating explication which reveals much of the subtle artistry of the poem, Professor Bate points out the absence from this poem of the oppositions, contradictions, and paradoxes so prominent in the previous great odes (and, we might add, in the narrative poems also):

But if dramatic debate, protest, and qualification are absent, it is not because any premises from which they might proceed are disregarded but because these premises are being anticipated and

[5] Two very worthwhile studies which militate against this view are D. S. Bland, "Logical Structure in the 'Ode to Autumn,'" *Philological Quarterly*, XXXIII (1954), 219–222; and B. C. Southam, "The Ode 'To Autumn,'" *Keats-Shelley Journal*, IX (1960), 91–98, although I do not share Mr. Southam's belief that the three stanzas "trace the progress of the season" into "earliest winter" (p. 93), but rather the progress of a day from morning through noon to late afternoon.

[6] For example, Bate, *John Keats*, pp. 581–583; David Perkins, *The Quest for Permanence* (Cambridge, Mass., 1959), pp. 290–294; and Harold Bloom, *The Visionary Company* (New York, 1961), pp. 421–425.

absorbed at each step. The result (in contrast to the "Nightingale" or the "Grecian Urn") is also a successful union of the ideal—of the heart's desire—and reality; of the "greeting of the spirit" and its object. What the heart really wants is being found. . . . Here at last is something of a genuine paradise, therefore. It even has its deity—a benevolent deity that wants not only to "load and bless" . . . but also to "spare," to prolong.

These resolutions are attained partly through still another one to which Keats's poetry has so often aspired: a union of process and stasis (or what Keats had called "stationing"). . . . If, in the first stanza, we find process continuing within a context of stillness and attained fulfillment, in the second—which is something of a reverse or mirror image of the first—we find stillness where we expect to find process.[7]

A few somewhat different views from these are in order here, I think, and some qualifications. The opposing premises that had injected debate and sustained duality into Keats's previous poetry are not *all* anticipated and absorbed in *To Autumn;* one premise in particular has been disregarded and kept out of the poem entirely, for its consequences already had been worked out earlier and its soundness found wanting: the premise that man can find more satisfying experience in intense daemonic ecstasies outside the customary human lot than he can find within its boundaries. The implications of this premise had to be worked out, tested, and very largely rejected before there was possible in Keats's poetry this successful union of the ideal (the heart's desire) and reality (actuality). For prior to this testing of the premise in previous odes and narratives Keats had sought the height of the heart's desire—what he kept on hoping would turn out to be the ideal

[7] Bate, *John Keats*, pp. 581–582.

—in daemonic experiences outside actuality, and had continued this hope and this wish right on into his writing of the great odes, in which it is subjected to its most severe testing and in which it begins to subside, as has been traced out. That is, man can find in daemonic experience only a minor addition to customary joys. Consequently, without his having made the emphatic rejection of this quest spelled out at this very time in *Lamia* and in the *Fall of Hyperion*, he could hardly have made so convincing a discovery of the ideal in the actual as is serenely expressed now in *To Autumn*, for he would have continued to search for the heart's desire beyond actuality, and he is pointedly and emphatically not doing so in this poem.

Moreover, I do not believe that a union of process and stasis in the sense of a resolution of them takes place in the poem. Most likely no such union of the two is possible, for they are not like Hegel's opposition between Being and Not-being, which can be resolved in Becoming (in process, that is); Keats's opposition is a more genuine contradiction between Becoming (process) and Not-becoming (stasis), and in his particular use of them in the poem he leans markedly toward stasis. The union of the two is achieved not by his resolving them but by his muting and reducing the evidences of process that appear in the poem to the minimum necessary to authenticate the materials of his picture as elements in a living world with a function there, so that they do not seem like the dead, dry specimens in a museum. Process is minimized and partly masked in the poem, leaving a total effect of living enrichments that linger and endure. Overemphasizing the role of process in the first stanza, I think, results in Professor Bate's asserting that in the second stanza "we find stillness where we expect to find process," when just the converse seems to be true; for we are led by the slowing and muting of process in stanza 1 to expect the remarkable near-stillness (for it is not complete stillness) amidst the harvesting activities in stanza 2. The same overemphasis of process perhaps also leads Professor Bate to see in the "last oozings" of the cider press "a hint that the end is approaching," though Keats has added "hours by hours," and to see as the pervading thought of the last stanza "the withdrawal of autumn, the coming death of the year." This seems out of harmony with the predominant effect which Keats skillfully maintains throughout. I believe that the beauties and values of the poem can be apprehended more clearly if it is read without major emphasis on the function of process and is viewed as Keats's consummate rendering of the long-developing anti-daemonic strain already in his poetry from the beginning.

The interwoven, careful artistry by which Keats cumulatively built up his remarkably sustained total effect is discernible at the outset in the opening line of the first stanza. With its key term "mellow fruitfulness" in the position of emphasis at the end, this line enunciates at once the theme of the whole poem and the aspect of that theme to be treated in the first stanza; for the structure of images of fulfillment displayed in the poem extends beyond the massed ripeness in the first stanza and moves on to the pleasant tasks of harvesting in the second stanza, and to the music made up of the sounds of autumn in the third. Even while enumerating with powerful concreteness the material things necessary to man that come to fruition in autumn, the speaker seems to be suggesting more than these; for throughout the poem all the concrete particulars that make up its total fabric are presented in the way in which they register upon a receptive human consciousness and are organized by that consciousness into a unified apprehension centering upon one overriding idea: that all these material things are nearing the completion of their ripening and maturing *in order to fulfill human needs*, not for the "slow smokeless burning of decay" or for the windblown replanting of new growth, which would be their destiny in the wilds. Though of necessity he has to present these ripening things separately one after another, he gives the effect of apprehending them all together in one manifold, yet in a way which does not detract from their strong individual connotations. They are made to fit together harmoniously by the modifying power of the poet's imagination as much as by his careful selection of them, as his rejected and variant readings indicate. The fact that they are being harvested and stored in granaries and bins *before* their ripening gives way to decay, emphasized in the first line of the second stanza, further sustains the central idea of their human purpose and the steady de-emphasis of transience and decay in the poem. The dominant impression is that autumn is a continuing and recurring outpouring of all that man needs, including suggestions of the spiritual as well as the earthly bread; and the use of "season" as the first word in this poem on "mellow fruitfulness" suggests its continual recurrence in the great cycle of nature, which helps to convey the impression of its lastingness:

> Season of mists and mellow fruitfulness,
>   Close bosom-friend of the maturing sun;
> Conspiring with him how to load and bless
>   With fruit the vines that round the thatch-eves run;
> To bend with apples the moss'd cottage-trees,
>   And fill all fruit with ripeness to the core;
>   To swell the gourd, and plump the hazel shells
> With a sweet kernel; to set budding more,

And still more, later flowers for the bees,
Until they think warm days will never cease,
   For Summer has o'er-brimm'd their clammy cells.

Now, having developed cumulatively the idea of "mellow fruitfulness" on the literal plane through the accrual of individual ripenings, and thereby having slowed the great process of birth, death, and rebirth to the minimum, he is ready to take up another aspect of the idea in the second stanza. Seldom before in a lyric poem has a second major section been so distinctly different and yet so indissolubly related to the first, making the poem evolve and yet reveal a tight unity of all its elements synthesized into one fabric. In the first line of the second stanza he reaches back as if with an enveloping hand, drawing together again the ripe fruits in stanza 1, emphasizing that they make up a rich "store" of good things needed by man, and thereby continuing the suggestion that they do not fade and decay but are gathered and retained to minister to man's needs over a long period and therefore will remain intact in their fullness: "Who hath not seen thee oft amid thy store?" At the same time that this line, with the full effect of the word "store," serves to tie the two stanzas together, it also enunciates what will be the theme of this second stanza—the perception of the very essence and spirit of the time in the pleasing human activities of harvesting and storing its substance. The individual images of harvesting are modified by the dominant idea that each task is satisfying and rewarding in itself to the performer and to any observer (i.e., to the "whoever seeks abroad" who "may find/ Thee" in lines 2–3 of the stanza), just as each maturing fruit in stanza 1 is presented as almost ready to give its fullness for man's sustenance. In perfect harmony with the marked slowing and muting of nature's great process in stanza 1, all these harvesters in stanza 2 have slowed their labors or have temporarily stopped them. But there is no dead and complete silence. The feminine thresher is "sitting careless" on a "granary floor," but her hair is "soft-lifted" in light movement "by the winnowing wind," an image also suggesting that the chaff itself, all streaming in the same direction in the wind, resembles the blowing locks of a mythological feminine embodiment of autumn, probably the most delicately handled instance of personification in English poetry. The breast of the harvester "on a half-reap'd furrow sound asleep" gently rises and falls in breathing, though the reaping hook is laid aside in stillness and thus "spares the next swath" and its "twined flowers." [8] The gleaner crossing the brook (evidently on stepping stones or footlog) has had to slow his pace perhaps to a complete stop, but slight movements are required to maintain his balance and thus to "keep steady" his "laden head," an image which echoes "granary" in line 2 and "thy store" in line 1 of this second stanza and through it the whole of the first stanza, which "thy store" had summarized before—the chain of reference constituting a pervasive linking up of basic imagery that is becoming symbolic. The word "granary" or synonyms of it had been a symbol of something beyond the physical in Keats's poetry from the time of *Endymion* and the sonnet *When I Have Fears* in early 1818. The second stanza of *To Autumn* closes with the patient cider-press worker watching

[8] As Professor Perkins states (*The Quest for Permanence*, p. 292), autumn is personified in various attitudes in the second stanza, but I cannot share his belief that "the dominant image is of autumn as the harvester—and a harvester that is in a sense another reaper, death itself"; that "the harvest is drawing to a close" (p. 293); and that "the notion of death is present [in the second stanza] to emerge more nakedly in the third stanza"—surely an overemphasis at least, although Keats's acceptance of earthly satisfactions in the poem embraces all that goes with earthly life.

"the last oozings hours by hours," an image which suggests again nature's unhurried outpouring of sustenance for man. I do not believe that these slow "last oozings" convey "a hint that the end is approaching," as Professor Bate has said, nor that "the pervading thought in what follows [i.e., in the final stanza] is the withdrawal of autumn, the coming death of the year"; for as the major idea of the stanza, that would be disturbingly out of harmony with the preceding two stanzas and with the carefully wrought total effect of the whole poem. If in the poem at all, the coming death of the year is a very minor strain, carefully muted and subdued, and the pain of it almost removed. To help the reader's imagination to take these "last oozings" of the cider press in just the right way, Keats added "hours by hours," bringing this image into line with the whole picture of the contentment that comes from contemplating autumn as a season of enrichments that linger and recur.

In sum, there is enough gentle movement amidst the massed stillness in the second stanza to indicate the presence of life, but no one in this harvest scene is presented in the act of strenuous exertion, rapid motion, or violent action; for the maturing sun and the season with "all its completions" have so conspired "to load and bless" man's earthly lot that no hurried and strenuous labors are necessary to gather in and preserve all this wealth. The degree to which movement is subdued and minimized in stanza 2 is exactly what we have been led to expect by the choice and modulation of details in stanza 1 and is in harmony with the total effect of that stanza and of the whole poem. The full stanza reads as follows:

> Who hath not seen thee oft amid thy store?
> Sometimes whoever seeks abroad may find

Thee sitting careless on a granary floor,
   Thy hair soft-lifted by the winnowing wind;
Or on a half-reap'd furrow sound asleep,
   Drows'd with the fume of poppies, while thy hook
     Spares the next swath and all its twined flowers:
And sometimes like a gleaner thou dost keep
   Steady thy laden head across a brook;
   Or by a cyder-press, with patient look,
     Thou watchest the last oozings hours by hours.

One of Keats's master strokes in this stanza is that another presence, delicately suggested, seems to linger unobtrusively about each one of these harvesters, observing, perceiving, understanding the significance of all. This shadowy presence, the "whoever seeks abroad" (line 13) that "may find/ Thee," does indeed find the essence, spirit, and deeper meaning of autumn conceived as fulfillment. That is, the seeker finds it within himself in his responses to all that is going on about him, and quite rightly; for autumn is really a matter of human perceiving and value-making placed upon the physical developments of the time; without this human perceiving and valuing, the great vortex of nature considered in its mere materiality does not have the meanings which the human consciousness alone can give it. These are the real subject of his poem. In this second stanza he has managed to move the center of interest away from the material details emphasized in stanza 1 and to express, without abstract terms but by sustained concrete images, something quite beyond the physical: the *idea* of what autumn is to the human spirit in purposiveness, fruition, lingering contentment, and manifold completions. This is chiefly what gives the poem an element of universality. Yet he has managed at the same time to carry over into stanza 2 the material ripenings of stanza 1 and to sustain them in a prominent secondary position while he gives first place to the workers in the field, for it is the ripening fruitage described in stanza 1 that they are harvesting and storing for human need. Thus he unobtrusively emphasizes the relationship between the physical ripenings and humanity by building that relationship into the structural framework of the poem as the basic link that unites the two stanzas intrinsically.

In stanza 3 Keats centers upon the music which the human ear apprehends in the pleasing sounds of autumn, and this third aspect of his over-all theme serves both to differentiate this final stanza from the preceding stanza and at the same time to unite it firmly to the whole. Just as the first two stanzas are sutured together by the retention in the second of elements of the first, so here the third stanza is further sutured to the second by the reference early in the third to the "stubble-plains" touched with "rosy hue" by the late afternoon sun; for "stubble-plains" recalls the harvesters now gone home to rest, who had been reaping in these plains in the second stanza. In this third stanza the cumulative presentation of sounds pleasing to human ears in early autumn is parallel in basic method to the presentation of massed ripenings in the first and the group of harvesters in the second. In the three stanzas taken together there is a steady progression from outpoured material substance toward nonmaterial satisfactions; from reveling in the literal ripe fruitage in stanza 1 the speaker moves on to enjoy the beauty of the harvesting tasks in stanza 2, and thence on to the even less tangible music of autumn made up by its pleasing sounds in stanza 3—the progression suggesting that the total picture has meanings beyond the literal.

At the beginning of this third stanza Keats asks the *ubi sunt* question that has rung down the centuries since the Latin lyricists, and this beginning has something to do with the tendency of interpreters to find transience and decay predominating in the stanza: "Where are the songs of Spring? Ay, where are they?" But Keats is obviously using the stock question for just the opposite purpose from the traditional one, for in the next line he does not give the expected stock reply, "Gone with the snows of yesteryear," or the like, but achieves both surprise and reiteration of his main theme by answering it differently: "Think not of them, thou hast thy music too." If a reader takes the implications of this reply sufficiently into account and not primarily the question itself, he will readily discern that there is very little of transience and decay in the rest of the stanza, and surely not the approaching death of the year as the pervasive thought; for the poem is progressing right along its main line of emphasis on the lingering contentment of the time now carried beyond material satisfactions. All years, of course, do end, but that is not depicted in this poem; rather, a *day* is ending slowly and serenely, without any expression of melancholy or regret, and this day is to be followed by another and another of the same mellow kind. Like the bees in the poem, the reader is made to "think warm days will never cease." In this last stanza the emphasis continues to center on the slow lingering of the season, and hence of the year, not on their fleetingness, although the living cycle of nature does involve birth, death, and rebirth. After the "surprise" answer to the *ubi sunt* question, the rest of the third stanza, paralleling the structure of the other two, is made up first of a few images that instantly recall the substance of the other stanzas, and then of a careful selection of the sounds pleasing to human ears in autumn—all in full harmony with the tone and atmosphere of the preceding stanzas:

> Where are the songs of Spring? Ay, where are they?
>   Think not of them, thou hast thy music too,—
> While barred clouds bloom the soft-dying day,
>   And touch the stubble-plains with rosy hue;
> Then in a wailful choir the small gnats mourn
>   Among the river shallows, borne aloft
>   Or sinking as the light wind lives or dies;
> And full-grown lambs loud bleat from hilly bourn;
>   Hedge-crickets sing; and now with treble soft
> The red-breast whistles from a garden-croft;
>   And gathering swallows twitter in the skies.

There may be a temptation here to press upon "soft-dying" and extend its implications, but the temptation should be resisted, for Keats applies the term only to the day; and the full context shows that nothing is expiring in a way that brings regret or sorrow and that the emphasis is not on the dying but on the mellow fullness of all. Similarly, we could press out of context "wailful," "mourn," "sinking," and "dies" and claim to have found strong evidence of death and decay; but again the full context militates against such a claim and an examination of the individual images within the context reveals that "wailful" and "mourn" chiefly suggest the sound of the small gnats' wings only and that if the two words refer to anything else they faintly call up a fitting accompaniment to the "soft-dying day," which is not to be mourned since it is actually "dying into life" in an oncoming day. It is only this sound of the gnats' wings that is "sinking" and only the light wind that "lives or dies." Only to a small degree, if at all, do these pleasing sounds constitute something of a dirge, and hardly one for the departing year, whose end is yet far off. Now dying has ceased to matter very much, an idea that has been unobtrusively building up since the very first word, "season," quietly suggested the continual recurrence of autumn at the same time that "mellow fruitfulness" in the same line announced that autumn was being conceived as the season of ripenings and fruitions. The whole body of the poem is developed within the scope of that conception. The cumulative effect of lingering enrichment that has accrued from the poet's slowing and muting of process, together with the effect of his having evolved nonmaterial satisfactions (the purposiveness of labor and the beauty of music) from their material bases in stanza 1, now conjoins with two other patterns of suggestion, coming to a head in the last stanza to elevate the whole structure into a complex natural symbol which extends the fulfillment found in earthly life to other seasons than autumn. First, the term "full-grown lambs" obviously implies that these were the new-born lambs of the spring, which is also true of the "hedge-crickets" that now "sing," the "red-breast" that "whistles," and the "gathering swallows" that "twitter." Many of them were born in the spring, grew up during the summer, and came to maturity in the autumn. This realization immediately brings the thought that such was the case with the ripe apples, gourds, and hazel nuts of the first stanza and with the ripe grain of the second; and since all these are being harvested and stored for human sustenance by the warm fireside in winter, all four of the recurring seasons of the year are involved and united in the fulfillment depicted in the whole poem.

The last glimpse at the "gathering swallows" effectively completes the whole picture, for this image brings to finality several patterns of suggestion running through the last stanza and a major strain that has been developing throughout the poem. As Professor Bate says, there are no reasons to believe that the swallows are gathering for the purpose of migrating.[9] But there *are* reasons for believing that they are gathering for another purpose fully in harmony with the total effect of the poem, as migration is not. Birds do not migrate during the mellow early autumn described in this poem; one does not need to allude to the extrinsic fact of its date of composition— September 19. They are gathering to take their places in a secure roosting place where they will be safe for the night. Birds are seen gathering for this purpose far more often than gathering for migration; they are seen doing so every day in the late afternoon and Keats has built the last stanza on the subtly hinted framework of a maturing day, in which the late afternoon is its autumn, its period of mellow richness parallel to the autumn season in the cycle of the year. Conceived as gathering preparatory to seeking their resting place for the night, the gathering swallows deftly complete the picture of the slowly concluding day in the last stanza and also that of the mellow fruitfulness extending beyond the literal which is set forth by the whole poem. Both pictures, one within the other, are simultaneously brought to serene completion in this final image of the swallows gathering for rest, which quietly recalls the preceding suggestions throughout the poem of stasis, security, enduringness, and manifold well-being.

This last fine touch of artistry that brings the poem to its proper close also helps to reveal that the totality has been steadily becoming symbolic while it was building up. Keats has made it powerfully suggest that the lot of common hu-

[9] Professor Perkins considers the swallows as gathering for migration (*The Quest for Permanence*, p. 294), as does Professor Bloom (*The Visionary Company*, p. 424).

manity, when considered deeply, is replete with all man needs in order to find life richly meaningful and satisfying. The poem is really about the spiritual as well as the material bread, although there is nowhere in it an abstract term for such values, for Keats's method of cumulative concretenesses and his uncanny sense of propriety led him wisely to keep to the concrete. But that the poem has meanings beyond the literal, that it is something more than mere description, seems beyond question. However, one should be careful not to over-state the degree to which it expresses meanings beyond what it actually presents. Perhaps the most accurate statement is a minimal one: the total structure is developed in such a way as to imply that in ordinary life at all times there are values which are nonmaterial and which point toward the spiritual, although they are never stated overtly. The enunciation of them gains in appeal from their being rendered indirectly through the symbolic aspects of the poem rather than being expressed allegorically or in the customary abstract terms. The poem is made up of concrete images and details from actual life nearly all of which Keats had used previously in similar contexts in other poems; and he had frequently juxta-posed daemonic elements to them in a way that clearly indi-cated that these images and details carry spiritual overtones, that they are a part of the sphere in which man finds the only true spirituality that he will ever know. *To Autumn* is simply the greatest and the most highly selected concentration of them imaginatively modified and woven together into a single matrix of great expressive power. In this new structure they seem to have the same antithetical relationship to daemonic elements as before; for although there is nothing daemonic in this poem, Keats's having completed *Lamia* so shortly before writing *To Autumn*, and his having reread it a week before and again in part on the day before, must have helped to impel him in reaction toward a fresh grasp of his long-sustained chief antithesis of the daemonic, the beauty of the actual world of men and things. He centered on it, and on it alone, with an intentness and concentration that enabled him to produce in the compact and controlled artistry of his last great poem the triumph of the anti-daemonic in his poetry and the most powerful assertion of the living beauty in the common lot of all—a fitting conclusion to the great odes and to Keats's poetry as a whole.

CHAPTER EIGHT   AT THE END
OF THE QUEST

Despite the vehement affirmation in *To Autumn* of the beauties and satisfactions to be found on the plane of ordinary human existence, there is no reason to believe that Keats had turned his back upon daemonic experience entirely. It remained for him a legitimate avenue, within judicious limits, for extending the range of aesthetic fulfillment. He still believed there were some steps, though "scanty" and "few," beyond the "bourn of care." But, quite obviously, in his recurring explorations beyond the beaten path of beauty, he had worked out something to his satisfaction and had arrived at some tentative conclusions, as is usually the case in every long-sustained endeavor by a man of integrity and intellectual honesty.

At the end of his daemonic quest, which coincided very nearly with the close of his productive period, he did not timidly draw back on moralistic grounds from the ecstatic region beyond our "mortal bars"; nor did he weakly despair of finding enduring beauty and satisfactions somewhere within the mind's possibilities. He had discovered that the structure of the human consciousness precluded a reliance on daemonic experience as a major element in human happiness; and he had discovered that his own imagination could make supreme beauty of objects in the ordinary world of phenomena. Here at the end of his career, daemonic beauty obviously does not matter so much as at the beginning of his preoccupation with it in *Endymion* or at the high point of it in *La Belle Dame sans Merci*. He has found the actual realm of men and things replete with meaning and happiness for human beings, as is firmly proclaimed in *To Autumn*, in which the previous expressions of this idea scattered throughout his poetry come together in a cohesive and strong expression of it that has the characteristics and tone of a distinct finale to the long-sustained conflict in his poems between the actual world and the daemonic, which had emerged as the major conflict in his poetry throughout his career. The attitude toward it which he had worked out for himself by September, 1819, seems to have been a lasting one, for in a letter two months later he implies that although he has not given up completely the kind of poetry that usually includes the daemonic, he considers it of much less importance and much less suited to his temperament. Back in the spring of 1818 he had written in the "chambers of thought" letter to J. H. Reynolds (May 3, 1818), "The truth is there is something real in the world." What he wrote to John Taylor on November 17, 1819, two months after having completed *To Autumn*, sounds like a full working out of the core idea in this sentence to Reynolds eighteen months before: "As the marvelous is the most enticing and the surest guarantee of harmonious numbers, I have been endeavoring to persuade myself to untether Fancy. . . . I and myself cannot agree about this at all. Wonders are no wonders to me. I am more at home among men and women." By this time he had surely afforded evidence of the truth of this assertion.

The finale to the daemonic strain in his poetry set forth in *To Autumn* and such utterances as these in his letters afterward does not mean that Keats was ceasing to be a Romantic writer and thinker, as might be erroneously assumed. There is a widespread tendency among critics to make such judgments of various writers of the period when they undergo crucial change of some kind, but these judgments are based upon a too narrow conception of what Romanticism essentially is. If there is any central current or common element in the varying manifestations of the Romantic temper during the early nineteenth century, and I believe there is, it surely must be found in the persistent drive that all Romantic writers made for greater and richer fulfillment of the individual self than the prevalent modes of perceiving, thinking, and doing during the preceding age had provided. The literature of the Romantic period is partly the record of this relentless drive for deeper enrichment of the psyche and partly the creation of new artifacts brought into existence by that fierce energy working through imaginative perception of experience and dynamic uses of literary form. These new artifacts in the various literary forms provide the bases for some of the new fulfillment and also point out the way toward more of it. In turning away from the daemonic Keats had neither ceased nor slackened in his quest for richer experience for the individual psyche than the preceding age afforded; he had merely changed the direction of his thrust and focused it upon "the very world, which is the world/ Of all of us,—the place where, in the end,/ We find our happiness, or not at all," as Wordsworth had said (*Prelude*, XI, 142–144). The remote corridors to daemonic beauty are esoteric paths open only to a few; but Keats proclaimed at just this time that a poet must be a "Physician to all men" (*Fall of Hyperion* I, 190). In his change of direction he was living up to the demands of that conviction, and his change is parallel, though not identical, to two changes that Wordsworth had made at different times in his career: his turning from political radicalism to nature during the 1790's and from mystical communion with nature to a deeper concern with humanity and the human world during the next decade. Like Wordsworth, Keats learned to make great poetry out of the activities, feelings, and language of ordinary men. But it was the transcendental powers of mind in both men that enabled them to make distinctive poetry out of materials from the common lot through their ability to respond to it, to be moved by it, to become involved in it, and to modify and reshape it. Keats was Romantic in the *degree* of his involvement, which he could carry to the point of self-oblivion, as Wordsworth could not, since he was not as highly endowed with "Negative Capability." Transcendentalism, the very heart of the deeper levels of Romanticism, is not limited to mysticism; "Negative Capability," or empathy, is transcendental because it entails more of mental activity than the sensory reception and analytical arrangement of data and therefore impels the mind to become constitutive of experience rather than merely recorder of it. From the first, Keats's poetry had been concerned with involvement—the involvement of the psyche with an object which powerfully activated the transcendental powers of realization and vibrant cognition latent in the mind. His change of emphasis toward the end of his career shows his capability of responding as deeply to objects in natural life that had the power to sustain his vision on that plane as he had formerly responded to objects that sent him soaring into the remote, glimmering beauties of the daemonic. The intensity and depth of involvement make both experiences Romantic because both bring a high degree of fulfillment beyond that usually allowed by the "lethargy of custom"; but the former is possible to more men, is more lasting, and is more capable of extension and recurrence. Though beginning early in Keats's poetry, this glorification of actuality reaches its apex of expression in *To Autumn*, in which he presents not merely an aggregation of sensory data from the autumnal countryside but a transcendental idea of all that autumn can mean to the human spirit; for many of the components come from the depths of mind alone—mind activated into creative constituency by the concrete objects in the harvest scene, not mind simply catching and reflecting sensory images of them derived from outside itself.

One of the significant aspects of Keats's poetry that becomes more clearly apparent through attention to his uses of the daemonic, although it has been increasingly noted in recent years, is that there is no extensive or significant neo-Platonic element anywhere in his poetry. He only "dabbled" in neo-Platonism briefly in Book I of *Endymion*, and thereafter in this poem it was usurped by the daemonic, which superimposed itself upon the neo-Platonic throughout the rest of the action, so that Endymion's spiritualization had to come through humanization, through growing closer to humanity and to the universals in the actual world, rather than through soaring away from it toward union with perfect "forms" or "essences" apart from it. Moreover, as has clearly become apparent, there is even less of the neo-Platonic in Keats's subsequent poetry than in *Endymion*. However, the daemonic in Keats's poetry served a somewhat similar function to the neo-Platonic in Shelley's, but with quite a different and more satisfactory result. That is, just as the recurring neo-Platonic element in Shelley's poems continually provided a second dimension beyond the mere reproduction of the surface of life, so did the recurring daemonic element continually provide another dimension in the poems of Keats, appearing even in the great odes as well as in the narrative poems. Complexity and depth were thereby added to the work of both men. But while Shelley on his neo-Platonic wings increasingly soared away from actuality and humanity, though all the time proclaiming that "intellectual beauty" would do man good (as indeed it would), Keats on the other hand continually diminished the daemonic element in his poetry, finally reducing it to the position of only a minor addition to the joys and satisfactions always available. As a result, Keats found the ultimately beautiful and real in the human world and within man's grasp, as Shelley emphatically did not. Near the end of the poem Endymion exclaims, "Say, is not bliss within our perfect seisure?/ O that I could not doubt!" (IV, 720–721). By the time that he found "Autumn bold/ With universal tinge of sober gold" all about him in 1819, and he in effect was about "to make an end" (*Endymion* I, 55–57) of his whole career, he had successfully erased all doubts as to finding contentment within our reach. In fact, the simple proposition "Beauty is truth," in the sense in which he meant it, is affirmed by the terminal events in his poetic life as well as in the final lines of his *Grecian Urn*.

Despite all the beauty and power of Shelley's idealism to those who will ferret it out, and they are few nowadays, here is surely one reason for Keats's steadily rising vogue and for Shelley's steady decline. Men are not comforted by repeatedly being told that their world is but a shadow of the real one.

The causes of Shelley's decline cannot all be ascribed to the effects of the prevalent empirical epistemologies that have all but vanquished idealism from our age; some of the causes can be found in the particular doctrine Shelley proclaimed and in the uneven texture of the poetic structures in which he proclaimed it. Partly because Keats's rejection of the daemonic as a major avenue to fulfillment repeatedly led him back to the world of common humanity as of first importance, Keats labored to polish, refine, and perfect the diction and imagery with which he rendered the beauties of the world of man and nature; but Shelley quite often did not carefully do so, inevitably impelled by his neo-Platonic quest to consider the other world of "forms" and essences the more important one. In contrast Keats reaped from his daemonic quest the great benefit of having another dimension in his poetry without incurring the commensurate defect of a separation from humanity and from the world in which men must live out their days. He used the daemonic in such a way as to give to his poetry an element of unearthly charm and at the same time to set off in sharper relief the beauties of the earthly world, the one in which it is surely best that men find some happiness rather than eternally to seek it in never-never lands afar.

Most important of all, clarification of the particular concept of the daemonic which Keats employed in his poetry provides significant help in the explication of the more difficult and complex poems. It especially helps to reveal specifically what is going on in *Endymion*, *La Belle Dame sans Merci*, and *Lamia*, in which it answers pointedly crucial questions; and it throws light on the artistry of the major odes, *The Eve of St. Agnes*, and some of the minor poems, such as the sonnet *As Hermes Once* and the verse epistles. At the same time an accurate perception of the sustained daemonic element in his poetry reveals surprisingly more unity and cohesion in the whole Keats canon than is usually attributed to it and shows that he was in actual fact working out a framework of ideas in his poetry, although not a preconceived one, which enables his work to speak to man more powerfully as a coherent body of interrelated poems than as single poetic structures, even though they have achieved high repute when considered individually. Tracing the function of the daemonic in them is one fruitful way of seeing their interrelation.

In sum, Keats's poems constitute a remarkable series of adventures in aesthetic experience. His own daemonic intensity and his controlled uses of daemonic effects play a major role in making them distinctive, powerful, and enduringly appealing. It was inevitable that the leaders of the aesthetic movement in the later nineteenth century should claim him for their own; but they saw only one side of what he was steadily working at during his whole career as he continually explored the nature of aesthetic experience. They missed entirely his deep humanity and his unbreakable commitment to the task of investigating the full range of the ways of beauty and of pointing out the intricacies of their human relevance.

INDEX

Aesthetic movement: ignored Keats's humanity, 179, 248

Allott, Miriam, 186, 188

Alpheus-Arethusa story: function of in *Endymion*, 55–57

Amadis of Gaul (15th-century romance): a source of Keats's daemonic, 19

Anatomy of Melancholy (Burton): a source of Keats's daemonic, 6, 18; conception of daemons in, 6; Keats's knowledge of, 6; plot of Keats's *Lamia* from, 18, 185, 190–191

Anima archetype (Jung), 20–21, 122–123; a "hook" for, 145, 198, 211; in *La Belle Dame sans Merci*, 145–148; similarities scored in *Palmerin*, 148. *See also* Collective unconscious

Animus archetype (Jung), 122; in the characterization of Lamia, 199. *See also Anima* archetype; Collective unconscious

Anti-daemonic: a major turning point in *Endymion*, 50; clarified in *To J. H. Reynolds*, 12–13; concept of, 4, 12; consummate rendering in *To Autumn*, 184, 216, 220–222, 239; first experience in *Endymion*, 50, 87; heightens beauty of actual, 12, 51–52, 56, 97, 216, 222; in *Ode on a Grecian Urn*, 182; part of major conflict in *Endymion*, 42–43, 50, 53, 99; triumphant conclusion to Keats's poetry, 240; value of reasserted, 110

Apollo: deification of in *Hyperion*, 72–73, 105, 211–212; sensation and thought united in, 72–73, 102, 105, 187, 211–212

Archetypal mythical hero: Endymion as, 94–95

Aristotle: essences in actual world, 39

Arnold, Matthew: quoted Keats for Celtic magic, 17–18

Art-for-art's-sake: a misunderstanding of *Grecian Urn*, 179, 248

Bailey, Benjamin: letter to, 70–71

Bate, W. J., 11, 152, 158, 174, 182, 185–186, 225–226, 227, 228, 231, 238

Beauty: principle of in all things, 77, 178–180
"Beauty is truth": explanation of, 178–182; meaning related to art, 180–182; proclaimed by Keats's life, 246; proclaimed in *To Autumn*, 221; related to "that is all/ Ye know," 180–181
Beyer, Werner, 1, 19, 186
Blake, William, 152; example of visionary poet, 16
Bland, D. S., 225
Bloom, Harold, 169, 225
Bordman, Gerald, 138
Bostetter, Edward, 125
Breyer, Bernard, 128
Bridges, Robert, 22
Brooks, Cleanth, 169, 171, 174
Brown, Calvin, 9
Brown, Charles, 117, 160
Burton, Robert: a source of Keats's daemonic, 6, 18; plot of Keats's *Lamia* from, 18, 185, 190–191
Bush, Douglas, 18, 87, 174, 186, 187, 188, 192, 210

Campbell, Joseph, 94
Chestre, Thomas, 137–138
Clarke, Charles Cowden, 18
Coleridge, Samuel Taylor, 71; on "Negative Capability," 11
Collective unconscious (Jung), 20–21, 145–148. *See also Anima* archetype; Jung
Colvin, Sidney, 22, 103, 158

Daemon: pre-Christian Greek conception of, 1, 4–6, 8–10
Daemonic dream: of Francesca da Rimini by Keats, 17, 119–123
Daemonic experience: as discussed in Plato's dialogues, 4–6; as mode of perception, 3, 10–13; as stage of ascent to ideal, 6–7, 23; as universal principle, 8–10; causes customary joys to fade, 12, 13, 60, 109, 120–123, 136, 146–148; differentiated from dreams, 17, 68, 69; differentiated from mystical, 15–16; differentiated from visionary, 16, 68–69; followed by deadening aftermath, 11–12, 32–33, 44–45, 50–51, 55–56, 60, 62, 109, 120–123, 136, 146–148; in Endymion's love of Cynthia, 27–28, 31–32, 48–49, 61, 81; in Keats's dream of Francesca da Rimini, 119–123; in *La Belle Dame sans Merci*, 128–148; in Lycius' love of Lamia, 198–206, 210–211; in *Ode on a Grecian Urn*, 176–179; in *Ode on Indolence*, 158–161; in *Ode to a Nightingale*, 172–174; in *Ode to Psyche*, 155–158; limited by structure of consciousness, 13–14, 109, 241–242; not the ordered and conceptual, 16–17; perilous for mortals, 10, 12–15, 44, 108–109, 145–149, 173, 198, 201, 211, 219–

220; possible to few, 243; price of, 55–56, 139, 148–149; proper worth of, 110, 149, 241–242; rejected by Endymion, 25, 45, 76–80, 97, 98, 100, 101, 119; related to Jung's collective unconscious, 19–21, 122–123, 144–146, 211; relaxes mind's order and unity, 10, 16–17; revulsion against in *Endymion*, 50–52, 76–82

Daemonic realm: as metaphor for act of consciousness, 7, 11–12; different from abstract ideal, 21; in *Ode to Psyche*, 155; nature of, 6–7, 12, 28, 75, 177; not where imagination works best, 12–13; pre-Christian conceptions of, 1, 4–6, 18; supplants mystical ideal, 24, 25, 41–43, 64, 98, 151–152, 155, 166, 177, 245–246; used structurally in odes, 157–158, 161, 165–167, 172–173, 177, 183. *See also* Daemonic world

Daemonic world: as concept of primordial joy, 7–9; as metaphor for act of mind, 7, 11–12; as objective correlative to state of mind, 7; best delineated in *La Belle Dame sans Merci*, 149; beyond proper bound of imagination, 13–14; beyond standard laws of knowing, 13–14; empty of enduring content, 177; in *Grecian Urn*, 178–179; in *Ode to a Nightingale*, 172–173; invested with glamour and appeal, 149; juxtaposed to human in *La Belle Dame sans Merci*, 148–149; nature of, 7, 11–12, 75. *See also* Daemonic realm

Daemonology: Keats probably heard friends discuss, 18

Daemons: pre-Christian conception of, 1, 4–6, 18; pre-Christian, debased by Christian theology, 4

Dante: his image of Holy Trinity, 96; Keats's dream of Francesca da Rimini in, 17, 119–123, 129–130

Demon: Christian conception of, 1, 4

"Demon Poesy": Keats's in *Ode on Indolence*, 2, 159, 161

De Moraes, Francisco: author of *Palmerin of England* (Portuguese romance of chivalry), 14

De Selincourt, Ernest, 22, 186, 187

Diana triad (Diana-Cynthia-Hecate), 56; as representative of knowledge in *Endymion*, 95; at the end of *Endymion*, 88, 93; becomes inclusive symbol in *Endymion*, 80, 95; change in Endymion's relationship to, 80–81; clarifies "triple soul" of Endymion, 89–92; Diana equated with Cynthia in *Endymion*, 87–88; has part in three regions of action in *Endymion*, 86; in sonnet *To Homer*, 85; lower mode, Hecate, in *Endymion*, 76, 84, 91; major emphasis in *Endymion*, 76, 84–92; more possibly intended in Endymion, 91–92; relationship to Endymion's spiritualization, 95–96; represents ideal in *Endymion*, 84–85, 87, 94; suggests three-fold setting in *Endymion*, 86; symbolizes ideas dramatized by incidents in *Endymion*, 91–92; why not clearly designated a trinity, 95–96

Dovaston, F. M., 139

Drayton, Michael, 23; Keats's indebtedness to for threefold Diana, 85

Dream: differentiated from daemonic dream, 17

Dunbar, Georgia S., 186

Evert, W. H., 1

Faery mistress: in chivalric romance, 137–141, 192, 213
Fairy lore: includes daemonic elements, 19, 137, 141, 192, 195
"Fellowship with essence": escalation not carried through, 97; five stages in, 36–41, 75, 92–93; late emendation in *Endymion*, 24, 35–36; meaning explained, 36–39; neo-Platonic meaning denied, 22–24
Finney, Claude L., 2, 22, 37, 126, 174, 186, 187
Fogle, R. H., 152, 169, 171, 174
Ford, Newell, 22–23, 37, 98

Garab, Arra, 9
Garrod, H. W., 4, 103; rearranged stanzas of *Indolence*, 160
Gittings, Robert, 158
Glaucus-Scylla story: purpose of in *Endymion*, 57–65
Gleckner, Robert F., 183
Goethe, Johann Wolfgang von, 8, 66, 176; concept of daemonic, 8–10; concept of daemonic resembles Keats's, 8, 10; his Faust resembles Keats's *personae*, 8; Keats's knowledge of, 7
Graves, Robert, 20

Hastings, James, 5
Haydon, B. R.: told Keats of daemonic inspiration, 2
Hazlitt, William: *Characters of Shakespeare's Plays*, Keats's scorings and annotations in, 73–74
Hermes-nymph episode: purpose of in *Lamia*, 192, 195, 203–204
Houghton, Arthur A., Jr., 14
Howe, P. P., 74
Hull, R. F. C., 123
Hunt, Leigh, 14, 15, 18, 120

Imagination: as potentially destructive agent, 14–15, 145, 148; bounds not to be transgressed, 166, 218; conflict of daemonic versus actual in Keats's, 3–4; constitutive of man's world, 167, 244–245; daemonic not its best sphere, 12–13, 106–107; in "purgatory blind" when beyond bounds, 106; its proper bound, 12–13, 106–107, 151; its synthesizing power in *Grecian Urn*, 174–175; modifying power in *To Autumn*, 229; relation to the concrete, 106–107
Initiation: Endymion's resembles archetypal, 94–95; nature of in *Endymion*, 74, 78–81, 94–95
Intellectual Beauty (Shelley): significance and function of, 16, 246

Jones, L. M., 182
Jowett, Benjamin, 6

Jung, Carl G.: archetypes of collective unconscious, 20–21, 122–123, 144–146, 198–199. *See also Anima* archetype

Keats, George and Georgiana: letter to, 72, 119–120
Keats, John
—*As Hermes Once* (*On a Dream*), 129, 151, 247; an account of a daemonic dream, 119–123; explicated, 121–123; relationship to *La Belle Dame*, 119–124; relationship to *Lamia*, 191; signature *Caviare* appended by Hunt, 120
—*Endymion*, 2, 26, 107, 108, 115, 119, 129, 141, 151, 157, 173, 210, 231, 242, 245, 246, 247; Alpheus-Arethusa episode in, 55–57; anti-daemonic major turning point in, 50; archetypal mythical hero in, 94–95; as quest for daemonic beauty, 23–25, 42, 43–45, 47, 53–54, 64–65, 76–79, 81, 97–99, 124; characters resemble those in other narratives, 212–215; conflict of daemonic versus actual in, 25, 31, 34–35, 42, 43, 47, 53–56, 64, 66, 76–77, 96–97; conflict of daemonic versus actual in Arethusa, 55–56; conflict of daemonic versus actual, turning point in, 64; conflict of daemonic versus anti-daemonic in, 43, 45, 50–53, 56, 76–81, 87, 97, 99; daemonic love of Glaucus for Circe in, 60–61; daemonic rejected in, 45, 64, 76–81, 97, 100, 101; daemonic supplants mystical ideal in, 24, 25, 41–43, 64, 98, 99; Diana triad symbolizes major ideas of plot in, 91–92; ending explained, 84–85, 92–95; "fellowship with essence," stages in, 36–41, 75, 92–93; function of daemonic summarized, 96–100; Glaucus-Scylla episode in, 57–65; Glaucus' story parallels Endymion's, 61; heroine similar to Keats's others, 191–192, 197; hero's fate linked to Glaucus', 62–64; includes imagery of *To Autumn*, 223; initiation in, 65–66, 74, 78–81, 94–95; initiation related to sorrow in, 74–75; neo-Platonism usurped by daemonic in, 24, 25, 28, 41–43, 93, 99, 245; recantation of daemonic quest in, 45, 76–79, 88; relationship to *Lamia*, 189; relationship to later poems, 98, 100; similarity to other narratives of Keats, 189; "Song of Sorrow" in, 69–77; spiritualization of hero in, 42–43, 52, 56–57, 64–65, 73, 92–94; threefold Diana in, 56, 80–81, 84–96, 88; three prevailing interpretations of, 22, 98–99; triple goddess as Universal Mother in, 97; "triple soul" explained by Diana triad, 89–92; "truth the best music" in, 92–94; unsatisfactory ending of, 83–84; various interpretations of, 22–23
—*Eve of St. Agnes, The*, 97, 151, 247; controlled daemonic atmosphere in, 111–118, 124; differing views of ending, 117
—*Fall of Hyperion, The*, 227; clarifies Keats's liking for *Lamia*, 219–220; close to *Lamia* in date, 217, 219; condemnation of obsessive dreams, 217, 218, 219; poet a sage and physician in, 215, 243; relationship of early lines to *Lamia*, 217–218, 219
—*God of the Meridian*, 103

—*Hyperion*, 103, 217; concept of reality in, 39; conflict of sensation versus thought resolved in, 72–73, 102, 105, 187, 211–212; deification of Apollo in, 72–73, 105, 211–212; intuitive knowledge dramatized in, 105

—*In a Drear-Nighted December*, 102–103

—*I Stood Tip-toe*, 157

—*La Belle Dame sans Merci*, 2, 98, 107, 108, 151, 161, 193, 210, 212, 242, 247; a culmination of previous developments, 124; *anima* archetype (Jung) in, 20; as a poem of daemonic experience, 128–148; autobiographical readings inadequate, 125–126; basic character of elfin lady in, 141–142; basic structure of, 129–130; contains imagery of *To Autumn*, 223; contrast between two speakers in, 133; date of early text in letter, 119–120; differing views of, 125–128; heroine not evil in, 141–144; heroine resembles Lamia, 197; heroine similar to Keats's others, 191–192; imagery of in *Endymion*, 82; influenced great odes, 149–150; isolation of the knight, 132–134; prototypes of elfin lady in, 137–139; relationship to *As Hermes Once* (*On a Dream*), 119–120, 124; relationship to *Lamia*, 189, 213–214; relationship to other narrative poems, 184; representation of nature in, 133–134; signature *Caviare* appended by Hunt, 120; significance of first speaker in, 131–136; similarity to other narratives of Keats, 189; suggested in *Endymion*, 45–46, 59–60, 62, 69, 78; symbol of rose in, 136–137; the knight's dream in, 144–146

—*Lamia*, 2, 97, 107, 139, 141, 149, 189–215, 220, 225, 247; *anima* archetype (Jung) in, 20, 198–199, 211; antithesis of *To Autumn*, 184, 221–222; Apollonius, character in: center of intelligence, 209–210, derogations of evaporate, 207–210, 212–213, Keats's attitude toward, 214–215, not representative of cold philosophy, 209–210, opponent of daemonic, 214, representative of good sense and balance, 209–210, significance and function in story, 187, 188, 205–214; autobiographical element professional, 215; Burton's account of, 190–191; characters resemble those in other narratives, 212–215; related to *Fall of Hyperion* and *To Autumn*, 217–220, 239–240; contradictory views of, 185–188; daemonic as complete way of life in, 203; Lycius, character in: his daemonic love and consequences, 201, 204–205, 206–207, severely derogated, 212, transposition of values, 205–206, 209; most irresistible heroine intended, 198; relation to other narrative poems, 184; similarity to Keats's earlier narratives, 189; story from Burton, 18, 185, 190–191; symbol of rainbow in, 210

—*Lines on Seeing a Lock of Milton's Hair*, 103

—*Lines Written in the Highlands after a Visit to Burns's Country*, 149; indicates proper place of daemonic, 108–110; shows revival of interest in daemonic, 124; states bounds of daemonic, 108–110

—*Ode on a Grecian Urn*, 103, 174–184, 221; date of, 158; end points to *To Autumn*, 182; essentially anti-daemonic, 182; relationship to *Melancholy* in idea, 177–178; relationship to narrative poems, 183; resignation in, 182; role in design of odes as group, 164, 168, 182–183; structure similar to *Ode to a Nightingale*, 165–168

—*Ode on Indolence*, 2, 158–165, 174; daemonic used structurally in, 158–159; date of, 158; "demon Poesy" in, 159–161; motto clue to interpretation, 159–160; role in design of odes as group, 168, 169, 182; second dimension of, 165; stanzas rearranged by Garrod, 160; suggests structure of other odes, 158, 165

—*Ode on Melancholy:* meaning and significance of, 69, 168; relationship to *Grecian Urn* in idea, 177–178, 181; replete with daemonic contradictions, 182; role in design of odes as group, 168, 182

—*Ode to a Nightingale*, 18, 158, 169–174, 177; "faerylands forlorn" in, 172–173; momentary death wish in, 170–171; nature of bird's immortality in, 171–172; relation to narrative poems, 183; role in design of odes as group, 168, 182; slow beginning of, 175; structure similar to *Grecian Urn*, 165–168

—*Ode to Autumn*, 98, 103, 150, 184, 219, 228–239, 241, 242; acceptance and resignation in, 166–167; adumbrations of in *Endymion*, 81–82, 223; antithesis of *Lamia*, 221–222; centered on one plane, 221–222; close to *Lamia* in date, 217, 220, 221, 239, 240; consummate embodiment of anti-daemonic, 216, 220–222; consummate rendering of joys of actuality, 224; culmination of pervasive strain, 224; differences from other odes, 220–221; enhanced by *Lamia* through contrast, 224; high point of the anti-daemonic, 216, 224; idea of recurrence in, 229; main idea in, 228–229; mood not transitory, 222–223; not a somber death song, 225; personification in, 231; relationship to *Endymion*, 98; relationship to *Grecian Urn*, 182; role in design of odes as group, 168, 183; similarities in earlier poems, 223–224; stasis and process in, 226–228; transcendental aspects of, 233, 244–245; use of *ubi sunt* theme in, 235

—*Ode to May:* poetry lessens pain of transience, 103, 107–108; splendor of the moment in, 103, 163

—*Ode to Psyche*, 164, 174, 182; daemonic element gives distinction to, 152, 155–157; date of, 150–158; first major daemonic lyric, 158; Keats's intention in, 154; role in design of odes as group, 168; structure of, 152–157

—*On Sitting Down to Read King Lear Once Again*, 105

—*Otho the Great*, 217

—*O Thou Whose Face Hath Felt*, 105

—*To Homer:* threefold Diana in, 85

—*To J. H. Reynolds, Esq.:* anti-daemonic clarified in, 12–13, 151, 218

—*To My Brother George:* daemonic spoils beauty of actual, 13–14

50; Keats's markings in, 14–15, 19, 139, 148, 181; on relation of art to life, 181

Pan: as bringer of universal knowledge (*Endymion*), 95; hymn to in *Endymion*, 26–27

Paradise Lost (Milton), 49

Parthenon: south frieze of and *Ode on a Grecian Urn*, 174–175

Perkins, David, 225, 231, 238

Pettet, E. C., 22

Philipson, Morris, 20

Philostratus, 185

Plato: concept of daemonically inspired poet, 2; concept of daemons, 4–6; concept of Ultimate Beauty, 6–7

Platonism: daemonic supersedes in Keats, 28, 41, 84–85, 97, 245–246; mentioned derogatorily in *Lamia*, 199. *See also* Neo-Platonism

Plotinus: daemonic and pursuit of Beauty, 7, 23

Praz, Mario, 1

Rainbow: symbol in *Lamia*, 210

Raysor, T. M., 11

Read, Herbert, 123

Recantation: in *Endymion*, 45, 76–79, 88; not final in *Endymion*, 110; not necessary in *Eve of St. Agnes*, 115; related to plot in *Endymion*, 79

Resignation: in *Endymion*, 68, 69, 74, 77–78, 81–82, 83; in Keats's great odes, 166–167, 177

Reynolds, J. H., 139

Roberts, John H., 186

Rollins, H. E., 190

Romanticism: conception of, 243–245

Sandys, George, 192

Schelling: discussed "Negative Capability," 11

Scot, Reginald (*Discoverie of Witchcraft*), 5

Sensation versus thought: conflict between resolved in *Hyperion*, 72–73, 105–106, 187, 211–212; solution late in coming, 101–102

Seward, Barbara, 136

Shakespeare, William, 23, 162

Shelley, Percy Bysshe, 18, 152; compared to Keats, 245–247; example of visionary poet, 16; Keats's probable knowledge of *Alastor*, *Hymn to Intellectual Beauty*, 18; reasons for his decline, 246–247; talking of Plato at Hunt's, 23

Sir Lanval (Marie de France), 138

Sir Launfal (Thomas Chestre), 137–138

Slote, Bernice, 186–188

Smithers, G. V., 138

A NOTE ON THE AUTHOR

Charles I. Patterson, Jr., is Professor of English at the University of Georgia. After receiving his doctorate from the University of Illinois, he was a Ford Faculty Fellow at Harvard University, and later a Fulbright Guest Professor at the University of Erlangen, Germany. Professor Patterson has published numerous articles in literary journals; *The Daemonic in the Poetry of John Keats* is his first book-length study since his Ph.D. dissertation on the Romantic criticism of prose fiction (1950).

UNIVERSITY OF ILLINOIS PRESS